The Anthropology of
GLOBALIZATION

The Anthropology of
GLOBALIZATION

Cultural Anthropology Enters the 21st Century

TED C. LEWELLEN

BERGIN & GARVEY
Westport, Connecticut • London

Library of Congress Cataloging-in-Publication Data

Lewellen, Ted C., 1940–
      The anthropology of globalization : cultural anthropology enters the 21st century / Ted
   C. Lewellen.
         p.   cm.
      Includes bibliographical references and index.
      ISBN 0–89789–738–2 (alk. paper)—ISBN 0–89789–740–4 (pbk. : alk. paper)
      1. Anthropology.   2. Globalization.   I. Title.
   GN27.L65   2002
   306—dc21   2001052793

British Library Cataloguing in Publication Data is available.

Library of Congress Catalog Card Number: 2001052793
ISBN: 0–89789–738–2
            0–89789–740–4 (pbk.)

First published in 2002

Bergin & Garvey, 88 Post Road West, Westport, CT 06881
An imprint of Greenwood Publishing Group, Inc.
www.greenwood.com

Printed in the United States of America

∞™
The paper used in this book complies with the
Permanent Paper Standard issued by the National
Information Standards Organization (Z39.48–1984).

10   9

Contents

Preface

Globalization is at the cutting edge of cultural anthropology at the turn of the 21st century. First, it opens new territory, challenging the bounded world of communities, localities, peasants, tribes, and cultures that has characterized anthropological research in the past. Second, globalization has become the point at which a number of theoretical trends have coalesced: interpretive anthropology, critical anthropology, postmodernism, and poststructuralism. However, this theoretical blending is often combined with a hard-nosed, pragmatic attention to empirical detail that suggests at least a partial resolution to the divisions that have split anthropology over the past decades.

This book draws together numerous disparate studies under the rubric "the anthropology of globalization." It thus may create an artificial unity, although, as I hope to show, there are already commonalities of viewpoint, agreed-upon assumptions about the nature of globalization and its effects, and well-developed topics within the globalization perspective, such as the studies of transnationalism and global identity.

The book is written for anyone interested in an overview of this frontier subject. Anthropologists and nonanthropologists who still equate globalization with globobabble may find that there is more here than has been widely recognized. Even anthropologists who are involved either directly or marginally in globalization research, or want to incorporate globalization into their future work, may find value in exploring the many trails already blazed by others.

Above all, I hope this book finds a place in the classroom. It could be used to structure a course on The Anthropology of Globalization (its thirteen chapters approximate the number of weeks in a full semester), or it could be used as a supplement in courses on anthropological theory, the anthropology of migration, the anthropology of identity, or other applicable subjects. I assume some background in anthropology, referring periodically to classical writings and to recent theoretical controversies. There is nothing, however, that should deter the nonanthro student who is willing to look up Franz Boas or Max Gluckman on the Web. The bibliography, though extensive, is by no means complete; there is an enormous amount of material out there. However, each chapter provides sufficient sources to create a substantive course.

While this is an overview, utilizing the ideas and research of many scholars, I have self-consciously tried to avoid an *Annual Reviews* survey-of-the-literature approach, which might mention several authors in the same paragraph and skim over a multitude of ethnographic examples very rapidly. The goal of such articles is to provide researchers with sources for further reading, and it is very valuable in that regard (in fact, I would like to extend a special note of thanks to *Annual Reviews of Anthropology* authors for their help in writing this book). However, my goal is to provide a broad, easily digested overview. As a result, I have concentrated on ideas rather than specific writers. Often, of course, particular ideas are closely associated with particular authors, and I have tried to give due attention to Arjun Appadurai, Michael Kearney, Ulf Hannerz, and Jonathan Friedman, among many others. Since I am a believer that the core of anthropology lies in ethnography, I devote considerable attention to specific studies, developing this material in as much depth as space allows. I have chosen these examples to represent a variety of cultures and geographical areas, but mainly because each illustrates, elaborates, or refutes a theoretical position. I open Chapter 12 with a globalized reanalysis of my own field work among the Aymara Indians of Peru, something I have wanted to explore for a long time.

A traditional line of stand-up comedians is, "Is there anybody out there I haven't offended yet?" Such might make an appropriate last line of this book. While I have tried to be fair in accurately representing the various authors and ideas, I have made no attempt at false objectivity. All theories are sifted through my own prejudices and assumptions, and I do not hesitate to critique or to present my views.

In some ways, this book is a sequel to my *Dependency and Development: Introduction to the Third World* (Lewellen 1995). That work was truly interdisciplinary, containing chapters on history, development theory, economics, politics, demographics, environment, and human rights. About the only appropriate discipline *not* included was anthropology. During the decade or so of research and writing, I had time to read only enough anthropology to keep up with my classes. As a result, when I refocused on anthropology, it was with a different knowledge base and theoretical orientation than that of some anthropologists. This shows up, for example, in a skeptical attitude toward the way that anthropology handles the subject of development and in the nonanthropological survey of globalization in Chapter 2. While those who want to get right to the anthropology may be tempted to skip this chapter, it is here that I lay down some of the foundations for the rest of the book, such as my contention that neoliberalism defines the present phase of globalization and that this was only made possible by the OPEC oil shocks of the 1970s. Throughout, I have tried to provide a background of data, say, on world migration rates, to set the scene for more specifically anthropological research.

This book by no means exhausts its subject. A truly complete overview of what has already been done in the anthropology of globalization would have to include separate chapters on gender, tourism, global factory labor, commodity chains, borderlands, environmentalism, AIDS and medicine in general, grassroots organizing, global cities, and human rights. I have tried to incorporate some of this material (gender, for example, receives specific attention in several chapters), but, in the end, I opted for a degree of depth on the subjects I have selected, rather than a greater inclusiveness.

A book like this owes its existence to literally hundreds of scholars, and I certainly thank them all. Funding from the Irving May Chair in Human Relations of the University of Richmond has been quite significant in making this book possible.

Chapter 1

Introduction: Who Is Alma?

Finally, it is necessary to emphasize the global character that productive processes assume in the maquiladoras, and the advantages and difficulties this poses for workers' struggles.

Norma Iglesias Prieto[1]

Alma was born in the small village of Cacahuatepec in the state of Oaxaca, Mexico. While she was still in primary school, her father sacrificed to buy her a sewing machine, in the hopes that as a seamstress she could escape a long heritage of poverty. However, she married young to a subsistence farmer who could barely eke out enough corn and beans from the wasted land to feed his family and almost immediately she began to have children, ultimately seven. At age 32, leaving her husband behind to continue to struggle on the paltry plot of land, she took her children and moved to Tijuana to join a sister-in-law who was part of a kin-based network in that border city.

After a couple of months working as a maid, Alma crossed the border illegally. In Long Beach, near Los Angeles, she was able to put her abilities as a seamstress to work in a small clothing factory, run by Cubans, that hired undocumented aliens. This and other similar jobs allowed her to enroll her children in school and to send money to her husband who had now moved to Tijuana and was living with her eldest son. After many trips back and forth across the border, periodically being caught by immigration and deported, she resettled in Tijuana and found work in one of the *maquiladoras* there.[2] The *maquiladoras* or *maquilas* are border factories owned by or closely affiliated with U.S. businesses and devoted to production for export to the United States. They mainly employ young single women willing to work for a few years at tedious, low-pay assembly jobs. Since the clothing *maquilas* require skilled labor, Alma was able to find jobs that paid enough to support her family, including an unemployed husband, and to send her children to school. The eldest daughter was trained as a nurse and another worked in an electronics *maquila* while studying to be a production technician.

Alma is one of many women described in Norma Iglesias Prieto's *Beautiful Flowers of the Maquiladora* (1997: 66–70). There is nothing unusual about her life; millions of women throughout the Third World[3] could tell similar stories. Yet she is one of the greatest challenges that cultural anthropology has had to face. In contrast to the tradition-bound, community-based "indigenous peoples" who have been the subjects of anthropological research throughout most of the 20th century, Alma is a thoroughly modern (or in some scholars' views, postmodern) woman. She moves easily between different worlds, almost between centuries, at home on the parched fields of Cacahuatepec or among the skyscrapers of Los Angeles. She is part of a global economy, employed in a sector created by the 1965 Border Industrialization Program and reinforced by the North American Free Trade Agreement (NAFTA). Her *maquila* jobs were created by the internationalization of finance and the peculiarities of a border between two states at vastly different levels of development. She grew up in a small village culture to which she maintains ties of kinship and sympathy, and she has lived in large cities in both the United States and Mexico. Most of her children were first educated in the United States and speak fluent English. Neither she nor they particularly identify themselves with the Mexican nation-state.

Who is Alma? Is she a "proletarianized peasant," to use a Marxist term that was popular a decade or so ago? Is she an international migrant or an internal urban migrant or, in contemporary parlance, a *trans*migrant? She is a woman, to be sure, but unlike most women studied by anthropologists, she is the primary earner for her family, working in an industrial sector that employs 80% females. Is she some sort of "hybrid?" to use the fashionable phrase of the moment. And what of her "culture?" This foundational term of anthropology usually means something like the set of values and symbols passed on from generation to generation. But what has she retained from her parents? What will she pass on to her already bilingual and bicultural children who will probably find a place in the world very different from Alma's and who since birth have been exposed to an endless inundation of television images and symbols from San Diego that boast of a world of unreachable wealth and adventure? In truth, of course, Alma is and has been many things, sequentially and simultaneously: woman, peasant, internal migrant, transnational migrant, skilled laborer, mother, family head, housekeeper, entrepreneur, Mexican, mestizo. The easy categories of the past seem oddly out of place in a world that is fragmented and in which space and time have imploded.

And subjectively, how would Alma view herself as she moves among these many roles and worlds? Where, if anywhere, would we find her identity? This was hardly even a question for anthropologists of the past who assumed that identity was coterminous with culture; one was simply Maya, Nuer, or Apache. Some postmodernists have portrayed the contemporary individual in terms of a "fragmented and schizophrenic decentering" (Jameson 1988: 351), but Alma, much to the contrary, seems a master at adapting to her multiple environments. If anything, it is her world, not she herself, that is fragmented, schizophrenic, and decentered. She is quite at home there.

Alma, of course, represents only one of myriad possible responses to the world at the turn of the 21st century. Others, caught up in permanent diasporas, may carry relatively intact cultures with them, creating enclave communities in new homes far from their places of origin, or they may reinvent themselves, passionately embracing nationalisms based on constructed histories and mythologies. Indigenous peoples in intact communities may commercialize sacred rituals for tourists. Threatened Amazonian natives may seek empowerment through blitzing their political representatives with e-mail or videotaping their negotiations with government representatives.

It is obvious, from even the most cursory glance at Alma, the degree to which anthropological "reality" has been an artifact of anthropological methods, especially participant observation fieldwork and the cross-cultural comparison of specific traits. Fieldwork has traditionally been community-based and ideally lasts at least a year or two, yet such research could hardly touch the routinized complexity of Alma's life. Traditional cross-cultural comparison would be forced to dismember Alma beyond recognition in order to fit her into narrow categories of kinship, gender, or profession suitable for statistical manipulation.

What are the "objective" (a term increasingly called into dispute) realities of a world that has been globalized in a way never experienced before? What are the constraints and determinisms of the processes of globalization for the individual and group? How do people experience and interpret this new world, and how do they accommodate or resist it? How do they make a place for themselves?

Alma challenges anthropology to step into the 21st century. Although the path is not particularly clear, a surprising number of fieldworkers and theorists have already gone a long way in mapping the terrain.

PART I

Globalizing Anthropology

Human society is in the process of being transformed to a degree possibly
not seen since the Industrial Revolution. The process can be summed up
by the term globalization.

Stanley Barrett (1999: 258)

Chapter 2

Slouching Toward Globalization

Globalacious, Globalasia, Globalatio, Globalemic, Globalescent,
Globalactic, Globaloney . . .

> Richard Wilk, "Globobabble"[1]

. . . what rough beast, its hour come round at last, Slouches towards Beth-
lehem to be born?

> William Butler Yeats, "The Second Coming"

"Globalization" has become *the* academic and media buzzword of the early
21st century. The most cursory of computer explorations, whether through
an on-line bookstore, FirstSearch, or any commercial search engine, will
turn up hundreds or even thousands of entries.[2] Considering that the term
was seldom encountered before 1990, this sudden ubiquity may set some
sort of record. Such trendyness might suggest a shallow fad and has already
given rise to satire, as the opening quotation shows. Obviously, a book titled
The Anthropology of Globalization might be expected to take the concept
seriously and to assume a degree of staying power.

Definitions of *globalization* are almost as legion as the number of experts
on the subject. To get our bearings, however, it might be worth starting out
with a bare-bones definition, which will be elaborated as we go along: *Contemporary globalization is the increasing flow of trade, finance, culture,
ideas, and people brought about by the sophisticated technology of communications and travel and by the worldwide spread of neoliberal capitalism,*

and it is the local and regional adaptations to and resistances against these flows.

This definition differs from most others in several respects. Many definitions encountered outside of anthropology are purely economic, such as "the growing liberalization of international trade and investment, and the resulting increase in the integration of national economies" (Griswald 2000), or—and this from a social scientist— "the cross-national flows of goods, investment, production, and technology" (Petras 1999). In contrast, my definition emphasizes not just capitalism but a very particular type of capitalism, not just economic flows but also cultural flows, and not just globalization but also regionalization and localization. (One "-zation" it significantly does not mention is homogenization.) Almost all definitions give some priority to the economic sphere, even if economics is viewed as only one part of a larger system. Some definitions include the decline or even disappearance of the nation-state, as its primary powers and functions are shifted to the international arena.[3] Whatever definition one employs, globalization must be thought of as an ongoing process, one with a long history. Thus, in describing globalization, it is useful to include the word "contemporary" or the phrase "current phase."

Globalization may be conceived as empirical fact, as theory, or as ideology. In reality, these blend together, but different researchers tend to emphasize one or another. Those who view globalization as a simple fact, or set of facts, point to quantitative data that show a world that is increasingly economically integrated; national markets have opened more than ever before to international, regional, and global trade; financial markets communicate instantaneously with any place in the world; transnational corporations disperse the processes of production and distribution to many different nations; labor markets are extremely fluid, ignoring national borders. As Don Kalb (2000: 1) puts it: "In principle [globalization] does not claim more than a geographic fact: people and places in the world are becoming more extensively and densely connected to each other as a consequence of increasing transnational flows of capital/goods, information/ideas, and people."

Whereas a globalization-as-fact approach assumes the data are self-explanatory, academic *theories* of globalization attempt to make sense of the data and to explain the internal logic of the system: how it came about, how it is structured, and what its effects are. There are postmodern theories that reject all metanarratives and insist that if globalization exists at all it will be found only in day-to-day practices at the local level. Marxist theories (which may also be postmodern) view globalization as the latest stage in the evolution of capitalism (Jameson 1990). Theoretical emphases vary, from the focus on postfordist flexible accumulation (Harvey 1990) to the identification of a global capitalist class (Sklair 1991) to the claim that the world is divided into mutually hostile civilizations (Huntington 1996).

Ideology adds a moral dimension to globalization theory. The dominant form of globalist ideology is that of economic neoliberalism, which we will look at in some detail in a moment. Neoliberalism is the semi-official philosophy of the United States government, of the World Bank, and the International Monetary Fund, as well as most university departments of economics and myriad political and financial organizations, such as the Trilateral Commission. It is the view that a certain form of global capitalism is good; if Third World countries carry out a few specific prescriptions, standards of living will be raised. Greater economic integration will ensure greater cooperation among peoples and countries, leading to world peace. There are also a multitude of ideologies that view globalization as a disaster, a system that is exacerbating inequality, marginalizing the poorest people and countries, and creating an increasingly concentrated elite of wealth and power (most anthropologists would probably lean in this latter direction).

[handwritten margin note: idea is the why or why not]

FROM SKEPTIC TO HYPERGLOBIST

In addition, we can delineate three distinct perspectives on the nature of globalization: the skeptical, the evolutionary, and the hyperglobalist.[4]

First is what might be termed the skeptical or so-what's-the-big-deal? thesis, namely that globalization either does not exist or has been vastly oversold. It might be noted that long-term migration—often considered a key element of globalization—affects only about 1% or 2% of the world's population and that earlier mass movements, say of the Irish, Italian, and Chinese to the New World in the 19th century, proportionately exceeded anything that is going on today when Western countries have imposed tight restrictions on immigration. The formation of political, economic, and military alliances, such as the European Community, NATO, and ASEAN, represent more a regionalization than a globalization, and the emergence and strengthening of ethnic groups and community-based nongovernmental organizations is evidence of a strong localization following the somewhat artificial and often authoritarian centralizations mandated by U.S. and Soviet alliances during the Cold War. If homogenization of culture is a criterion of globalization, as many in the media claim,[5] then how do we explain the explosive increase in ethnic politics, religious fundamentalism, and local organizing? In most larger countries, 80% or more of production is still for domestic consumption (Burawoy 2000a: 338).

[handwritten margin note: are we in a pd. of localizat, post-globalization]

A second point of view might be termed *evolutionary*. Globalization is a reality, but it represents a change in degree, not in kind. The processes that we now see as distinctive have been emerging over centuries and represent no significant break with the past, nor are they transforming world structures in any revolutionary manner. Transnational corporations, often considered the engines of globalization, have been evolving since the great joint stock companies of the early colonial period. What we see is not something new but just the working out of the logic of capitalist expansion. Culturally, Westernization may have been more of a factor for a greater percentage of indigenous peoples in the 18th and 19th centuries when colonizers had the power to create entirely new Europeanized elites in Africa and Asia. Politically, the period after World War II, when the United Nations was formed, might be seen as a greater period of globalization than anything that is happening today. Thomas Patterson (1999: 2) points out dismissively that "contemporary descriptions of the global world emerging today are stunningly similar to modernist accounts from the 1890s or early 1900s." If our present constructs of globalization seem fresh, it is only because we have forgotten or are ignorant of many similar processes taking place at the turn of the 20th century, which was also a time of imperialism via the consolidation and internationalization of capitalism and finance. Many critics claim a much earlier genesis, suggesting that globalization has been going on at least since the 16th century (a paleontologist might legitimately make a claim for a *much* earlier date).

Finally, the *hyperglobalization* thesis is that the world is experiencing something entirely new, fundamentally different than anything that has gone before, which will ultimately transform the nature of human life on earth in very radical ways. Economically, the collapse of the Soviet Union and the dissolution of socialism as a serious alternative have given rise to a third stage of capitalism—first preindustrial, then industrial, and now postindustrial (or to use a term to be discussed in a moment, *postmodern*). Globalization represents not a smooth evolutionary sequence but a rupture with the past, a disjuncture, a fragmentation in the course of history, a new era. A key element is the deterritorialization of production and finance. Transnational corporations, many of which control more wealth than most countries of the world, purchase both raw and finished materials from all over the globe, distribute the process of manufacture in many different countries, and have worldwide advertising and distributional networks that reach into the most remote tribal and peasant communities and the most impoverished shanty towns. Finance is even more fluid; almost entirely divorced from the existence of precious metals or hard cash, computerized electric money flows instantaneously and everywhere via satellite. Indeed, communication is a central element of this new era. Transnational corporations, combined with global organizations (the United Nations, the World

Bank, the International Monetary Fund) and treaties (GATT, the Law of the Seas, the Montreal Protocol), assume functions formerly belonging to the state; even policy and decision making becomes deterritorialized. The ideology and practice of consumerism, the driving force of capitalism, is spread through movies, television, radio, billboards, and the Internet, breaking down traditional cultural values based on kinship and community.

It is too easy simply to assume the blind-men-and-elephant perspective. As the reader may recall, each blind investigator feels a different part of the elephant—tail, trunk, leg—so each assumes a different reality; the elephant is like a rope; no, it is like a snake; no, a tree. . . . (It might be noted that in this metaphor, although each is only partially correct, there *really is* an elephant.) The position taken here is that globalization is a reality, *but so are regionalization and localization.* While sympathetic to the evolutionary argument, I will argue that what is new is, first, that neoliberal capitalism has achieved an unprecedented global dominance and, second, that regionalism, localization, and globalization now form a single, unified system, more closely interrelated than ever before. Eric Wolf (1982) has convincingly documented the degree to which even the most remote society was affected by the capitalist mode of production, but what is occurring today is somewhat different; influences once felt as distant, abstract, and incomprehensible are quite immediate, the links more clearly visible, the presence of the global experienced more directly.

THE EMERGENCE OF A GLOBAL WORLD

While various scholars disagree about the nature of globalization and, therefore, how and when it began, there is some agreement that the present phase of globalization is closely tied to, if not defined by, expansionist capitalism. Capitalism is an economic system of private ownership of property and the means of production; distribution is based on the profit motive and takes place within a free, or relatively free, competitive market in which supply and demand determine, or are supposed to determine, price. Capitalism emerged several times in the past—in ancient Mesopotamia, for example, and during various periods in China—but Western capitalism can be traced back to the early 16th century in Europe. This is, of course, the great period of ocean exploration and of the solidification of the nation-state; the spread of empire and the growth of capitalism proceed in close symbiosis from the very beginning. Today's globalization was inherent in capitalism's birth.

European feudalism began to self-destruct almost as soon as it was firmly established in the 11th century. The feudal system, based on rent bondage and labor tribute to a landlord, was challenged by the growth of commercial fairs, guilds, urbanization, and the emergence of a commercial class. Fortunes brought back from the Crusades established huge commercial banking families, first in the Italian republics then in Holland and England, and these families helped finance the consolidation of centralized states. The discovery of America greatly increased Europe's wealth and power; between 1521 and 1600, 18,000 tons of silver and 200 tons of gold poured into Spain alone.[6]

The economic philosophy of mercantilism that developed was based on the notion that the state was strong to the degree that its coffers were laden with precious metals, which could buy armies and ships. The ideal was to take in money but avoid, as much as possible, paying it out. The state was the center of economic exchange, at least at the higher levels; the wealth of the state was supposedly ensured through strong laws regulating trade, minimizing imports of any goods not used in production, and maximizing exports of finished goods. Colonies, which supplied cheap labor and raw materials, could trade only with the mother country. Within the European state, craft production by guilds existed side by side with incipient small-scale capitalism, based on wage labor.

Eric Wolf, in his seminal *Europe and the People Without History* (1982)—perhaps the first true anthropological study of globalization—documents the profound and lasting impact of these processes on indigenous peoples. According to Wolf's analysis, the dominant mode of production of prestate native peoples was "kin-ordered," that is, it was the lineage or clan that determined the division of labor and decided what would be produced and how it would be distributed. There was no concept of private property. The mercantilist "tributary mode of production" was imposed by European conquest: Property remained in the hands of the indigenous peoples, but they were required to use that land, and their labor, to supply wealth to the conquerors. The encomienda system employed throughout Spanish America gave overlords, or *encomenderos*, rights to Indian labor within a certain region, although theoretically they did not really own the land (many of these encomiendas later turned into fully owned haciendas or plantations). In many Asian and African colonies, high taxes had to be paid in goods, and laws forced specific percentages of native land to be used for export production. In early Canada, the French imposed an equally effective, if somewhat less brutal, form of tributary economy. Indians were made dependent for their very survival on European manufactured goods, which could only be obtained through the exchange of beaver pelts. The transformation from kin-ordered to tributary mode of production affected nearly every aspect of indigenous life—breaking up lineages, shuffling leadership, causing migrations to new territories, and, in North America, creating exterminative warfare as beaver (and later, bison) diminished and Indian tribes fought each other for trading networks and shrinking resources (Blick 1988).

Joint stock companies, financed by individual investors and private businesses but directly controlled by the state, were a natural progression of the mercantilist system. These often huge organizations, of which the British East India Company and Hudson Bay Company are the best known, were transitional. They were more than economic enterprises; they established long-term European communities in foreign lands, created their own class systems, and acted as surrogate governments complete with their own armies and navies. On the one hand, as official representatives of their home governments, obligated to trade only with the mother country, they were firmly mercantilist. On the other hand, they were corporatively owned by multiple private investors and—given the length and difficulty of communications—relatively autonomous, so in many ways they were the direct precursors of today's transnational corporations.

Mercantilism and capitalism were never clearly demarcated, and the former simply merged into the latter over a few hundred years. Wolf saw wage labor—the transformation of work into a commodity to be bought and sold like any other commodity—as a defining quality of capitalism. By this criterion, true capitalism did not really become firmly established, even in Europe, until the first industrial revolution in the mid-18th century. If capitalism is defined more broadly, as private ownership of the means of production and competitive trade for profit, it began much earlier. It is hardly necessary to split hairs on this issue since there was a period of centuries when tributary production overlapped and merged with capitalist production; in fact, semi- or wholly mercantilist tributary systems continued in many parts of the world until the collapse of colonialism in the latter half of the 20th century. Wherever capitalism became the dominant form for indigenous peoples, further transformations of culture, social structure, economy, and politics were inevitable. Whereas tributary systems had created broad classes of surplus takers and surplus producers, under capitalism class stratification along lines of wealth, race, and ethnicity became increasingly elaborated. Native property was privatized in European hands through outright land theft or legal maneuvering: In El Salvador, land was confiscated if not turned to coffee production, which was all but impossible for most peasants since it takes five years for coffee plants to produce their first crops, and natives lacked the capital to survive that long before seeing the benefit of their efforts. Throughout the colonies, huge commercial plantations replaced tributary lands. Bereft of land, native peoples were forced to work for minuscule wages. As money became the single universal value, local handicrafts were wiped out by the availability of cheap manufactured imports. So-called *comprador* elites, whose economic allegiance belonged to their European employers and benefactors and not to their own country's welfare, were established in positions of rule. In contrast to mercantilism, in which the state controlled the economy, in capitalism the function of the state was to protect private property, encourage business, open new territory to exploitation by corporations, and use its military might to promote and protect overseas private interests.

Perhaps the primary insight of Wolf's history of indigenous peoples is that the large majority of them stopped being indigenous a long time ago. Those who anthropology has been blithely fitting into primal classifications, such as band, tribe, and chiefdom, have long histories of transformation through interpenetration and interaction with powerful outside forces. In many cases, the processes of devolution overcame any internal evolutionary forces directed toward more complexity. The slave trade, for example, collapsed complex state societies into the "primitive tribes" later studied by anthropologists as indigenous (Friedman 1994: 1–14).

As viewed by Immanuel Wallerstein (1974), the result of European expansion was a world capitalist system based on a division of labor between core, periphery, and semi-periphery. The core—the industrialized countries—employed capital-intensive production to create manufactured goods to be sold around the world. The task of the periphery was to supply raw materials and cheap labor to the core and to provide markets for core products. The semi-periphery countries combined features of both the core and periphery, mediating between the two. Although Wallerstein was a major influence on contemporary globalization theory, much of what he describes has already changed or is in the process of transformation. The division-of-labor structure is based on an industrialized core and a pre- or nonindustrial periphery. Today, the core has moved into a postindustrial phase and to a great extent the periphery, even some of the poorest countries, has taken over the function of manufacture and the refinement of raw materials. The neat functional integration of world system theory seems increasingly simplistic given the rapid transfer of industrialism and mass consumerism to the Third World, the unfettered fluidity of financial flows, and worldwide media saturation.

THE MAKING OF NEOLIBERAL GLOBALIZATION

While the evolution of global economies has been going on for a long time, neoliberal globalization is a relatively recent phenomenon that dates only to about 1990 and results from the convergence of several different factors. All of the elements were in place well before then: Neoliberalism became official U.S. policy with the Reagan presidency beginning in 1981; the transfer to postfordism in the West was coming along well, and the technological innovations in transportation and communication had already shrunk the world significantly. However, to turn neoliberalism from an American economic philosophy into a global structure required two massive changes: the end of superpower rivalry and the acceptance of neoliberalism by the Third World. By as late as the mid-1980s, neither of these was even remotely accomplished.

The debt crisis of the 1970s and the lost decade of the 1980s was crucial to the incorporation of the Third World into the neoliberal system. At that time, almost all of the governments of the less-developed countries had adopted some degree of import substitution, attempting to protect indigenous industries from foreign competition via high tariffs or outright bans on certain imported goods. Foreign investment was tightly controlled and foreign ownership often prohibited. A few countries—mostly among the poorest of the poor—were outright communist, but most others were attempting some sort of third way between capitalism and communism. The communist bloc countries traded preferentially among each other, and Soviet trade was often based less on supply and demand than on political and strategic considerations. With the exception of already relatively well-developed countries with strong ties to the United States, there was little inclination—and much antipathy—to transforming economies along neoliberal lines.

The primary, though by no means only, cause of the debt crisis was the oil shocks imposed by OPEC (Organization of Petroleum Exporting Countries). In reaction to the 1973 Arab-Israeli war, OPEC countries took control of the pricing and production of their oil, which until that time had been largely under the control of Western multinational corporations. Prices for oil increased by 400% in 1974 alone and kept climbing. As huge amounts of petrodollars poured into OPEC coffers, the money was put into American and European banks to be recycled. Partially to pay for oil and partially for development (which seldom materialized), countries borrowed prodigiously from private banks and major multilateral institutions at variable rates. In the early 1980s, the whole system collapsed, leaving the countries heavily overindebted. The International Monetary Fund (IMF), originally designed to promote free trade among Western nations after World War II, stepped in to offer loans designed to pay enough interest on the debt to keep the country from default. World Bank loans, targeted for development projects, imposed similar strictures. When accepting an IMF loan, the country must sign a conditionality contract promising that it will make certain structural adjustments. It receives the money over time as these adjustments are made.

The structural adjustments are, of course, textbook neoliberalism. We will take a look in a moment at exactly what that means. The point here is that the IMF and World Bank found themselves with powers that would have been the envy of the most rapacious emperor of Imperial Rome, namely the power to dictate the economies of almost all of the developing countries of the world. As long as the USSR was a superpower, some countries could hold out by trading with the communist bloc. With the collapse of the Soviet Union in 1989, not only did communist-aligned countries lose their trading partners, but corrupt U.S. allies, who had been propped up by American aid in exchange for their militant anticommunism, suddenly found themselves abandoned. Not only communism but socialism and all the other third way variations were left with no support all. Even Russia was subject to neoliberal pressures in order to get loans (comprised partially of money transferred from Third World aid), with well-known disastrous results. While a few Third World countries, notably Chile and Brazil, embraced neoliberalism with apparent enthusiasm, most were pulled into the fold almost literally kicking and screaming; structural-adjustment riots, strikes, and even revolutions became common. The Southeast Asian industrial tigers, Singapore, Taiwan, South Korea, and Malaysia, signed on partially because they were ready to; these countries had developed strong industrial economies through policies that were totally at odds with neoliberalism—extensive government intervention, import substitution, state-owned enterprises—but had been so successful that they now felt ready to compete in the rough-and-tumble of a laissez-faire global market (Lewellen 1995: 117–121). After just a few years of neoliberalism, their economies were in deep trouble, but they seem to be making a comeback.

In short, the present phase of globalization has existed only since 1990. The evolutionary argument that this is a late stage of capitalism, the result of a smooth and inevitable evolution, is debatable, since without the oil shocks, the resultant debt crisis, and the collapse of Soviet communism, Third World countries would not have been forced into the neoliberal system.[7]

Whether previous globalizations existed is to a great degree a matter of semantics, of definition (though, of course, definitions derive from theory and ideology). Wallerstein applied the term world system to ancient empires, such as those of Rome and China. The best case for an earlier Imperial globalization is the period between about 1870 and 1914 when largely uncontested colonialism was at its peak; this was, however, quite different from today's globalization, which is defined largely in terms of relatively free trade among nations (colonial empires tended to trade within themselves) and technological innovations in communications and transportation. Many of the *processes* of contemporary globalization, such as the ubiquity of electronic media and the spread of consumerism, have, of course, been going on for a long time before 1990, so anthropological studies of the globalization of cultures and peoples may date back several decades.

NEOLIBERALISM

> Globalization and neoliberalism are, at present, the only games in town.
> William Loker[8]

It has been argued that neoliberalism is crucial to the current definition of globalization. In its most fundamental aspect, neoliberalism is simply the idea that trade should be unfettered by government regulation. This seems innocuous enough. However, until recently, the vast majority of Third World countries were being managed on completely different principles and according to completely different philosophies. Most Third World states operated on the assumption that their domestic industries, small and large, needed to be protected from international competition. For example, Pedro, a shoemaker in Lima, Peru, runs a shop with ten employees; he produces a fairly decent product on low-tech equipment. However, if Peru is inundated with lower-cost, more stylish, and more durable shoes from, say, China, Pedro is out of business. Multiply this by thousands of entrepreneurs who are unable to get their businesses off the ground and 10,000 farmers who cannot produce crops cheaper than they can be imported and one can see the problem. In the world market, bigness, technology, and the cheapest labor have the advantage. If Pedro and all those like him remain in poverty, there is not enough wealth among the masses to create effective demand for goods, so what is produced within the country is targeted for export, and what is imported is mainly luxury goods for the upper classes. The result is a weak domestic economy that endlessly reproduces itself, never reaching a point of self-development. Another problem has been that transnational agriculture or mining corporations remove far more resources and profits than they put back into the country.

Basically, this is a conflict between domestic capitalism and international capitalism. To solve it, some countries turned to socialism, others to various hybrids of socialism and capitalism, and others to protected capitalism, but most placed strong restrictions on imports and tried to control foreign investment. Governments assumed ownership of major resources and industries with the promise that profits would be used to serve the people. With a few notable exceptions, such as South Korea and Taiwan, these attempts to create strong domestic economies did not achieve expectations,

[handwritten margin note: protectionism is ideal if you can be self-sufficient → natural resources which now US has already extracted]

and some were disastrous failures. Reasons for failure varied, but usually were related to statism and overcontrol by the government, with accompanying corruption and inefficiency.

Neoliberalism, in contrast, shifts the strategy for development from inward-oriented policies directed toward national self-sufficiency to outward-oriented policies designed for maximum integration into the global market. Ideally, the government should be removed from the economic sphere, allowing the market to work for itself (in practice, of course, extensive government intervention is required to rapidly transform an economy). The primary requirements of the neoliberal model are the reduction and removal of tariffs and quotas and the elimination of barriers to foreign investment, allowing free trade, especially via transnational corporations rather than the government, to regulate the economy. Other required structural adjustments include a severe reduction in fiscal deficits, privatization of nationalized corporations, the decontrol of prices including the elimination of subsidies, and the decontrol of exchange rates and interest rates (Loker 1999).

The underlying theory is a combination of the classical policies of Adam Smith's self-adjusting market and David Ricardo's comparative advantage. Forgotten are Smith's insistence that the invisible hand of supply and demand be tempered by morality and that in formerly closed countries the opening of markets to foreign goods be done very gradually in order not to "deprive all at once many thousands of our people of their ordinary employment and means of subsistence. The disorder which this would occasion might no doubt be very considerable" (Smith 1976 [1776]: 469). Russia, which was forced to rapidly transform its economy along neoliberal lines in order to get desperately needed loans, does indeed have "very considerable" problems. The Southeast Asia successes are often cited as prime examples of neoliberalism, which is odd since the development of these countries followed a far different model that included import substitution, government ownership, price controls, and extensive and ongoing government involvement in almost every aspect of the economy, from land reform to industrial production. Whereas the Southeast Asian model was pragmatic and flexible, with new changes being made as old policies were outgrown, neoliberalism tends to be more of a cookbook approach to be applied, irrelevant of the culture, history, society, and level of development of the country.

Proponents of neoliberalism point to high-level statistics, much the same way that early development theorists used gross national product as a measure of success. On closer examination, however, even claimed successes are few—Chile, Brazil, and Peru are often cited. The Southeast Asia tigers are regularly claimed as exemplary, which ignores the fact that the financial crisis of the 1990s occurred shortly after these previously rapidly growing economies abandoned earlier policies and adopted more purely neoliberal regimes.

Neoliberalism favors the rich and, since anthropologists usually study the poor or lower middle classes, a near consensus has emerged that neoliberal adjustments undercut domestic production prices, cause unemployment, create sweatshops that utilize underpaid child and female labor, disrupt families, disempower peasants, and encourage environmental despoliation.[10] Nevertheless, neoliberalism is not without its mass appeal. Many of the countries to which it is applied have had too much state intervention in the past, often by violent and corrupt governments; as economic power is moved out of the hands of the bureaucracy, new opportunities arise for domestic entrepreneurs. Government-owned industries were often (though by no means always) inefficient and run by political cronies of the regime in power, so little of the promised profits ever made their way back to the people. As miserable as they are, transnational factories in Third World countries often pay more and have better working conditions than domestic factories. In some countries, skyrocketing inflation has been brought under control.

The score of minuses and plusses is more mixed than either side wishes to admit; arguers both pro and con will never lack for examples to prove their points or disprove the points of their opponents. Although neoliberalism wants to be a one-size-fits-all model, in reality it does not have the same effects in any two countries because it is always laid over pre-existing structures, histories, and cultures. What appears at the macro level as a logical set of neutral economic principles turns out, on the ground, to be as subjective, political, and contingent as any other set of policies. It is at ground level—down there on the subsistence farms and in the back alleys of shanty towns where the anthropologist resides—that neoliberal globalization takes on tangible form.

THE NATURE OF GLOBALIZATION

The terms modern and postmodern can be extremely confusing, not least because in the past modern pretty much meant contemporary, rendering postmodern either nonsensical or, at best, futuristic. In the globalization literature, one will often find one scholar using the term modern for the same phenomena for which another employs the term postmodern. Most confusing, however, is that the term postmodern can refer to two quite distinct things: (1) an empirical condition or (2) a set of artistic, literary, and social theories. For some analysts, these two are mixed together, so that postmodern theory becomes a means for analyzing the postmodern condition. In what follows, I would like to keep these separate; the postmodern *condition* does not necessarily have anything whatsoever to do with postmodern *theory*.[11]

The postmodern condition can only be comprehended relative to modernism, which in turn is best understood in contrast to what came before. If domestication of plants and animals is considered the first great revolution, then it is a revolution that lasted more than 5,000 years. All great states and empires of the past were built upon the surpluses provided by intensive agriculture. The industrial revolution, which passed through at least three phases and is closely associated with the rise of capitalism, shifted the basis of political power from agriculture to manufacturing. The modern era may be considered the period from about 1770 onward when industrialization, centered in Europe and North America, fundamentally transformed political, economic, and social structures. As people's livelihoods came to depend not on family-owned or share-cropped farms but on wage labor in a fluctuating market, individualism replaced communitarianism as a primary value. Formerly agrarian workers needed to adapt to labor specialization and to acclimate to high labor mobility and to working ten- to twelve-hour days at routinized occupations. Science and technology became primary determinants of social change.

The Enlightenment provided the philosophical legitimization and guidelines for these processes. For Enlightenment thinkers, rationalism replaced religion and superstition. An understanding of nature through science, and the application of that understanding in the form of technology, would inevitably and in linear fashion lead to progress. Positivism, basically the idea that no statement was validated until proved empirically (or, in its more extreme formulation, that no statement could be *meaningful* unless it was susceptible to empirical verification) promised that once-philosophical questions might be subject to objective answers. The social and political worlds were amenable to goal-realization in the same way that the physical sciences were. Democracy, based on the rational participation of the governed, was the end point of political development.[12]

This broad, stereotypical portrait of Enlightenment philosophy is routinely repudiated by contemporary theorists as if these values were universal; however, it should be noted that these ideals and practices never, right from the beginning, went unchallenged. I am suspicious of attempts to generalize the cognitive maps or discourses of entire epochs; there are always multiple competing ideologies, and the claim that one particular set of ideas is dominant necessarily rests on a very selective use of sources. Many influential theorists—not the least of which were Karl Marx and Frederick

Nietzsche—bemoaned the dehumanization and alienation of these processes and were contemptuous of the concept of progress. The religious reaction against Darwin's evolutionary theory was profound and continues to this day, and our Founding Fathers were quite distrustful of democracy (a term they seldom employed). It might also be noted that the cloaks of rationalism and scientism were, and are, regularly donned as camouflage for the most egregious irrationalisms: pseudo-scientific IQ studies used to justify draconian immigration laws, Velokovskian "astronomy," the crackpot eugenics of the Nazis, and, in Russia, Lysenko's theories, which just about destroyed Russian agriculture for decades. The scientific bandwagon will always carry its load of circus clowns. In any case, at the very apex of futurism—the early 20th century—we see a concerted intellectual reaction against Enlightenment certitudes, emerging as the surrealism of Dali, the disillusion of lost generation writers like Hemingway, and the antiprogress cynicism of Charlie Chaplin's *Modern Times* and William Faulkner's Snopes novels.

The high modernism that appeared after World War II was based to a great degree on what has become known as fordism. This actually emerged much earlier; David Harvey (1990) dates it precisely to the year 1914 when Henry Ford introduced the five-dollar, eight-hour day at his Dearborn, Michigan, assembly plant. But fordism did not fully come into its own until the latter half of the 20th century. Most of these trends were long in developing, dating into the 19th century: the standardization and objectification of clock time (which always moves forward and is the same for everyone); the conception of space as something useable, malleable, and capable of domination; the notion of labor as a commodity to be bought and sold in a labor "market." These various trends coalesced, laying the groundwork for a very particular type of business-political-social structure. Industrial management was organized in a fixed hierarchical arrangement. Labor became deskilled, in the sense that assembly line work required the most minimal of actions, repeated over and over again. The worker had to be socialized into long, tedious hours of routinized movement, for which he would be rewarded with a middle-class income, unthinkable a generation earlier (and with which he could purchase a Ford of his own). Since anyone could do any of the required assembly line jobs, individual workers were as interchangeable as the bolts on the car (at first, the labor turnover at the Dearborn plant was 40% to 60% per month!). The sheer hugeness of finance and production and the need for planning years in advance required new forms of state intervention, protection, and control. The commodification of assembly line products gave rise to a commodification of mass culture. All this worked together as a single more or less unified system—one that could be exported anywhere that an assembly line could be constructed.

The radical transformation of this form of industrial modernism, with its rigid hierarchies and linearities, becomes evident in the United States in the 1960s when the number of workers in industrial production—that is, those who physically *make* something—dropped below 50% of the workforce. What was emerging, and is now fairly accomplished, was a service-and-information economy to replace the industrial economy. *Postfordism* is much more fluid than what preceded. While First World countries remain oligopolies (just a few major industries dominate production in particular areas, whether cars or breakfast cereals), the hierarchies are less rigid. The transnationalization of almost all major businesses has removed some of the centrality of the state as protector and regulator. According to Harvey, this era of "flexible accumulation"

rests on flexibility with respect to labor processes, labor markets, product, and patterns of consumption. It is characterized by the emergence of entirely new sectors of production, new ways of providing financial services, new markets, and above all, greatly intensified rates of commercial, technological, and organizational innovation. (Harvey 1990: 147)

Postfordism is one aspect of what has come to be known as the *postmodern condition*. Another aspect is the compression of both space and time. Jet travel and satellite communications have made the world increasingly smaller relative to the time it takes to converse or to travel over long distances. Whereas modernity was a period of homogenization of culture and consumer goods, the postmodern era promises a world of difference, of almost infinite access to goods for the most individual tastes. Three or four television channels have given way to literally hundreds. The world of the Internet, which is evolving with a rapidity almost inconceivable a decade ago, is one in which every individual can indulge his own taste in choosing interest groups, chat rooms, or mail-order sellers. With more and more work being done at the home computer, on the car phone, or on the laptop computer on the plane, the cubicle environment is giving way for many to a deterritorialized workplace, where the office clock no longer determines linear time. The fixed and predictable walls of our lives are dissolving, giving way to heterogeneity, fragmentation, and contingency. One of the most radical changes since, say, the 1950s is the degree to which leisure experience is commercially mediated to every conceivable individual taste. Malls are experiential palaces, not just shopping places; adventure tours can take the traveler anywhere, even to the top of Mount Everest; elaborate arcade games almost erase the distinction between virtual reality and reality itself; theme parks funnel the lust for excitement into zones of commercialized fantasy that are both exciting and safe. The rapidity of these changes seems to be increasing.

THIRD WORLD MODERNIZATION

What has just been described is largely, so far, a First World phenomenon. However, the subject matter of anthropology has traditionally been the Third World or indigenous groups, such as Native Americans, embedded within industrial societies. The *maquiladora* world of Alma is more akin to fordism or prefordism than to *postfordism*; because fully industrialized countries are exporting their manufacturing to the Third World, many "underdeveloped" countries are only now entering early industrialization, complete with all the accompanying ills of child labor, environmental devastation, long and dismal working conditions, and labor-management conflict. It should not be supposed that this is some general developmental stage, similar to United States or European stages of development, as was proposed by the modernization theorists of the 1950s and 1960s (Rostow 1960). Each country will experience industrialization uniquely, depending on its peculiar history and social structure. The point is that the postmodern condition of deterritorialization, receptivity to indiscriminate media inputs, and cultural hybridity applies mainly to middle and upper classes, which together comprise no more than 20% of the populations of the more impoverished Third World countries. While everyone experiences globalization to one degree or another, the postmodern condition described above is very differentially experienced, if at all, by many or most Third World peoples. This needs to be emphasized because, to a great degree, postmodern theory dominates the anthropological study of the Third World; when no differentiation is made between theory and empirical condition, it is up to the reader to keep the two distinct.

The stereotypical condition of modernity, or postmodernity, that has emerged largely from sociological studies may be summarized in such terms as space-time compression, consumerism, commodification, and individualization. Within anthropology, however, the concept of multiple modernities has taken hold. As anthropologists increasingly pay attention to the "subaltern voice"—the viewpoints of postcolonial peoples and the ways that modernization is subjectively experienced by the world's underclasses—it is evident that different peoples react to global inputs in very different ways. While everyone seems to have some concept of modernity, in the technological sense, if in no other, the ways that modernity is perceived, reacted to, and idealized are often quite unique. The standardized image of modernity provided by sociologists and economists is based on the Western experience.

Within anthropology, even the idea of multiple modernities has been challenged as the inappropriate application of a metanarrative (high-level theory or model) to local cultures (Englund and Leach 2000). This complaint is new only in its particulars. There has probably never been a student of anthropology who did not go into the field for the first time with a head full of wonderful classroom theories—structural-functionalism, evolutionism, cultural ecology, you name it—who did not quickly find that on-the-ground realities did not fit very well, if at all, into pre-established molds. The link between general theory and the minutiae of everyday living has always been complex, uncertain, and contested (some postmodernists solve the problem by repudiating general theory altogether). It should be no surprise that a field researcher specifically seeking modernity, of whatever shape, within a Fijian tribe or among Andean peasants, might be in for a frustrating time. The solution might be to view globalization and modernity not as models to be imposed in a cookie-cutter fashion, not even as a theories, but simply as *context*, and even then as merely one aspect—not necessarily the most significant one—of a holistic context that includes colonial history, ecological situation, cultural continuity, and class structure. What can no longer be ignored is that, for even the most remote of peoples, there are global inputs that form some part of the environment and that must be reckoned with.

GLOBALIZATION-REGIONALIZATION-LOCALIZATION

While any system will have some sort of internal logic—or theories would not be possible—this logic is almost never determinative. One way to understand the evolution or transformation from one system to another, such as a state-centered system to globalization, is as a shift in the type of choices people are likely to make. Some sets of alternatives become more likely, some less likely. I do not wish to get into the complex issue of the difference between cause and constraint here, except to say that I favor the latter. The billiard-ball causality favored by early environmental determinists does not take into account the wide range of behaviors possible within *any* human system. Except in relatively rare cases, such as land reform or war, changes come about through a shift in the probability distribution of certain activities. The establishment of a new factory will provide opportunities for labor that did not exist previously, but most people will continue in the occupations they had before. Lower-cost transportation will encourage many to travel, but most people will stay home most of the time.

What might be clumsily, but accurately, described as globalization-regionalization-localization (Table 2.1) should not be considered a dialectical system in the Marxian sense. These are not conflictual opposites

Table 2.1
The Local/Global Continuum

	Micro	Meso	Macro
Integration	Fragmentation	Mid-level integration	Unity
Economic	Marginalization of tribal and peasant economies. Increased labor migration and factory labor in Third World.	Regional common markets: NAFTA, European Community. At a lower level, the nation-state.	Global neoliberal capitalism promoted/enforced by World Bank, IMF, U.S. policy. Decentralized MNCs and financial flows.
Institutions	Local-level neighborhood, community, ethnic, feminist, environmental, and human rights organizations.	Regional political/economic/cultural organizations: OPEC, ASEAN, OAS.	United Nations, World Trade Organization, World Bank, IMF. NGOs: Amnesty International, Red Cross, Greenpeace.
Cultural, Ideological	Indigenization, diaspora communities, detribalization, ethnicity, post-peasantries, transnationalism.	Huntington's "civilizations." Transnational religious and ideological integration, such as Islamic fundamentalism.	Global consumerism. "Coca-Cola culture." Media: films, news, television. Democracy. Gender awareness.
Identity	Increased ethnicity, transnationalism, hybridity, nationalism.	Transnational-regional identities: Arab, Caribbean, Afro-American, Islamic.	Global awareness.
Political	Ethnic politics, nationalism. Diminishment of state-centric power leads to increased localization of politics. NGOs fill former state functions.	Democratization adapted to state political cultures, class systems. Arab/Islamic antidemocratic models. Organizations: NATO, ASEAN.	Spread of western democratic models. Global economic and political organizations take over many functions of the state.
Conflict	End of Cold War and collapse of USSR release nationalist/ethnic conflicts.	Huntington's "fault-line" wars. International intervention in local wars.	UN peace-keeping interventions. Diminishment in wars between states.
Theoretical	Postmodern focus on micro processes and repudiation of "metanarratives." Globalization is an illusion.	Globalization as a continuation of long-term processes; nothing new. Huntington's "civilization" theory.	Globalization today is different from anything before; ideology of neoliberal capitalism.

that will ultimately blend into some sort of synthesis; rather, the three gradations are simply different aspects of one system and thus form relatively permanent interrelationships. NAFTA, for example, both derives from and reinforces the processes of globalization. On the one hand, it is a defensive reaction against the laissez-faire trade of neoliberal capitalism and an obvious response to regional organizations elsewhere. On the other hand, it encourages numerous global processes, especially in Mexico where we see the transformation of women's labor, the transfer of technology and finance, and the internationalization of trade.

This said, there are some fairly obvious determinative aspects of the global-regional-local system. The most blatant are the structural adjustments required quite specifically of Third World countries by the IMF and World Bank and de facto by other lending institutions, trade organizations, and First World governments. While these structural adjustments are negotiated country by country and are not as rigidly ideological as they are often portrayed, they basically force all countries into a single model of development. The spread of technology, especially communications and computer technology, is also inevitable, a given of the global system. There is nothing inevitable about the effects at the local level, however. While neoliberal capitalism may be hegemonic (a term much overused) at the global scale, locally it works very differently in different social, cultural, and historical contexts. This book will give numerous examples of a wide variety of local-level responses to global processes—migration, gender-role transformations, nationalism, the emergence of new or revitalized ethnicity, revolution, riots, the assumption of transnational and even global identities, and religious revivalism. There is no such thing as a passive response to globalization. People protest, adapt, invent, accommodate, assimilate, make alliances, whatever. Specific responses will be constrained—not determined!—by the global system, but only in conjunction with local history, culture, the physical and social environment, leadership, and individual decision making.

This is why anthropology is so important to the study of globalization. Just as one cannot predict who, individually, will be killed in Memorial Day auto accidents based on yearly accident statistics, so it is not possible from the higher level to predict downward, except within very general parameters. To understand globalization, we must study it at the level of real people who imagine new lives, make plans, travel, form networks, assume identities, and socialize their children. Global ethnography is not a contradiction in terms; it is the only way to understand.

Against Futurism

Despite a tendency on the part of globalization theorists to add layer upon layer of interpretation, a certain amount of theoretical humbleness may be called for. One way to think about globalization is to attempt to prophesy the future. What will the world look like in the first decades of the 22nd century? I would suggest that life will be so profoundly different than anything we can even contemplate that such prediction is absurd. Had we lived in 1900 and predicted a century in the future based on then-present trends, we might have—if we were optimistic—looked forward to progress through industrialization. Trains had crossed the United States since 1869 and there were incipient automobiles, suggesting a revolution in transportation. Electricity was common in some cities, and movies, though a mere curiosity, had already been invented. Industry was breaking down farm culture and stimulating urbanization. Thus, much might have been predictable. What would have been *impossible* to predict based on these trends? Just about everything of significance: two world wars, atomic power, the collapse of the colonial system, the emergence and decline of Russia as a superpower, the Cold War, the United Nations and the World Bank, routine jet travel, space exploration, the Third World debt crisis, environmental devastation and the rise of a global environmental movement, the emergence of China as a world power, organ transplants, the discovery of the structure of DNA (with all that that might signify), satellite communications, the rise and collapse of communism, global warming, the computer and the Internet and much more. Today, change—technological, cultural, political, economic—is occurring faster than it ever did in the 20th century.

One accurate prediction is possible, however: Whatever we think about globalization today will turn out in the long run to be short-sighted and perhaps (or even probably) grossly wrong.

With this disclaimer in view, it is incumbent on the present generation to try to understand the structure and forces that are going on *now*, and this will require some radical changes—already well along—in the way that anthropology does business.

Chapter 3

The Anthropology of Globalization

Globalization . . . is not entirely new and does not necessarily demand a
reinvention of anthropology.
Priscilla Stone, Angelique Haugerud, and Peter Little[1]

It takes only the merest acquaintance with the facts of the modern world
to note that it is now an interactive system in a sense that is strikingly new.
Arjun Appadurai[2]

As we have seen, the present phase of globalization embodies a convergence
of a number of separate but interrelated factors: postfordism, innovations in
technology—especially those related to communications and travel—neoliberal economic ideology, the debt crisis and the resulting power of the
World Bank and IMF to impose structural adjustments on Third World countries, and the collapse of the Soviet Union, which left capitalism virtually unchallenged. Similarly, the emerging anthropology of globalization
represents a convergence of a number of interlinked changes in the anthropologist's scholarship, especially in subject matter, theory, the conceptualization of culture, and the ways that data are collected and analyzed.

Globalization represents a significant break with anthropology as traditionally practiced, partially because the primary empirical technique of participant observation fieldwork tended to bring the bounded community to
front and center. The focus of anthropology has inevitably been the "local,"
pretty much defined as the amount of territory one anthropologist could cover

in some depth in a year or two. There have been significant exceptions. Neo-evolutionary theory and cross-cultural statistical analyses via the Human Relations Area Files were very broad in their sweep, but even these tended to maintain the band, tribe, community, and lineage as the basic units of analysis. Edmund Leach's seminal *Political Systems of Highland Burma* (1954) compared a number of overlapping systems in a much larger area than was usually studied at the time. Eric Wolf's *Europe and the People Without History* (1982) and Peter Worsley's *The Three Worlds* (1984) were revolutionary in assuming a truly global perspective, but both also remain anomalies within anthropology since they were written at a time when such grand theorizing was already being challenged. Even today, globalization studies seldom, if ever, assume Wolf's or Worsley's global viewpoint, but tend, rather, to focus on the effects of globalization on specific groups or within particular subject areas, such as identity or development. A major difference from the past is in the definition of the groups studied. Whereas traditional anthropology looked at bounded cultures and communities, globalization theorists are more likely to be interested in transnationals, diasporas, nations that are scattered in many countries, and deterritorialized ethnicities. There is an increasing self-consciousness of the degree to which the community and the local were artifacts of the participant observation method.

This does not mean that such fieldwork and narrowly circumscribed studies are going to be washed away in a tidal surge of globalization. As a glance through any professional journal, such as the *American Anthropologist* or *Current Anthropology*, will show, focused studies on particular groups is still the norm and will undoubtedly remain so. Globalization is not about to become the dominant paradigm of cultural anthropology, although it seems to be emerging as an important subdiscipline. The true importance of the globalization perspective is not that it is some rapacious new orientation that is going to gobble up the rest of anthropology, but rather that it provides an alternative way of understanding and opens the field to subjects previously ignored. Any study can be globalized, but most probably should not be, at least to the extent that globalization becomes the heart of the analysis. Globalization is always there, however, as a layer of contextualization that can add depth to even the most tightly focused ethnography.

"At least as long as I have been in it," writes Swedish anthropologist Ulf Hannerz (1996: 4), "Anthropology has been in the process of being 'rethought,' 'reinvented,' 'recaptured.'" The not-too-arbitrary chart of Anthropological Periods (Table 3.1) suggests some of the more significant reinventions. Like all such classifications, this chart needs to be taken with a rather large grain of salt; the periods overlap considerably, are often prefigured long before they actually kick in, and continue for decades after they have lost their centrality.

Table 3.1
Anthropological Periods

	Time	Focus of Interest	Dominant Paradigms	Major Theorists
Formative	Late 19th century	Savage, barbarian, civilization	Cultural evolution	Tylor, Frazer, Morgan
Classic	1900–1945	Primitives: bands, tribes, chiefdoms	Historical particularism, structural functionalism	Boas, Malinowski, Radcliffe-Brown
Modern	1945–1980	Peasants, urban shantytowns, underdeveloped societies	Modernization theory; later, dependency and world systems theories	Wolf, Worsley, Harris
Transitional	1980–1990	Anthropology itself	Interpretive anthropology, critical anthropology, postmodernism, poststructuralism	Geertz, Clifford and Marcus, Jameson, Foucault
Global	1990–	Transnationals, diasporas, nations, ethnicities	Vocabulary and selected assumptions of postmodernism	Appadurai, Hannerz, Friedman, Kearney

Source: Roughly based on Kearney 1996: 23–41.

Above all, two things need to be kept in mind. First, unlike the situation in the natural sciences where a single paradigm dominates any given period (Kuhn 1970), in anthropology there will be several paradigms at the same time (a paradigm is a broad perspective and set of assumptions within which multiple theories can exist). Second, while journal publications require some sort of theoretical elaboration, most anthropologists would hardly be considered ideologues of any particular viewpoint; as Stanley Barrett (1999: 276) observes, the standard within the field is a sort of "no-name anthropology" in which theory is secondary to data collection and to tracing correlations and causes.

In any case, I found Kearney's (1996: 23–41) broad, pseudo-archeological classification of formative, classic, modern, and global to be heuristically useful. Kearney dates the global from the "second Cold War," starting with U.S. involvement in Vietnam. While he is correct in emphasizing the importance of the Cold War to anthropological interests and funding, I believe that the more defining character of this period for anthropologists is the collapse of the colonial system and the emergence of a Third World of postcolonial states (Kearney is a Latin Americanist, and there colonialism has been a dead issue for over a century). I have added a Transitional period, which seems to me, for good or ill, to be one of the most important periods in anthropological history. It was—and continues to be—a period of self-criticism characterized by fierce battles about the nature of anthropological representation. In the scope and intensity of its rejectionism, this period echoes the Boasian revolution against the 19th century evolutionists and the post-World War II reaction by process-oriented theorists against a spatially bounded, synchronic structural-functionalism. Much of the current globalization literature is a direct result of this radical rethinking, although, as we shall see, in practice the results have been fairly moderate.

YES, VIRGINIA, THERE *IS* AN ANTHROPOLOGY OF GLOBALIZATION

Two earlier global paradigms were extremely influential in anthropology: *dependency theory*, which postulated that Third World "underdevelopment" was not a primal condition but rather the result of the historically evolving structure of capitalism, and *world system theory*,[3] which viewed nations in relation to their placement within a global division of labor between core, periphery, and semiperiphery (see Chapter 4). A major reason that these orientations never really gained a central prominence in anthropology was that the viewpoints were postulated at such an altitude that it was difficult for the ethnographer to apply them to the on-the-ground realities experienced in the field. If dependency theory and world system theory were too stratospheric for anthropological use, then what is the anthropologist to make of globalization, which is even more comprehensive in scope than either of its predecessors?

Paradoxically, perhaps, many anthropologists have felt quite at home with globalization. First, globalization emphatically does not denote top-down analysis. If, as I argued in the previous chapter, globalization, regionalization, and localization comprise a single, unified system, then it is as valid to look at that system from the local perspective as from the higher one. This is done by examining ways that global forces impinge on the local communities or even households and individuals, by showing how the individuals and groups react defensively or adaptively to global threats, and by showing how people use and, within the local setting, even alter global forces. With the emergence of identity as a major focus of study for anthropologists, globalization reaches down even to the psychosocial level of analysis. Second, while globalization may be conceived as a theory, it is not necessarily so, and therefore need not determine the theoretical perspective. Globalization can merely mean a set of data about market forces, transnational flows of people, distribution of foreign aid, commodity chains, and so forth. Such information may be invaluable, if not essential, to contextualizing what is happening with individuals and groups. Third, unlike modernization theory, dependency theory, and world systems theory, culture is a key component of globalization discourse; far from being excluded, the anthropological voice is badly needed. Fourth, not only anthropologists but also sociologists, political scientists, and some economists have seen the primary problem posed by globalization to be how to connect the macro to the micro and vice versa. This challenge offers an interdisciplinary bridge that connects anthropology with other academic disciplines.

Finally, globalization might be conceived not as a radical departure for anthropology, but as a natural next step. Historically, anthropology has wavered between the high-level analysis of, say, diffusionism and evolutionism, and the intense specificity of community-focused ethnography. The virulent repudiation of structural-functionalism, with its bounded communities and ahistorical approach, opened the way for theories emphasizing process, fluidity, agency, and overlapping and multidimensional networks. For anthropology, globalization is not the radical disjuncture claimed by some postmodernists, but rather the addition of another level of analysis, a recognition that people and the world they live in are just a bit more complex than we have credited.

THE SUBJECTS OF A GLOBALIZED ANTHROPOLOGY

In terms of subject matter, globalization is already normative in anthropology, as the briefest perusal of the bibliography of this book will reveal, but so far the term does not designate any overarching consolidation or coherence. Almost any study can incorporate a bit of global analysis, at least in the sense that no culture or community is completely isolated from transnational influences and world capitalism. However, if we seek out those areas of anthropology where there has emerged a degree of self-conscious unity, that is, where a group of scholars tends to recognize common themes and a common vocabulary and to build upon each other's work, then only a limited number of subject areas really fit. The fields of development (or antidevelopment) and identity cover both local and transnational effects of globalization. Beyond these, we can, without too much harm, classify other fields under two broad categories: those subjects dealing with transnational migration and those dealing with globalization's effects on people who stay within the boundaries of their own countries. Extensive work has already been accomplished on diasporas, refugee populations, and transnational migrants. The global-local is represented by studies of tribal communities, peasants, and those who, like Alma, work in global factories of the Third World.

What I have just described is the structure of this book. In establishing this classification, I have been acutely aware of the violence done to reality. If there is a single major theme to emerge from globalization studies so far, it is that everything overlaps, flows into, and blends with everything else. Probably the most used concepts in the field are the multiple variations on *fluidity* and *hybridity.* It is impossible to discuss peasants, for example, without also discussing identity, migration, gender, and development. What aids the artificial separation of these into chapters is that each favors only one or two theoretical orientations.

The anthropology of development. Anthropology recognizes two broad definitions of development. The first is similar to the way that other social science disciplines, such as economics and political science, conceive the term, that is, as industrialization, modern communications, and growth of gross national product. The term has both a descriptive and prescriptive sense; descriptively, it means almost the same as modernization, a broad process that may be planned or fortuitous and may have negative as well as positive effects. In the more prescriptive sense, it suggests "progress," such as better nutrition and health, perhaps the emergence of democratic institutions, and some degree of income equality. Few anthropologists have adopted this idealistic meaning; to the contrary, most ethnographies that deal with the issue have demonstrated how development tends to destroy indigenous cultures, disrupt communities, and marginalize individuals. Since these studies have little in the way of a theoretical center, this type of anthropology of development has not been a significant theoretical influence in anthropology. A second form of development anthropology is simply applied anthropology, that is, anthropologists working with development agencies to induce planned change at the community level. While this form of professional anthropology has also been undertheorized, in the 1990s it came under the influence of the poststructuralist ideas of French philosopher Michel Foucault. Both field-workers and academic critics of development employed Foucault's theories of knowledge and power to reveal deep-rooted problems within the very "discourse" of development leading, in some cases, to a virulent repudiation of development altogether.

Identity. Surprisingly, perhaps, identity was not a focused concern of earlier anthropology. Looking back to Ruth Benedict's *Patterns of Culture* (1989 [1934]), which came out of the Culture and Personality school, people are seen as locked within the identity of the group. A person was Hopi, Kwakiutl, or Dobu, and that was that. National character studies essentialized identity on a much larger scale. For the British structural-functionalist, who emphasized the boundedness of cultures, questions of Nuer or Andaman Islander identity would have been met with incomprehension. Those days are long past. Boundaries were never as solid as once believed, and globalization has weakened or dissolved many boundaries that did exist. The question that we started with—Who is Alma?—is at the heart of the study of globalization. In seeking the answers to this question, anthropologists have had to employ words like hybrid, Creole, transnational, ethnic, and postpeasant. Gender roles are also being radically transformed. Globalization has stimulated an explosion of nationalisms demanding their own sovereignty and challenging the whole idea of the nation-state. As the subjects of anthropology move back and forth among different life-worlds, take on different roles in different places, and absorb new ways of thinking and imagining through the mass media, identities that might once have appeared simple, obvious, and coherent are now seen to be enormously complex.

Migration. Cross-border migration has many faces. It is the Guatemalan woman who hires a *coyote* to take her across the border into Texas where she can join distant relatives in a mostly Guatemalan exile community in El Paso. It is the wealthy Palestinian businessman who routinely flies to New York from his home in Jordan, where he was born. It is the Rwandan Hutu refugee living on the edge of starvation in a camp in Burundi, terrified to return home as long as Tutsis hold power. It is the thoroughly Americanized woman from Calcutta getting her graduate degree in biology at Princeton while studying for her naturalization test. It is the Egyptian laborer working in Kuwait and sending his wages back to his family in Alexandria.

As with the study of identity, the anthropological focus on migration is relatively recent. Of course migration itself reaches back to the origins of humankind in Africa and its spread throughout the world. Within historical times, there have been migrations of vaster scale and with greater structural impact than anything going on today. However, modern high-tech transportation coupled with a truly global labor market have brought about a routinization of transnational migration that has no real equivalent in the past. A Haitian immigrant to New York no longer need assimilate into some sort of dominant white-Anglo-Saxon-Protestant culture when she can regularly return to Haiti at little cost and can maintain contacts with family by phone and e-mail as though they were across town. Pakistanis work in the Arab countries of the Middle East on such a routine basis that such trips are closer to commuting than to migrating. Some high-emigrant states are beginning to conceive of themselves as deterritorialized, encouraging either permanent or circular migration because of a dependence on remittances. Diasporas form vast multicountry networks held together by the common dream of a lost homeland.

Global-local. Global forces and structures impinge on societies and communities in different ways, depending on a multitude of factors: local histories, religions, social structures, local leadership, and the like. There are myriad different ways that people can respond to the same global input. Thus, analysis from the global level to the local level cannot be predictive except within parameters so broad as to be either amorphous or obvious. As a result, far from globalization making local-level, bottom-up studies anachronistic, it makes such studies essential. Although some anthropologists call for a dethronement of participant observation fieldwork, what really may be needed in some cases is for such fieldwork to be extended to more than one site and to be supplemented with other kinds of inquiry, such as archival research or interviews with official development agents. The very concept of local has become ambiguous; for a traveling Hong Kong executive with a transnational corporation, the "local" may be offices and hotels in many different cities. Networks of agricultural workers that extend from central Mexico to northern California create a shifting and transitory concept of local. Even the most stay-at-home family will be inundated with images and ideas via television and radio, expanding the imaginative local outward indefinitely.

Work is transformed by global processes as women who formerly labored in the household and subsistence fields are increasingly preferred by Third World factory managers. Two of the main subjects of traditional anthropological study, tribal peoples and peasants, are undergoing radical changes. The very term "tribal" is itself under fire because of its association with primitivism and its connotations of boundedness and isolation. Some natives in the Amazon jungle are now using video cameras and the World Wide Web politically to publicize their conflicts with the Brazilian government and are aligning themselves with international human rights organizations. Peasants have become highly mobile and work at so many different jobs outside of agriculture that it has been suggested that the term be replaced with postpeasant.

These subjects, which will be examined in some detail in this book, hardly exhaust the topics that anthropologists have studied in relation to globalization. Gender is the most crucial subject area that lacks its own chapter, but I found that consideration of this topic is so all-pervasive that I have tried to integrate it into several chapters. Some other subjects that have caught the eye of the anthropologists of globalization are the spread of AIDS, the international sale of body parts for transplant, children conscripted in war, global cities, and transnational religious movements. While this book is necessarily limited in scope, I hope to at least point a direction toward some of the possibilities.

ANTHROPOLOGICAL THEORY AND GLOBALIZATION

> [A] new, all-embracing problematic may be crystallizing around global-ization, articulated with capitalism, and informed by the tenets of postmodernism rather than the Enlightenment.
>
> Stanley Barrett[4]

The theoretical language and basic assumptions of most anthropological globalization studies are what I would term pragmatic-postmodern. This rather stark statement is meant to be less controversial than it may appear. Probably very few theorists of globalization would describe themselves as postmodern, nor would they subscribe to the extreme antiscientific, cognitive-constructivist notions associated with the more radical statements of this position. A progression has occurred within anthropology in the direction of a mellowing of extreme positions and a synthesizing of multiple once-separate philosophies.

What I am here calling postmodernism—for want of a better word and because this term has always been sufficiently vague to include a range of disparate ideas—is a blending of four different trends: interpretive anthropology, critical anthropology, poststructuralism, and postmodernism proper (Table 3.2).

What these have in common is their rejection of ideas associated with the Enlightenment and positivism. Thus, as a group, they are sometimes referred to as postpositivist, a term that works fine in philosophy but which I reject—for reasons to be addressed in a moment—as all but meaningless for anthropology. Each of these theoretical positions is undergirded by layer upon layer of philosophy. Since most anthropologists are not philosophers, there has been a tendency to skim off the *usable* ideas. Thus, we regularly find the type of "thick description" associated with Clifford Geertz (1973), but not Geertz's idea that an ethnography should be judged as a literary work; indeed, most seem convinced that their interpretations reflect some degree of objective reality. The postmodern taboo against grand theory, metanarratives and essentializing often goes hand in hand with pronouncements so generalized and universalized as to make the most traditional Marxist blush. An antiscience bias seems to exist side by side with some outstanding empirical field research. Thus, the postmodernism that has emerged is a largely pragmatic one: If it works, use it; if it does not, ignore it.

Table 3.2
"Postmodernism" in Anthropology as a Convergence of Four Theoretical Trends

	Defining Attributes	Key Terms	Major Work
Interpretive Anthropology	• Method of "thick description" requires intensive empirical fieldwork; rejects possibility of scientific objectivity; all interpretation is situated • Ethnography as literary text • Analyzes symbolic systems to understand cultures as experienced • Seeks to express point of view of "others" rather than of researcher	Thick description Text Paradigm (cultural) Systems of meaning	Geertz, *The Interpretation of Cultures*, especially, "'Deep Play': Notes on a Balinese Cockfight"
Critical Anthropology	• Anthropological representations reveal more about ethnographer than people studied • Lack of reflexivity leads to false sense of objectivity • Anthropology situated in colonialism, postcolonialism	Reflexivity Crisis of representation Situated knowledge	Clifford and Marcus, *Writing Culture: The Poetics and Politics of Ethnography*
Postmodernism	• Contrasts Enlightenment modernism (progress through rationalism, technology, science) to postmodernity • Against all "grand theory" and "metanarratives" including science, which has become a privileged narrative • Subjectivity, impressionism emphasized over false objectivity • Rejects distinction of high and low culture • "Reality" is socially constructed; knowledge is relative	Hermeneutics Deconstruction Fragmentation Discontinuity Hybridity	Jameson, *Postmodernism, or, the Cultural Logic of Late Capitalism*
Poststructuralism	• Studies discourse of historical time periods and institutions • Focus on epistemology and language • Rejects Lévi-Strauss' structuralism's universal claims • Emphasis on power as inherent in all discourse	Discourse Power/knowledge Gaze	Escobar, *Encountering Development*

Only a few years ago, the battle between the proponents of emics and etics, idealism and materialism, modern and postmodern seemed intractable. The two sides could not have been farther apart. The very basis of postmodernism was a total distrust of scientific objectivism; the very basis of the anthropology-as-science crowd was an equally passionate distrust of intuition. Now, like boxers who have made it to the fifteenth round but are too tired to do much more than hang on to each other and grunt, the two opposing sides in this once epic fight have been reduced to occasional painless jabs. Postmodernism is only winning on points; some of the best globalization studies I have come across, especially in economic anthropology, are in the traditional scientific mode (e.g., Phillips, ed. 1998; Haugerud, Stone, and Little, eds., 2000). By and large, however, the social-scientific point of view—the forming of testable and operational hypotheses, the collection of quantitative data, and the employment of statistical analysis —is underrepresented in globalization studies. Because most globalization studies are so imbued with either conscious or unconscious postmodern assumptions, it is essential to take a closer look at the theories underlying these assumptions.

Can you use the sci. meth. for social science

Postmodernism

While a certain empirical postmodern *condition*—by whatever term one wants to use—seems widely conceded, postmodernism as *theory* is more controversial and has led to some acrimonious conflicts. The Department of Anthropology at Stanford University split into separate departments over this issue, and it stimulated considerable debate over the editorship of the *American Anthropologists*, the primary journal of the American Anthropological Association.[5] Marvin Harris (1999a: 13), a major theoretician of the old school, jokes that whereas his standard text *The Rise of Anthropological Theory* was referred to by two generations of students as RAT, perhaps a new volume would be in order, to be called FAT—*The Fall of Anthropological Theory*. Postmodernists, on the other hand, dismiss Harris's materialist perspective as an outmoded remnant of a well-discarded Enlightenment scientism. Postmodernism (or "pomo" as its critics dismissively call it) had become a sufficiently pejorative term by the mid-1990s (just as positivist was a term of dismissal from the postmodern side) that many who had originally embraced the position were now calling themselves poststructuralists or critical theorists or were abandoning cultural anthropology for cultural studies or for science and technology studies.

To what extent was postmodernism in anthropology designed to account for the postmodern *condition*, so far as it exists in the Third World? The answer is—not much. Postmodernism started as a school of architecture and spread as an artistic and literary response to postindustrial society, that is, the society of the First World. The concept of postfordism, as both an economic and a sociopolitical phenomenon, is most applicable to the wealthier countries that have passed through the Second Industrial Revolution, that now have only a small (often very small) percentage of their populations working in agriculture and manufacturing, and that have shifted from the processing of materials to the processing of information: education, entertainment, law, advertising, computer software development, and so on. This does not apply to much of the Third World, which is still relatively pre- or nonindustrial; agriculture, mining, imported manufactured goods, and street-vendor "commerce" in the informal sector may dominate the economy. Such countries are most definitely not some earlier version of the United States. Each country or region or even community has its own dynamics, which are a unique combination of the traditional, the national, and the global. Although postmodernism may critique Western domination, and its relativistic philosophy has been amenable to many Third World scholars, it was *not* developed to deal with some postmodern condition in the Third World. As a result, there is no particular reason to privilege postmodern theories. On the other hand, many of the subdisciplines that have emerged to deal with the Third World, such as identity studies and the discourse analysis of development, derive from some aspect of postmodern theory and would view, for example, Alma's mobility and lack of cultural rootedness as part of the fragmentation of the postmodern condition.

Defining Postmodernism

Probably no two writers agree on the defining characteristics of postmodernism. Given the numerous influences, ranging from literary theory to linguistics to studies of the practice of science, any attempt to find *the* underlying unifying element that defines postmodernism is doomed to elicit many cries of "But that doesn't apply to me!" For Marvin Harris (1999b: 153), "the most prominent and important" aspect of postmodernism "is the disparagement of Western science and technology." For others, the main focus is the rejection of grand theory, metanarratives, essentialism (the attribution of a priori or universal traits, such as a common human nature), and of any description of objective reality that fails to take into account the way that reality is cognitively or socially constructed. Such ideas have led to accusations that postmodernism implies a degree of relativity that renders any kind of authoritative statement impossible. It should be noted, however, that the question of relativity is a controversial one even *within* postmodernism.[6]

I would suggest that what is common to postmodernist anthropology is, first, its attention to the cognitive and the epistemological, and second, its rejectionism, both of which have many precursors in the history of anthropology. Whether or not postmodernists accept that there is a real world separate from our interpretations, they emphasize that the world is cognitively constructed differently by different peoples at different times. Culture may be interpreted as a process of negotiating meaning. This calls into question any claims of objectivity, even within the physical sciences. Indeed, modern science is only one type of human rationality, though one that has been privileged over other forms through the hegemonic globalization of Western technology, culture, and economy. Equally legitimate traditional knowledges have been marginalized or obliterated in the process. Within anthropology, all classic ethnographies that claim objectivity may be reassessed as literary texts that might tell us more about the author and his culture than about the people he or she was studying.

On the one hand, language is inadequate to express reality, and, on the other hand, it is through language that we create reality. Thus the dominant discourse (in its broadest sense, the limits to thinking and acting within a given historical period) must be deconstructed in order to reveal inherent presuppositions and assumptions. Power is suffused through all discourses and institutions, including science, especially the social sciences. In the very process of objectifying, classifying, and studying other cultures, we are assuming a position of power over them. Ethnologists must be acutely aware of this power. The written ethnography needs to make clear the always-partial, always-distorted position of the field-worker and provide the voice of the people being studied. If reality is culturally constructed, then truth (always with a small "t") is specific to particular historical periods and particular cultures. This means that grand theories that attempt to generalize to all humankind or to characterize some global system or structure must be soundly repudiated. History, as formulated within the Western tradition, *imposes* order on the past to make sense of it. Looked at from this perspective, both history and the contemporary world appear fragmentary and discontinuous. *Is this productive - how is this applied and has does this contribute to society?*

A few postmodernists have pushed relativism to virtual nihilism and have been accused of rendering any moral stance or any change for the better impossible. On the other hand, if objectivity is unattainable, then the scientists' clear distinction between the descriptive and prescriptive breaks down. Not only is morality not excluded from investigation, it *should* be considered. The way is open to legitimize what might be called agenda-driven theory, that is, theory in which a conscious goal is to increase the self-esteem of a certain group, to raise public consciousness, or to improve the welfare of people. This would apply to aspects of feminist studies, Afro-centrist studies, and to the entire antidevelopment movement. Proponents of such morality-driven research would claim, first, that *all* theory is agenda-driven, even if it is not acknowledged as such; second, that conscious recognition of the moral component of research might obviate the harmful effects of, say, racist IQ claims; and, third, that such theories have pointed research in productive and revealing directions that might otherwise have been overlooked.

Postmodern Rejectionism

In some ways, it is easier to describe postmodernism by what it rejects than what it endorses. Arguably, just about all progress in anthropology has come through data collection; right from the beginning, theory has often tended to be rejectionist rather than cumulative, that is, instead of a new theory building upon or elaborating a previous theory, each new theory jettisons the previous one, in what might be called the throwing-out-the-baby-with-the-bathwater syndrome, or what others have referred to as "slash-and-burn anthropology" and "intellectual deforestation."[7] Franz Boas's rejection of 19th century cultural evolutionism was absolute; he wanted no part of Tylor's and Morgan's unilineal stages (their metanarratives, to use contemporary terminology). In contrast to England and France, where academic department chairs at prestigious universities would establish paradigms for the entire discipline, within the United States, the norm has been simultaneous multiple theoretical enclaves, often with relatively little dialogue among them. A nonlinear neo-evolutionism based on ecological theory might exist side by side with group-personality studies or with ethnoscience's attempt to examine linguistic categories as the crucial keys to culture. If any perspective can be said to have dominated American anthropology after 1900, it would be structural-functionalism, imported from England, which held sway for two decades after the 1940s. The rejection of structural-functionalism was as vehement and total as Boas's repudiation of cultural evolutionism. To replace it, emphasis shifted from static, closed community structures to individual agency, process, change, and interaction within the larger nation-state. A few minor theoretical movements—general systems theory, action theory, game theory—sputtered along for a few years before dying out and leaving little residue. Lévi-Strauss's structuralism seemed exciting for a time, but today seems as archaic as last year's rock star; indeed, it has been most fervently repudiated by the poststructuralists who are Lévi-Strauss's direct heirs but who object to his essentialist claim to have discovered basic organizing principles of the human mind.

Postmodernism, at least in its stronger versions, picks up on this traditional rejectionist tendency within anthropology. It is unique mainly in the *degree* of its rejectionism. What does postmodernism reject? Specifically, it rejects all grand theory (cultural materialism, structuralism, structural-functionalism, materialist versions of Marxism), ecological and biological explanations of human behavior, all claims to objectivity in representing other cultures, hypothesis testing and other applications of the scientific method, and all essentialisms (including the attempt to find universals of human nature or of gender behavior, whether based in biology or cross-cultural regularities). Difference and complexity are favored against unifying or simplifying theories. This is a hefty load to leave by the wayside.

The more general villains of the postmodern drama are the Enlightenment and positivism. The Enlightenment envisaged progress toward a better world as emerging from the applications of reason, science, and technology. Positivism ostensibly embraces a correspondence theory of reality; that is, there is something truly out there, separate from ourselves and our perceptions, that we can describe, at least in rough approximation, through the neutral and objective methods of science. The laws of nature can be mathematically formulated.

While Enlightenment values and positivist philosophy really did and do exist, the problem with choosing these as the primary malefactors for anthropology is that, of all the disciplines, anthropology never really bought in to either in any big way. Twentieth-century anthropologists have been deeply suspicious of the concept of progress. Even neo-evolutionists have preferred terms like complexity, nucleation, or intensification—never progress. If anything, there has been a tendency to idealize traditional societies, to see the hunting-gathering Bushmen, for example, as the first leisure society or to proclaim the ecological superiority of subsistence horticulture over intensive agriculture. What freshman anthropology student has not been assigned "Steel Axes for Stone-Age Australians" (Sharp 1952), which demonstrates how the introduction of even the slightest new technology can be disruptive to happy primitive people.

Positivism has fared no better than the Enlightenment in cultural anthropology, at least outside of how-to methodology books. Anthropology's guiding paradigm, if it can be said to have one at all, is cultural *relativism*. Granted, there have been a few attempts to establish science-like Laws, but they were never taken seriously for very long. While hypothesis-testing has been one tool of fieldwork, much if not most ethnography has always been descriptive or interpretive. In other words, to attack Enlightenment progressivism and positivist objectivism as the dominant paradigms of anthropology is to set up a straw man whose primary function is to be knocked down. As Herbert Lewis (1999: 726) observes, the postmodernists had to "invent something that never existed in order to dominate it. Their version of anthropology—their invented anthropology—has served to 'otherize' and marginalize anthropologists and anthropological knowledge."

Given this brief history of anthropological rejectionism, one might wonder if theory is really an accurate term for ideas that can be dropped like so much excess baggage along the side of the road. Perhaps something like "intellectual fad" would more fit the reality. The satire "What's Hot, What's Not" (Table 3.3), which was originally published in *Anthropology News* in 1999, offers a sardonic but serious look at the faddish and rejectionist nature of contemporary anthropology.[8] While it is true, as the table shows, that the postmodern vocabulary is "in" today, perhaps more so in globalization studies than some other fields of research, as we shall see, the widespread acceptance of this vocabulary does not denote a similar acceptance, nor even knowledge, of all of the theory that underlies it.

Is Postmodernism Really All That Post or Modern?

The question remains: Why has such a large part of anthropology welcomed postmodernism with more enthusiasm than has any other social science? One answer might lie, paradoxically, in that, despite postmodernism's rejectionism, most of its tenets have a long history within anthropology. The postmodern emphasis on difference, rather than cross-cultural commonalties, finds its precursor in Boas's historical particularism, and this is reinforced by the intensity of the fieldwork experience, which is often hard to reconcile with universalistic theories. Ruth Benedict's classic *Patterns of Culture*, once vilified as an example of poor scholarship and pseudoscientific stereotyping, anticipates postmodernism's emphasis on the cultural construction of reality. As noted above, cultural relativism, in its sense of trying to experience the world through the eyes of others, has been a mainstay of anthropology since the early 20th century. The very idea of culture, while now under question, is not that different, at least in some of its myriad permutations, from Foucault's concept of discourse or Bourdieu's notion of habitus.[9] Whatever poststructuralists may think of Lévi-Strauss, he did bring epistemology—a concern usually relegated to philosophers—to the forefront of anthropology. Also, Lévi-Strauss rejected the Popperian claim that verification had to be empirical; he insisted that his work be judged by whether his model fit the evidence better than alternative models.[10] This challenged empirical hypothesis testing as

Table 3.3

What's Hot, What's Not in Anthropology

Ever since Franz Boas's denunciation of 19th century evolutionism, it has become traditional for each succeeding anthropological theory to totally repudiate the previous theory, leaving no residue to contaminate the new, more enlightened viewpoint. Among the theories that have been utterly surpassed are diffusionism, cultural evolutionism and neo-evolutionism (routinely, several times), group personality studies, and structural functionalism. Postmodernism carries on this great tradition. The following "What's Hot/What's Not" chart may help neophyte anthropologists avoid some damning anchronisms.

Hot	Not
Postmodern discourse	The Enlightenment[i]
Science and Technology Studies	Science and technology
Micronarrative	Metanarrative, grand theory
Discourse[ii]	Talk, speech, paradigm, theory, culture, society, language, dialogue, argot, in-group jargon, communication, episteme, historical period, conversation, chit-chat, chew the rag, shoot the breeze
Foucault, Derrida, Baudrillard	Harris, Turner, Geertz
Fragmentation, discontinuity	Cause and effect
Gender	Women
Deconstruction	Analysis
Situated knowledge	Archimedean point of view[iii]
Hybridity	Biculturalism
Post-development discourse	Development[iv]
Hermeneutics	Analysis
Subjectivities	Reality
Alan Sokal	Hitler, the Anti-Christ
Reflexivity	Thought
Heisenburg Principle	Newtonian physics
Bishop Berkeley	Samuel Johnson
Knowledge claims	Knowledge
Power/knowledge	Power, knowledge
Crisis of representation	Representation
Self-reflexive micro-discourse on the impossibility of writing culture from an Archimedean viewpoint	Ethnography

Notes:

[i] It would be difficult to find an anthropologist after Morgan who bought into anything remotely resembling the Enlightenment ideal of progress through rationalism and technology. Nevertheless, it is absolutely essential to begin any argument with a repudiation of Enlightenment thinking.

[ii] All new paradigms reqiure one all-purpose word. "Discourse" replaces "function" and "adaptation."

[iii] This is a point of view from which the object can be seen in its totality. No sane person, with the possible exception of Archimedes, ever espoused such a thing, but along with the Enlightenment and positivism this perspective is sufficiently erroneous that it must be repudiated at every opportunity.

[iv] Development is dead. The World Bank is concerned.

Source: Originally published in *Anthropology News* (1999). Reproduced by permission of the American Anthropological Association.

the primary means of verification. Indeed, there is little in postmodernism that does not find some antecedent in earlier anthropology.

The Pluses and Minuses of Postmodernism

The values of postmodernism, especially for studies of globalization, lie in its critique of the unwarranted reality claims of traditional ethnographies, in making anthropologists aware of the processes by which cultures negotiate reality, in revealing how cultures once thought of as static or primal are constantly in a state of self-creation, in exposing the subtleties of power as it is suffused through language and institutions, and in steering anthropology in directions of research that we might otherwise have missed, such as the importance of identity construction in understanding ethnicity and nationalism. Postmodernism demands that the subaltern be given a voice, that we try to understand the world through the eyes of our subjects. It points out the arbitrariness of our classification systems and forces us to recognize the degree to which categories like tribe or peasant suggest firm boundaries around groups that are fluid and malleable. While I find a need for grand theories, postmodernism rightly reminds us that these are heuristic devices to help us understand, rather than external realities. We are cautioned to remember that knowledge is situated; no matter how objective our data, it represents a particular point of view.

The primary weakness of postmodernism, it seems to me, lies in the lack of criteria for validating statements. A reader has the right to ask of any nonfiction text, "Why should I believe this? What are the criteria by which I should judge this to be truer than what others say on this subject?" I am not sure how a postmodernist would respond to this, except to say, perhaps, that in even asking the question I am misunderstanding postmodern epistemology. The scientist, on the other hand, responds, "Check it against the facts." But if facts are mere cultural constructions, and if scientific claims are as negotiated as the cultural truths of religion or ideology, the very basis for *any* validation is called into question. The postmodern critique of the *physical* sciences, to a great degree subsumed under the rubric science and technology studies, has been extensively analyzed and rebuked by the scientists themselves.[11] The social sciences are very different from the physical sciences,[12] and attempts to replicate hard-science laws or mathematical certainties have been more detrimental than helpful, but one thing both the natural and social sciences hold in common, or should hold in common, is a firm skepticism toward intuitions and interpretations that are neither derived from nor testable by systematically gathered data.[13] Philosophically, even such bare-bones positivism as this is unbridgeably anathema to postmodernism. In actuality, however, many anthropologists regularly apply postmodern concepts in the interpretation of meticulously collected empirical data that are presented as fact.[14]

What is impossible in radical postmodern philosophy—namely the blending of materialist, social-scientific practices with postmodern assumptions—is actually quite routine in practice. Realism, defined as the belief that entities exist independently of our perceptions or theories about them, can be reconciled without a great deal of difficulty with the postmodern emphases on reflexivity, situated knowledge, and social constructionism (Maxwell 1999). Once it is accepted that reality places constraints on our interpretations—a fairly basic proposition—replicable validation procedures become both possible and essential. As Charles Hale (1997: 570) aptly observes, the "polarized divide—between postmodern theoretical observation and materialist reassertion—has grown steadily less important, and less useful, as an organizing framework. . . . [M]ost of the interesting, forward-looking research already has set its sights squarely beyond this divide, incorporating insights from both sides while rejecting the extreme terms of the polarization itself."

RECONCEPTUALIZING CULTURE

Culture is at once anthropology's most vital and most discredited concept. . . . Culture, notoriously resistant to specification or definition, has not been so much an object of study as the ground upon which other issues can be addressed.

Nicholas Thomas[15]

> The starting point . . . will be to revise the concept [of culture] so that it reflects the heterogeneity and fragmentation generated by globalization and cut the concept down in size so that it does not promise more than it can deliver.
>
> Stanley Barrett[16]

> [C]ulture is not a self-evident category and can certainly never be used to account for any other aspect of reality.
>
> Jonathan Friedman [17]

In the Congo,[18] popular music helps unite 300 distinct ethnic groups. During the 1920s through the 1940s, a guitar-based Afro-Cuban style, the Congolese rumba, emerged. Itinerant solo musicians were hired by the first recording studios, and by the 1960s some twenty such studios formed the basis for a music infrastructure, complete with a star system of professional groups. By the 1970s, rumba had evolved into *"la musique moderne,"* which borrowed from Afro-American soul music and expanded outward to become a standard for all subsaharan Africa, helping to create a sort of pan-African identity. Dance musicians signed contracts with corporate sponsors and with distributors in Paris and Brussels. Live concerts and television appearances stimulated the sale of cassettes and records.

While never as popular as reggae, a particular type of Congolese music, *soukouss*, gained international prominence outside Africa, especially in Europe. Musicians became culture brokers, spreading a simplistic and impressionistic version of Congo culture far and wide. Absolutely crucial to the popularity of *soukouss* was its ethnic origins; it was successful precisely because of its exotic identification with the mysterious Congo: *"C'est la vraie musique Africaine!"*

However, this particular style was unknown in the Congo itself! There, complex lyrics, usually with encrypted political messages, were typical. *Soukouss*, which needed to avoid offending anyone and had to contend with listeners speaking different languages, emphasized rhythm, reducing lyrics—if they existed at all—to a few banal stanzas about love and heartbreak. Concerts usually included attractive, semiclad women dancers, thus playing to European stereotypes of Africans as exceptionally erotic and as possessing natural rhythm. Neither the international stars themselves nor the Congolese people saw any problem with this. Since they did not define themselves nor their music in Western terms as imbued with some essential or authentic identity, the concept of selling out was meaningless (White 2000).

This amusing curiosity brings up a number of serious issues regarding "culture" in an age of globalization. Can culture be manufactured from scratch? Can it become a commodity to be bought and sold like any other commodity? Is this an example of Congolese, or at least African, culture, or is it more accurately an example of the homogenization of world culture, here in the form of an entertainment created to Western expectations? If the Congolese do not have any self-conscious sense of culture, is the very application of this concept to them no more than a Western anthropological imposition?

The Debate Over "Culture" Goes on (. . . and on . . . and on . . .)

Perhaps one generalization about culture is possible: Nobody likes the concept, but few want to do away with it altogether. As a result, it is endlessly debated, criticized, and redefined. Since the 19th century, when culture was associated with broad stages of civilization, the concept has gone through numerous permutations, usually many at the same time. Early 20th century theories defined culture as those superorganic aspects of humankind that could not be reduced to the biological or psychological. Virtually everything was cultural: language, art, mythology, ritual, the ways that colors were classified. Alfred Kroeber restricted the concept to symbolically meaningful systems of ideas and values; it was separated from behavior, which might be evidence of culture but was never culture itself. Neo-evolutionists and cultural ecologists, viewing culture as an adaptive strategy, tied the concept less to specific groups than to broad categories, like band and tribe or hunter-gatherers and horticulturalists.

More recently, there has been a tendency to see culture as cognitive and symbolic, as systems of meaning. Pierre Bourdieu's (1997) *habitus*, an unconscious internalization of the objective structure of society that confines action within narrow limits, is a substitute for the American concept of culture. Foucault's concept of discourse (see Chapter 4) also has many of the characteristics of culture. Increasingly, culture is conceived "as coming not 'from above' versus 'from below' but instead . . . 'from within' versus 'from without'" (Kearney 1996: 167). Culture, so conceived, involves a constant contestation of power between individuals and their social milieus.

Postmodernists have been ambiguous about the culture concept. While the idea of culture is not incompatible with postmodernism's constructivist bent, it does imply a defining property of groups of people that can be considered essentialist. Postmodernists might tend to view culture entirely as a construction of the observer, with no real objective referent. Appadurai (1996: 12) objects to traditional ideas of culture on the grounds that they denote a sharing, agreement, and boundedness among people who may live within the same society but at very different levels of power, wealth, and knowledge. What is needed is a more flexible concept that can make room for individual variation and for the multitude of new imaginings that come from the media.

Globalization presents numerous challenges to traditional concepts of culture. Whatever else culture has been in the past, it was usually considered something that differentiated one group from another, an identification of otherness. To the extent that culture has been one of anthropology's primary categories of enclosure (Nuer culture, Kwakiutl culture, peasant culture), the plasticity of boundaries today makes the concept even more abstract and amorphous than previously. If the traditional Boasian, relativistic image was of a world-mosaic of cultures, each of equal value, the effects of globalization suggest more a mosaic of plastic tiles that are melting in the sun, becoming fluid, running into each other. Jonathan Friedman (1994: 211–213) objects that even a runny mosaic metaphor suggests a degree of boundedness that never really existed. If globalization is "the social organization of meaning," as he defines it, then it was never circumscribed.

Global Homogenization or Fragmentation?

> sono kakki wa buronkusu,
> tsumari hippu hoppu ga saisho ni
> hakken sareta basho,
> soko kara umi o koe nihon ni mo
> tobihi shita no de aru.
>
> (That vigor came from the Bronx,
> the place where hip-hop was
> first discovered,
> from there, across the ocean, to Japan
> a spark flew and lit a fire.)
> Japanese hip-hop lyrics[19]

> Sushmita Sen [Miss Universe] and Aishwarya Rai [Miss World] have become role models for many of the college girls. . . . Did you know Jyoti Basu's niece entered a beauty contest here!? . . . The Communists will shout objectification of women when it's other people's women—but when it's their own daughters, it's a different story.
> Indian informant to anthropologist Dimple Suparna Bhaskaran[20]

The rapid development of what would become a substantial fashion and beauty industry in India after 1991 coincides with a massive multinational corporate investment in the business. While female beauty has always been valued, now it came to be, like Congolese *soukouss* music, a commodity to be sold to the widest possible market. This required intensive advertising campaigns, fashion shows, pervasive television images, and beauty pageants. The government saw beauty as a way to promote India to business and to tourists. It encouraged the Miss Universe contest, which involved a series of corporately sponsored preliminary competitions: Miss Beautiful Eyes, Miss Beautiful Smile, and the like. Regional winners would compete in the national Feminina Miss India contest in Bombay, which would lead to the Miss Universe and Miss World pageants. In 1994, Sushmita Sen became the first Indian Miss Universe, and her rival for the Miss India crown, Aishwarya Rai, became Miss World. They were feted at a state reception attended by the President and Prime Minister, and became ambassadors for India.

Bypassing some of the deeper feminist implications, is this an obvious example of cultural imperialism, of the extension of Western conceptions of commercialized female beauty to India? Perhaps, but that is not the way the author of this study interprets it. Bhaskaran (1998: 107) sees the current beauty industry as "the construction and reproduction of normative gender and sexual identities [that] are deeply tied into the patriarchal institutions of kinship-making, and embody and inform the practices of state-making, nation-building and the rhetoric of authenticity." Or, in Sushita Sen's words, "A woman is one who shows a man what love and caring is all about. That is the essence of woman" (quoted 112). While the beauty contest itself has a Western origin and Western corporate sponsorship, it takes on a different meaning than similar contests in the United States, which are increasingly promoted as empowering liberated women who have college degrees and professions and aspire to serve humanity (in a recent movie satire, *Miss Congeniality*, all of the contestants proclaimed "world peace" as their fondest desire). In India, in contrast, existing patriarchal roles are reinforced. Women are represented as symbols of the traditional nation, in which women's sexuality is still bounded, taboo, dangerous, something to be owned and managed by men.

A study, by Xiaoping Li (1996: 205–262), of the recent emergence of a similar fashion and beauty industry in communist China, complete with professional modeling and beauty contests, has a similar theme; while the outward manifestations are globalized-Western, the underlying meanings are Chinese and can be tied into a deep history of cultural attitudes toward evolving female roles. While in the long run, Western fashions may foster strategies of resistance against patriarchy, the immediate effect is part of a process of disempowerment, of return to a precommunist form of patriarchy, in which "the traditional gender hierarchy has been reinforced." Conventional gender roles are thus recast "into the sexist occupational structure of the new market economy" (216).

Hip-hop music that came out of the American urban Black ghetto found a niche among rebellious middle-class young people in Japan. However, there it was connected with *karaoke*, which had its origins in Japan and diffused to the West. Ian Condry (1999), the author of a study of Japanese musical borrowing, notes that it is necessary to make a distinction between the transnational cultural "market" and the local "scene." The global market is relatively indiscriminate, based largely on considerations of profit, while the local scene remains historically and culturally rooted.

A similar theme emerges from Daniel Miller's (1997) study of business and consumerism in Trinidad. In contrast to the pure transnational capitalism of neoliberal ideology, his analysis reveals a more organic capitalism at the local level. Although the Trinidad economy is thoroughly embedded in the global system, and IMF structural adjustments are supported by both the government and the people, the reality is a fluid, interactive, and unpredictable system that functions on a different rationality than that of capitalism-in-theory. This is as true, if not more so, for large companies as it is for the penny capitalist on the street corner. In contrast to the principle that markets respond automatically to supply and competitive pricing, the local economy is heavily consumer driven. Consumers inject all sorts of symbolic values into products that may have little to do with quality and price, and as a result, business people who administer subsidiaries of transnational corporations constantly chaff against the universalized prescriptions, based on pure capitalism, of their parent companies. For example, there is a tendency to view goods coming from the United States, Europe, and Japan as higher quality and local goods as lower quality even when objective measures reveal little difference. While China is considered a "worst-quality" country, right down there with Trinidad itself, shiny peanuts from China are highly valued, apparently for their shininess rather than their taste. Soft drink manufacturers must constantly compete to produce brands that can be tied to gender or ethnicity. Increasingly, people take their identities from the things that they purchase.

What these studies have in common is the theme that the issue of cultural homogenization versus fragmentation is a complex one. In some of its early manifestations, globalization was held to be coterminous with homogenization. Just as in old modernization theory (with which neoliberalism has much in common), traditional society would inevitably be absorbed by development, so Western cultural hegemony would inescapably overrun non-Western cultures. If there is any consensus about anything in anthropology, it is that this viewpoint is flatly incorrect. Ethnography after ethnogra-

does it homogenize culture/society
or create/redefine new ones

phy has revealed fragmentation and differentiation—increasing ethnicities, nationalisms, retribalisms, and the like.

This may itself be an artifact both of traditional anthropological thinking and of postmodern influences; contemporary anthropologists are theoretically disposed to look for difference not similarity, resistance not accommodation, transnationalism not assimilation. Friedman (1994: 10–11) points out that there are numerous examples of cultural *devolution* unaccounted in evolutionary theories—cultures such as those of Hawaii, North American and Peruvian Indians, and Congo pygmies that have lost much of their original autonomy and complexity as they are absorbed into the margins of dominant cultures. Brumann (1998: 499) remarks that, although there is a consensus among anthropologists that no cultural convergence is observable, "there are good reasons to assume that the total repertoire of cultural forms in the world has been shrinking for some time."

It is perhaps appropriate to introduce here a simple and obvious principle (which I will return to in my conclusions), which is sometimes overlooked in theoretical generalizations: *Some do; some don't*. A great many *individuals* are indeed being absorbed into a sort of globalized, mostly Western culture and so are some groups of people. By and large, specific cultures are inevitably transformed by changes in technology, mobility, and more porous and malleable boundaries, but rather than being absorbed by some global culture, *they* do most of the absorbing.

There seem to be two spheres of culture. At the global level is a depthless Coca-Cola culture consisting of relatively unintegrated traits. The most significant of these traits, and the one most important to global profits and therefore most promoted, is consumerism. Other traits, not all of them Western, are factory work-time, music videos, women's fashion, T-shirts, Kalishnikov rifles, white weddings, television and radio soap operas, Chinese food, bilateral kinship, acceptance of diverse gender roles, and the worship of technological innovation.

The specific-culture level is more unified, more holistic. It has historical depth, even if that history is constantly reinvented. If we take a cue from ecological anthropology, we can say that culture is adapted to its environment. Of course people do not always have the capacity to pick and choose what traits of Coca-Cola culture they want. If a factory is built smack in the middle of Maya country or a massive advertising campaign for McDonald's is aimed at Russians, they have no alternative but to respond in some manner; rejection itself is a choice. Also there are many aspects of global culture that may not be accessible, such as automobiles in a very poor country or certain television programs. By and large, however, there is a lot of discretion available at the local and individual level to take what is perceived as useful or desirable and

[handwritten: G. entities are always put against a backdrop of current/disparate culture and thus transform into something unique]

reject what is not. Whatever trait is taken in, however, will most likely assume a meaning different—perhaps quite different—from that which it has in its place of origin. A television set, for example, can be used not as a communication device but as a prestige item for dowry or bride price; images coming through the television may be interpreted in a completely different manner than intended (Friedman 1994: 203). In an impoverished shantytown in war-shattered Nicaragua in 1989, on those random days when electricity was available, I joined my host family in watching an extremely popular Brazilian *telenovela* about the trials and tribulations of rich people in Rio; I still wonder what strange resonances these images and voices were stimulating. Not all adopted traits will be transformative. Cultures are as capable of compartmentalization as of hybridity. Brumann (1998: 501) argues that in Japan, compartmentalization has become the dominant mode of appropriating Western culture; a much deeper indigenous culture remains relatively untouched by it.

Continuing the cultural ecology metaphor, we might assume that within broad parameters similar physical and social environments give rise to similar cultures. On the surface, the life of a middle-class advertising executive working in midtown São Paulo or Singapore may not be that different from that of a similarly employed New Yorker. The transformations of society associated with global processes—global cities, routine long-distance travel, huge farms devoted to export agriculture—create roughly similar environments in many parts of the world. However, to the extent that consumerism is the dominant cultural force of globalization, enculturation in global culture will occur to the greatest degree among those with sufficient money to buy into the consumer ethic, namely the middle class and the elite. Those economically marginalized by global processes or prevented from participating in such processes by deep-rooted religious values will more likely increase their sense of cultural autonomy and differentiation, perceiving global culture as a threat or simply as irrelevant to their lives.

Even in the most Westernized setting, globalization is not laid over some cultural tabula rasa. As Aihwa Ong (1999) observes, Asia has its own deep multicultural heritage that sets all sorts of cultural constraints on global processes that valorize mobility, flexibility, and consumerism. The "cultural logics" of transnational global processes ensure that transformations, adaptations, and resistances will take place in intricate ways, for example, in China's maintenance of an "authoritative Asian" political model, while at the same time it opens itself to neoliberal globalization.

Given its shallowness and fragmentation, global culture is never manifested in any pure state, but only in interaction. To the extent that culture is generated and lived locally, global culture exists only through other cultures.

TRANSFORMING FIELDWORK AND METHODOLOGY

In the end, the most valuable contribution of the anthropologist is the rich detail of the ethnographic method. Combining the voices of the Guatemalan migrant and her parents, the Oaxacan vegetable producers and their educated children, the rain forest Amerindian villagers, and the indebted Dominican farmer, we can begin to discern the many meanings of globalization.

Peggy Barlett[21]

Now, with the studies of the transnational and the global, [anthropology] may face the final test of its tools.

Ulf Hannerz[22]

Norwegian anthropologist Øivind Fuglerud's study *Life on the Outside: The Tamil Diaspora and Long Distance Nationalism* (1999)[23] resulted from more than a decade and a half of "fieldwork" in multiple official and unofficial capacities. In the 1980s, he worked for the Norwegian Red Cross organizing the reception of refugees, most of whom were Tamils escaping the war in Sri Lanka. Later, as a regional advisor to Asia for the Norwegian immigration service, he made several trips to Sri Lanka with various research institutions, nongovernmental organizations, and colleagues. During these trips, he visited the home communities of the Tamil diaspora and interviewed both government officials and internally displaced refugees. After leaving his official positions, he did nearly a year's participant observation fieldwork among Tamil refugees in Norway.

While this represents an exceptional case, in that Fuglerud had long been professionally employed in the field in which he would later do anthropological work, it is suggestive of some of the challenges of globalized research. Travel to multiple locations is not unusual, nor is joining volunteer organizations. In her study of Cambodian immigrants in the United States, aside from doing fieldwork in a diaspora community in Fall River, Massachusetts, Lydia Breckon (1998) worked with several international agencies, including the Cambodian American National Development Organization, and followed her subjects on their return visits to Phnom Penh.

Anthropological fieldwork has a long history. Although 19th century evolutionists are disparagingly referred to as armchair anthropologists, Lewis Henry Morgan studied the Iroquois Indians of New York state firsthand, emerging with one of the earliest scientific descriptions of a matrilineal kinship system. Franz Boas insisted on fieldwork, but conducted his research on the Kwakiutl of Vancouver Island on day trips out of a hotel in a nearby town, relying heavily on key informants to collect a huge and rather indiscriminate mishmash of information.[24]

Bronislaw Malinowski's revolution in methodology was probably as much a result of his "Introduction" to *Argonauts of the Western Pacific* (1961 [1922]), in which he described what would become known as his participant observation methodology, as to his analysis of the Trobriand Island Kula Ring. "Imagine yourself," he says, "set down surrounded by your gear, alone on a tropical beach close to the native village while the launch or dinghy which has brought you sails away out of sight" (4). In one fell swoop, the Anthropologist as Hero was born. By the time Malinowski's diaries were published in 1967—revealing a normally lustful, chronic hypochondriac given to periodic outbursts of racist vitriole against the natives—his method was already thoroughly established, not only as the anthropological standard for research but also as a required rite of passage for entrance into the anthropological inner circle. The Malinowskian archetype of the researcher, usually a male (despite Margaret Mead's fame) braving it through a year or more all alone among the natives is still dominant today and has become one of the defining qualities of American anthropology. Two major effects of this have been that, first, the arena of research, and to some extent the arena of theory, was by default reduced to the size of the studyable community, and, second, the more exotic the research the greater the prestige—a prestige that would pay off in the academic job market.

While participant observation fieldwork will undoubtedly remain an important method in cultural anthropology, it is being viewed either as one alternative method among others or as a method that should be a part, not the whole, of the research process (Gupta and Ferguson 1997). This is especially true for globalization studies, which may require following migratory networks across borders or interviewing immigrants in both their home and host communities. Participant observation was a matter of necessity for lone researchers with time constraints and limited budgets. It was justified by the fact that the communities studied were relatively stable; in most cases, the people had spent their lives in that place. More and more, however, anthropologists are turning to highly transient phenomena, people constantly on the move or communities that only exist for a brief period. For example, Liisa Malkki (1997) speaks of the need to extend anthropological research to "accidental communities of memory," people briefly united by traumatic events such as refugees in camps, disaster victims, civilians or soldiers in war. Rather than being joined by class or culture, such groups are bound by temporary need and the intensity of shared experience.

Postmodernist Influences

The impact of postmodernism on fieldwork is great (Marcus 1995). There was always a canyon-size gap between the reality of fieldwork and the scientific strictures of manuals of field methodology. A university colleague in the physics department at my university once commented that the typical physicist neither knows nor thinks much about method and that he would not know a null hypothesis if it bit him on the butt; rather, in physics, researchers simply do what they have to do to find out what they need to find out. Anthropologists have often discovered that gathering information in the field is similar, an art of the possible. Even the most systematic and social-scientific fieldwork has always been a matter of openness and improvisation. Critical theory, which shook up the profession in the 1980s, called into question the objectivity of anthropological fieldwork, in some cases (rather grotesquely, I think) reducing classics of participant observation to literary texts. For better or worse, this self-reflexivity about the role and situatedness of the anthropologist has had the effect of deromanticizing fieldwork and loosening up expectations, such as the requirement for holism, that were never entirely realistic.

Perhaps the most important contribution of postmodernism is its insistence on a redefinition of the groups that are the subject of anthropological research. "Cultures," "communities," and "local" no longer occupy well-defined territories, but are spread all over the place and sometimes constantly change shape. Within such ill-defined structures, the typical long-term face-to-face fieldwork may be inadequate or inappropriate. Another contribution, which dates back to the Manchester School and to systems theory, is the insistence that the surrounding environment be part of any study. Part of that environment will always involve power, often in subtle and complex ways, and this power will be infused throughout the people being studied even if relationships appear on the surface to be horizontal and egalitarian.

The subjects of anthropological globalization studies are less likely to be communities or cultures than translocalities, border zones, migrations, diasporas, commodity chains, transnational corporations, foreign aid agencies, tourists, refugees, cyberspace, the influences of television and other communications media, the international processes of science, or commercialized art. In the past, there has been a tendency in anthropology to focus on the subaltern; globalization, however, often shifts attention to elites who are most able to take advantage of opportunities for travel and consumerism, such as wealthy Hong Kong businessmen or scientists. While groups of people remain the focus of all study—anthro, after all, means people—sometimes not just one group but multiple groups might need to be studied. This could be the case with studies of development, in which different aid agencies and governmental and nongovernmental organizations as well as targeted subjects could all be considered (Ferguson 1994), or in commodity chain analysis where the production, processing, distribution, and marketing of, say, Brazilian grapes might be traced from the farmer to the consumer thousands of miles away (Collins 2000).

New Techniques of Investigation

Sociologist Michael Burawoy experimented with ground-up approaches to globalization by having a group of doctoral dissertation students globalize their research (Burawoy, et al. 2000). While several of the ethnographies were only moderately successful, mainly because the projects were not initially conceived as globalization studies and thus there was a tacked on feel to the analyses, the technique that was standardized is instructive. Following the extended case method innovated by the British Manchester School under Max Gluckman in the late 1950s, the researchers replaced the fixed concept of "community" with the more versatile concept of "field," which embraced not only those being studied, but also their social world as it extended outward in time and space. From the microforces within the group, the level of analysis was shifted to macroforces, higher level structures, causes, and constraints. Such a shift might imply a top-down determinism that objectifies globalization, making such forces seem inevitable. To counter this, they viewed the macrostructures as cognitively constructed and focused on the ways that people resisted, adapted, or transformed such structures at the local level. There was a deliberate attempt to trace relations of power as it moved back and forth between macro- and microlevels.

Multisited field work is often a necessity in transnational studies. Numerous studies of the Mexican-U.S. border area routinely research both sides of the line. Labor migration research will probably require observations and interviews in both the home communities and distant immigrant camps. Often it is not the end points that are most important to the research, but what is in between. Network analysis, which had its heyday in the 1960s and 1970s and went out of fashion, is being resuscitated as it becomes increasingly evident that networks are absolutely central to understanding migration. Networks may change form kaleidoscopically, have multiple beginning and end points, and create new destinations, making reasearching them extremely difficult.

With all these demands, a problem of anthropological depth arises. The major value of long-term participant observation fieldwork has always been the degree to which a culture could be experienced in its fullness. Because answers to interview questions can be determined by the ways that the questions are phrased, and people routinely lie or tell the interviewer what they think she wants to hear, gathering information can require a long period in a single setting as the researcher circles in on the data. It may take a great deal of time in one place before the researcher even has any idea what to research. The requirement to research more than one site imposes a number of very practical considerations of time and money. Language facility may also be a problem; the very definition of diaspora is that people who relate to a single homeland reside in not just one but many different countries. It is all very well to insist on rigorous standards at every point, but the reality is that tradeoffs will have to be made between breadth and depth of research.

One obvious solution is more collaborative work. Teams of researchers, often utilizing graduate students, can cover different aspects of a subject and be in many places at the same time. Perhaps the best-known team in anthropological globalization studies at this writing is that of Linda Basch, Nina Glick Schiller, and Cristina Szanton Blanc, who have jointly published multiple articles and two books (Basch, et al. 1994; Glick Schiller, et al. 1992). Although their fieldwork is done separately on Caribbean and Philippine migrants to the United States, they have blended their data and theoretical analyses into a seamless whole that has been foundational in establishing transnational studies as a major subdiscipline within anthropology.

Gupta and Ferguson (1997: 38) call for bringing in a multitude of "other forms of representation" besides fieldwork: "archival research, the analysis of public discourse, interviewing, journalism, fiction, or statistical representations of collectivities." Also field research need not end when the anthropologist leaves the field; it is now both inexpensive and easy to maintain contact with a few informants via letters, telephone, perhaps short-wave radio, or e-mail.

In Defense of Participant Observation

The legitimization of multiple forms of anthropological research should not be considered a denigration of participant observation, although it is often phrased that way.[25] Critical anthropology has become almost a subdiscipline in itself, and it was inevitable that sooner or later its jaundiced eye would fall on fieldwork. However, it might be suggested that there are good reasons, aside from the romanticism and sense of adventure that often draw students to the field, why participant observation has become so central to anthropology. There is still no other means of gathering some types of information in depth. Certainly one of the most important contributions of this type of research should be applauded by postmodernists, namely, participant observation research almost inevitably makes hash out of theory. Those tidy structures, functions, development prescriptions, discourses, and the like can dissipate quite quickly in the chaos of daily life in an alien culture. This process of tearing down, only later to build back up, is essential to understanding the priority of the real, the sense that anthropology is about people first—which can be too easily forgotten when theory is divorced from what it is trying to explain. Such fieldwork also gives the possibility of bottom-up theory construction, something that has been neglected in an age of Foucault, Bourdieu, and a resurrected Gramsci, and also gives a sense of the range of variation within groups. Critics may rail against the idea of participant observation research as a rite of passage, but it is precisely that; as the sophisticated PhD or doctoral student finds himself in the position of an innocent child, he is forced to discard the baggage of unthought ethnocentrisms and look at the world anew. The process of rebuilding oneself, of growing up into another culture, may be the only real way of approximating those "subjectivities" so central to postmodern understanding.

In a globalized world, anthropology needs to be more than it has been. A sufficiently wide range of data-gathering and analytical techniques should be available to fit the research methodology to the subject, rather than the other way around. One gets from the recent critical approach to methodology, however, the sense that all techniques are equal and nothing should be valorized over anything else. While participant observation should no longer be a defining or essential element of cultural anthropology, we might think long and hard before too far diminishing its importance.

Chapter 4

Development, Devolution, and Discourse

> The term ["development"] is so imprecise and vulgar that it should be stricken from any proper lexicon of technical terms.
>
> David Apter[1]

Not long ago, development occupied that privileged place in the lexicon of the social sciences presently held by globalization. As is the case with the present usurper, there was little agreement about what development meant. There were passionate assertions that it would save mankind and equally passionate accusations that it was a postcolonial conspiracy to maintain Western hegemony over the Third World. Some believed that development would bring about equality between peoples and nations, while others held that it was increasing inequality. Macroeconomic statistics proved that development improved the lot of the masses, and microeconomic statistics proved that it impoverished the masses. Some scholars contended that it would raise Third World women out of poverty, and others asserted that it condemned them to even greater poverty. The claims and counterclaims for and against development were so similar to those now being applied to globalization that one might well assume that one concept has simply replaced an earlier one. Indeed, some economists, especially those who see free-market forces as the primary engine of world betterment, seem to assume that globalization is just development writ large. This is unfortunate: Globalization and development are very different concepts.

"Development . . . is a user-friendly term," notes Jan Knippers Black (1999: 15), "having virtually as many potential meanings as potential users." It may be conceived as all but synonymous with modernization (as that term used to be employed in the singular), that is, industrialization, technological development, increased literacy, and the like. In this sense, it is mainly descriptive. Development is more often meant prescriptively, as a process, usually applied at the national or community level, by which people's lives are improved and life-chances enhanced. The form of such enhancement and how it will be achieved varies whether one is an economist (growth in GNP and perhaps equity), a political scientist (democratization, grassroots mobilization), or a social scientist (empowerment of the poor, access to jobs and health services). Development was always something that was in process or that would happen in the future, but only to the "underdeveloped" or "developing" countries of the Third World. The First World, by definition, was already developed.

Globalization is much more all-encompassing. Development is something that happens (or does not happen) *within* globalization. Globalization has thus replaced development only as the latest faddish buzzword, not as a concept. Much to the chagrin of a coterie of social scientists who seem to have expected development to disappear, it remains the foundation concept of the World Bank, the UN Food and Agriculture Organization, the InterAmerican Development Bank, a host of nongovernmental organizations, and most Third World governments.

While the difference between development and globalization should be kept clear, the two are closely interrelated. To the extent that development is considered as directed change, it is usually transnational organizations—whether official or NGOs—that do the directing. Prior to the emergence of globalization as an analytic model, development was a key point of articulation for the anthropologist between the local and the transnational.

THE DEVELOPMENT OF DEVELOPMENT

Some scholars trace the modern idea of development precisely to President Truman's inauguration speech on January 20, 1949, in which he referred to Latin America as "underdeveloped" and thus in need of the altruistic largesse of the United States.[2] In reality, the idea of development, if not the term, is implicit in Enlightenment ideals of progress, but there is some justification for the claim of a recent genesis because during the colonial period what are now called underdeveloped nations were seen as appendages of the mother country, with the primary functions of supplying raw materials and cheap labor. Any type of development that would retard these functions or permit the colony to compete with the mother country was systematically prevented. However, by the mid-20th century, Latin America had been decolonized for over a century, and it is here that we find some of the most fertile ground for theories of development. As early as the 1920s, Haya de la Torre and José Carlos Mariátegui were debating North American and European Marxists about "economic evolution," land reform, and public education (Mariátegui 1971 [1928]). Shortly after the founding of the United Nations, one of its committees, the Economic Commission for Latin America (ECLA), articulated theories of underdevelopment and development that had been germinating for decades. Their division of the world into a wealthy *core* and underdeveloped *periphery* would become the basis for later dependency theory.

This said, Truman's 1949 speech is as good a benchmark as any for the United States' entrance into the development business. Until the colonial system collapsed in the 1950s and 1960s, such efforts had little practical meaning beyond the Americas. Right from the beginning, the U.S. concept of development was tied closely to national security and anticommunism, just as was the Marshall Plan. Altruism is very nice, but if it costs money that must be voted for by Congress, there must also be benefits to the donor; development would remove the underlying appeal of communism while tying governments and militaries to the United States.

At first conceived entirely as growth of gross national product (with the emphasis on gross), the concept of development rapidly accumulated more and more layers of meaning until by 1966 Jagdish Bhagwati (1966) would describe the objectives of governments as "a high rate of growth of income, an egalitarian distribution of income, fuller employment, the development of backward regions, the creation of strategic industries and the reduction of reliance on foreign trade" (105). A typical economic definition of the 1970s might be: "A national economy is considered developed if it has high levels of internal differentiation, integration, and energy consumption, employs scientific technology in production, and has a high level of labor productivity" (Bornschier, et al. 1978: 645). Noneconomic goals might include democracy, governmental stability, and high rates of literacy.

THEORIES OF DEVELOPMENT

Modernization theory is strongly associated with W. W. Rostow's *The Stages of Economic Growth* (1960) in which the author detailed six stages, derived from U.S. and European development, that would lead from "traditional society" to an "age of mass consumption." This unilineal stage model was simplistic even for that time, but many of the basic ideas that would become a more complex modernization theory were implicit in Rostow's formulation. The *Third World* (a term coined in France in 1952) was characterized by dual societies, one traditional and one modern. As the modern sector developed, it would grow away from the traditional sector; income disparities between the two would increase rapidly, and the traditional would be left as a cultural and economic backwater. Growth of the modern sector, at least until the point of "take-off" or self-generation was accomplished, would come from the diffusion of capital, technology, and education from the developed world. The main problem facing the underdeveloped country itself was to remove the cultural and material barriers to development: fatalism, illiteracy, superstition, primitive technology, paucity of transportation and communications infrastructure, and lack of individualism, "achievement motivation," and the capitalist entrepreneurial spirit.

As early as the 1960s, it was becoming evident that, despite massive transfers of aid, technology, and multinational corporate investment, most countries were not developing. While there was impressive growth in terms of macroeconomic statistics, these statistics were distorted by a handful of countries, such as Brazil, which was experiencing an economic "miracle." A closer look revealed that benefits of modernization were very unequally distributed (Brazil ended up with the worst income distribution in the world). The problem, then, might not be that the countries *lacked* something, but rather that they were embedded within in an international structure that historically created their poverty and continued to maintain it. This was the basic idea of dependency theory. Andre Gunder Frank (1969) made a distinction between *un*development and *under*development; the former was an early stage of evolution similar to Rostow's "traditional" society; the latter was created by the exploitation of "satellites" by a "metropolis." Within anthropology, Eric Wolf's *Europe and the People without History* (1982) would get rid of the concept of *un*developed altogether; there were no pristine societies, because *all* had been affected by colonialism, neocolonialism, and imperialism. The ECLA model of an exploitive and controlling *core* and a subordinate *periphery* would be given historical depth by Immanuel Wallerstein (1974) who traced the system back to 15th century Europe. His world system theory is often considered separate from dependency theory, but might best be conceived as part of a wider dependency paradigm. Wallerstein added the idea of *semiperiphery* nations that mediated between core and periphery and embodied attributes of both.

In accord with the social sciences' conventional throw-out-the-baby-with-the-bath-water approach to theoretical revolutions, the dependency perspective now seems wholly discredited. This is unfortunate, because such unqualified rejection fails to distinguish between its empirical basis and its speculative and ideological analysis. It is quite true that the high level of abstraction made dependency theory difficult to apply in particular cases, and the economic emphasis on a world division of labor undervalued the importance of political factors, culture, and raw military intimidation. Most telling, dependency theory failed to predict, and then required increasingly baroque analysis to explain, the rapid development of several southeast Asian countries. The prescriptive solutions usually called for socialism and/or delinking from the capitalist system, which turned out to be either self-destructive or impractical. Finally, the functional division of core, periphery, and semiperiphery now seems highly simplistic even strictly within the sphere of economics; it has given way to a much more complex, multidimensional system[3] of interaction based not on raw material production versus manufacture, but on low-tech manufacture versus high-tech manufacture and factory production versus information processing, combined with attention to international finance, media technology, and local culture. In short, the predictive value of dependency theory ranged from not very good to nil. This said, the most radical idea of the dependency paradigm is in some ways more empirical than theoretical and remains foundational to many contemporary perspectives; underdevelopment, by whatever term one prefers, is not an initial condition but was *caused*—and continues to be caused—by relations with the developed countries.

For a while, *articulation theory* offered promise. This was especially promoted by Marxist anthropologists beginning in the 1970s. In contrast to the view that capitalism simply overwhelms preexisting forms, articulation theory posits that when precapitalist economies come in contact with capitalism, both are transformed, often in unpredictable ways. The two modes would be fused within the identities of individuals, leading to such hyphenated concepts as peasant-proletarian. This helped bridge the dichotomizations inherent in earlier theories: capitalist/precapitalist, developed/underdeveloped, modernization/dependency. Instead of being barriers to capitalist development, traditional economies and the people within them interacted symbiotically through labor and commodity markets (Kearney 1996: 82, 98–104). Such ideas continue to be valuable, for example, in analyzing the "Confucian capitalism" and "alternative modernity" of contemporary China (Li 1996: 72–74). While analytically useful, articulation theory was limited in its scope, mainly to economic and labor studies. With the emergence of postmodernism, with its radical self-reflexivity and its shift to more cognitive constructivist approaches, such materialist models were becoming passé.

The gradual collapse of dependency theory, which dominated the social sciences for decades, left a theoretical vacuum in anthropology that it would be up to the poststructuralists to fill, if only temporarily.

DEVELOPMENT ANTHROPOLOGY VERSUS THE ANTHROPOLOGY OF DEVELOPMENT

We have already noted that the general term "development" has multiple meanings. To add to the confusion, the phrases "development anthropology" and "the anthropology of development" mean very different things, and to make matters worse, in the 1990s, a group of antidevelopment anthropologists redefined these phrases to fit their specific arena of controversy (see Table 4.1). For the moment, we will use the terms in their more conventional formulation.

Table 4.1
Two Competing Sets of Definitions that Distinguish "Development Anthropology" and "Anthropology of Development"

	Conventional Definitions	Discourse Analysis
"Development Anthropology"	Applied anthropology: practitioners working with development agencies. Neutral connotation.	Applied anthropology: practitioners working with development agencies. Strongly negative connotation.
"Anthropology of Development"	The anthropological study of development in the very general (but controversial) sense understood by economists and other social scientists: poverty reduction, improvements in health and nutrition, empowerment of women, political democratization, etc.	The critique of development in general and applied anthropology in particular.

To oversimplify (but not by much), development anthropology refers to *planned change introduced by outside agents, usually at the community level.* By this definition, development anthropology is nearly identical with applied anthropology, that is, the work done by anthropologists employed by development agencies. As John Bennet (1990: 183) observes, "when anthropologists speak of development, they usually mean what the field representatives of the foreign aid agencies mean: particular projects in particular places, affecting particular populations and regions." In other words, development is conceived as *local* and *planned*.

The "anthropology *of* development," on the other hand, defines its key term in the broader, more inclusive sense of the social sciences in general. *Development* refers to *changes, planned or unplanned and at any level of society, through the processes of modernization, such as industrialization, increased communications, and increased use of technology.* Within anthropology, development of this sort has largely been perceived in a negative sense.

It is routine to begin any anthropological book or article on development with a rejection of the idea of development as "progress." There is some justification for this. Development has quite often been devastating to the indigenous peoples studied by anthropologists.[4] However, national, regional, and global statistics are not consistent, revealing that development is highly uneven. It is certainly true that peoples and cultures have been wiped out, entire ecosystems have been destroyed, and inequality between and often within nations is increasing. On a world basis there are declines in per capita grain production. Although the proportion of those living in extreme poverty is steady at about 20%, the absolute numbers are growing. On the other hand, in gross terms, we see increased life expectancy, better nutrition, higher literacy rates, and a significant emergence of democracy (UNDP 1993: 12). It is obvious that development benefits some and devastates others, empowers some and disempowers others, provides employment for some and marginalizes others, creates democracies in some places and military dictatorships in others.

Destructive Development: The Orang Asli of Malaysia

A lifestyle, so leisurely and so gracious that, thankfully, it can be enjoyed by only a select few.
Advertisement for the Sultan Aziz Shah Golf Course, Malaysia, built on lands formerly occupied by the Orang Asli[5]

Malaysia is one of the rapidly developing countries of Southeast Asia, with the stated goal of attaining a GNP, personal income levels, and consumption rates equal to those of Europe by 2020. In the process, the Orang Asli—an overall term for about nineteen separate groups of indigenous peoples—have suffered impoverishment, loss of independence, and social breakdown.

Often referred to as "originals," the Orang Asli comprise 1% of Malaysia's population of 16 million. As the smallest and most marginalized of

Malaysia's main groups—others are Islamic Malays, Chinese, and Hindu Tamils from South India—they have found themselves with little power to retain their lands or defend their lifestyles. Occupation by foreigners is hardly new; they suffered through centuries of domination, as Indians, Portuguese, the British, and, briefly, the Japanese occupied the Malay Peninsula. Through it all, the native peoples were able to maintain their cultures and economies based on fishing, foraging, horticulture, rice farming, and trading. Before the 1950s, most lived in relative isolation. It was only with decolonization and the formation of the Federation of Independent Malaysia in 1957 that the state's goals of development set in motion the processes of cultural genocide.

In direct contradiction to the Malay Constitution, which gave the Orang Asli full rights as citizens, the Aboriginal Peoples Act of 1954 handed control of their lands and communities over to the government. State doctrine called for the rapid assimilation of indigenous peoples into the modern market economy. They were stripped of rights over the land that they had always farmed or hunted; state offices would not even sell them land. Domination was so complete that in the 1970s the state began a program designed to convert all natives to Islam.

Given Malaysia's ideology of rapid development based on Western models, primary production through the exploitation of land was seen as essential to creating the capital and savings required to build an industrial infrastructure. Logging became second in importance only to oil in the country's export earnings. In 1962, three-quarters of the Malay Peninsula was covered with rain forest, which rapidly disappeared as loggers removed 300,000 hectares of forest per year throughout the 1970s and 200,000 hectares per year in the following decade; a limit of 149,000 hectares per year was established only after the disastrous effects of deforestation became abundantly obvious. Although clearcutting was illegal, the logging of a third of the trees led to removal of as much as three-quarters of the canopy that prevented the torrential rains and scorching sun from eroding the thin tropical soil. Logging roads caused even more devastation, interrupting drainage and creating mosquito-breeding ponds and swamps. In addition, state encouragement of plantation agriculture and the creation of golf courses and tourist complexes further razed the forests. With their ecosystems destroyed, the Orang Asli were forced to work for wages, usually at the lowest possible pay, in jobs that were sporadic and unreliable. Ironically, most of these jobs were precisely in occupations created by the industries—logging and plantation agriculture—that had demolished their livelihoods.

The government's answer to the problem was "regroupment," that is, re-settlement. As is usual in such cases (including many Indian reservations in the United States), reserves were established only on lands that no one else wanted, often virtual wastelands. Natives who had traditionally depended on constant movement for foraging, trading, or slash-and-burn cropping were forced into sedentary lifestyles. People for whom independence was a primary value were brought under direct political control of the state. The elaborate infrastructure promised for the resettlement communities seldom exceeded a few plank houses reserved for government-appointed commu-nity leaders. Education never went beyond three grades, and modern medi-cine existed only at a very low level.

The predictable results have been high levels of poverty, extreme de-pendence on government handouts, alcoholism, and domestic breakdown. The Orang Asli were previously a peaceful people, but violence has become increasingly common, almost always involving alcohol abuse. Prostitution is prevalent, and women are subject to the molestation and sexual harass-ment of outsiders.

The Orang Asli are not against development. Interviews reveal little de-sire to return entirely to traditional ways. Most have assumed many of the values of the dominant culture; they desire money, houses, modern medi-cine, good jobs, and education. But so far, development has left the Orang Asli by the wayside (Dentan, et al. 1997).

Development Anthropology—Directed Culture Change

Development anthropology, that is, applied work with change agen-cies, had a truncated start after World War II when many anthropologists were hired briefly by the International Cooperation Agency. The domi-nant theoretical orientation in anthropology at the time was struc-tural-functionalism, which emphasized unity and stability; it would take the forceful repudiation of this theoretical position before change, includ-ing induced change, could find a firm place within the culture of anthro-pology. Also, the 1950s and 1960s were the period of decolonization, requiring a reorientation from the category "colonial" to "underdevel-oped." The modernization paradigm, dominant at the time, held that de-velopment would take place in linear stages and come about through the West supplying the capital and technology that traditional nations lacked. This was to be accomplished on the large scale, through massive foreign aid to build hydroelectric plants and to improve export agriculture, and through multinational corporate investment. There was little room within such a view for anthropological cultural relativism; indigenous societies did not need to be understood, they needed to be changed.

By the 1970s, it was widely recognized that optimistic projections for development had not been realized. Even where industrialization took hold, the norm was sectoral development; wealth would be highly localized, resulting in internal colonialism, in which one city or region would hold almost all political and economic power while draining the resources of the rest of the country. Peasants were often the hardest hit, as the growth of rationalized export agriculture, quite often assisted by foreign aid, displaced millions of formerly subsistence peasants, forcing them into the shanty towns of burgeoning cities or onto the most marginal lands. Meanwhile, within anthropology, the collapse of the colonial system had replaced "structure," "function," and "stability" with a new vocabulary that emphasized "process," "change," and "agency."

In 1973, the Foreign Assistance Act was rewritten by Congress, shifting the goals of development from growth of GNP to equity and moving the focus of development from the industrial sector to agriculture. This provided inroads for more professional anthropologists to be hired by aid agencies as advisors and researchers. Although their influence was limited, especially in the planning process, by the 1990s, anthropologists were an accepted and important part of the development apparatus. At the same time, the top-down, techno-economic approach of the World Bank was stimulating some difficult-to-ignore criticism from numerous human rights, environmental, and feminist organizations. The emergence of "participatory development," gender analysis, and environmental sustainability further legitimized, at the highest levels, much that anthropologists had been saying all along. In addition, anthropologists could bring a new respect for local-level knowledge and practices. Huge and complex development bureaucracies, such as the World Bank and the United States Development Agency, often move at a glacial pace as ideas sift down or up through the myriad levels of the hierarchy, and channels of financial flow have to be rerouted. As we will see, even when change does take place, the aid industry that is supposed to deliver the goods may be so unwieldy that little of value can get through.

Applied anthropologists working for development agencies can make a number of significant contributions. First, they can educate technical and economic specialists about the structural and cultural complexities of local communities and can try to elicit respect on the part of the development agents for indigenous knowledge systems, often built up over hundreds of years and adapted to the particular environment. Second, they can at least plead for long-term research, avoiding the down-and-dirty, drive-by approach that the culture of technocratic efficiency often considers optimal. Anthropologists may assume leadership of multidisciplinary development teams, in which considerations of culture can become central to the project (Horowitz 1996). Since development often creates or exacerbates gender inequalities, anthropologists can make considerations of such issues a crucial factor in planning. Finally, anthropologists can critique the development agency itself, examining its internal "culture" in terms of assumptions, biases, and conflicts.

Participatory Development in Brazil

Participatory development is often claimed as an ideal, but it is not easily achieved. The goal is to form horizontal associations, composed of those directly affected, that can suggest directions of development and that can implement their own improvements. A recent anthropological assessment of a major World Bank project in northeastern Brazil exposed many problems with this model, while suggesting ways that they might be overcome.

Perhaps the primary findings of the study, which involved participant observation fieldwork, structured interviews with association leaders and members, and various statistical surveys, was the importance of identifying and utilizing existing structures. One part of the project involved building two dams and canals to irrigate 900 hectares. However, forming the native associations was highly problematic. The anthropologists discovered that traditional communal work groups, called *bandeiras de trabalho*, had died out in many regions but, unknown to the developers, were still operating within the project area. Had the project utilized this already existing cooperative structure, it might have had greater success.

Another major problem was the difficulty of creating egalitarian, horizontal associations that cross-cut the asymmetrical and vertical associations formed by the patron-client system. Many peasants are used to relating to the outside world through an exploitive system called *coronelismo*, literally referring to regional bosses. In return for labor, services, surplus goods, and political support, the *coroneis* would make loans of seed, provide assistance with legal problems, and act as brokers with a government that was extremely remote to most peasants. With the growth of the power of the state and with new ideas being spread through the media, many of these patron-client relations had lost their force, but such allegiances were still prevalent. Associations that threaten these local structures may be blocked or sabotaged by the patrons. Also, since *coronelismo* has traditionally been the main form of association known to peasants, ostensibly participatory associations may be structured along similar lines;

members might expect the leader to make all decisions and to disperse benefits in return for loyalty. The temptation for corruption is always present in such situations.

It also became evident that few association members were really interested in the good of the community or the group. Most joined only if they and their families would benefit personally and remained only as long as such benefits seemed likely to be achieved. Thus, it was difficult to hold together ideological associations with long-term or abstract objectives. Participatory development worked best when the returns for the individual were clear and when the project had concrete short-term goals.

One of the surprises to emerge from interviews with association leaders was their respect for women participants. Many interviewees expressed the belief that women had "more of an associative mentality" than men. Partly, this seemed to derive from Catholic church organizations that incorporated women. Also, because men were often away, either as temporary or semipermanent migrants to the cities, women provided a continuity otherwise impossible.

"Participation" and "sustainability" often seem like such admirable goals to development administrators that they expect the target populations to immediately buy into them. However, societies are always vastly more complex than is evident from the outside. This is why the anthropological perspective and anthropological research may be essential to the successful implementation of development projects (Costa, Kottak, and Prado 1997).

DISCOURSE AND DEVELOPMENT

Starting in the early 1990s, with the theoretical vacuum left by the post–Cold War collapse of dependency theory and world-system theory, a new challenge to development anthropology emerged under the rubric of poststructuralism (often equated with or seen as a subdivision of postmodernism), giving rise to an impressive number of books and articles.[6] The primary influence on the poststructuralist critique of development is French philosopher Michel Foucault, the author of about fifteen books and numerous essays over a period of thirty years. In books such as *Madness and Civilization* (1988 [1961]), *The Birth of the Clinic* (1973 [1963]), and *Discipline and Punish* (1995 [1975]), Foucault shows how sovereign power, once centered in the monarch, was replaced by a more insidious form of disciplinary power, diffused through institutions and through the processes by which individuals internalized and accepted their own domination. Power is not only inherent in insane asylums, prisons, and the military, as is obvious, but also is suffused through society like the capil-

lary action of the blood system (Sheridan 1980: 217). By extension, the colonial era of blatant top-down power has given way to an era in which the
Third World (itself a social construction created by the West after World
War II) is controlled not by overt subjugation or repression, but by subtle
forms of disciplinary domination that are infused throughout the very institutions that are supposed to be helping.

The key term *discourse* has a special and complex meaning within
Foucaultian analysis; it refers to the ways that speech, writing, and even
thought and action are constrained within any particular historical place and
period. To some extent, discourse can be defined by its "rules of exclusion."
These include the prohibition against certain statements and practices and
the opposition between what is considered reason and unreason. Anything
that does not fit within the dominant discourse is excluded as false, assuming it is conceivable at all. In addition to these external rules, many others
are internalized, such as "principles of classification, ordering, and distribution" (Foucault 1972: 216–220). The dominant discourse of an age (which,
in his early writings, Foucault refers to as an "episteme") is assimilated by
the individual, so that it is virtually impossible to think outside of it; it becomes an aspect of one's very being. Since there is no universal human nature, the discourse of each age in a sense determines what it is to be human.
Discourse defines truth for a specific period; there is no metadiscourse that
serves as the arbiter of some higher truth (such as might be claimed for science or, at earlier times, for Christianity). Other discourses exist alongside
the dominant discourse, but they are marginal and subjugated. Power, then,
in the sense of control over thought and action, is not merely an incidental
aspect of discourse; it is at its center, a part of its essence.

Arturo Escobar (1984–1985: 377) emphasizes two of Foucault's insights
that are especially pertinent: "the extension to the Third World of Western
disciplinary and normalizing mechanisms in a variety of fields; and the production of discourses by Western countries about the Third World as a
means of effecting domination over it." In addition, he notes that "some of
the most important contributions of post-structuralism to the understanding
of development . . . are the emphasis on the production of subjectivities; the
link between expert knowledge, power and the state (governmentality); and
a different set of political criteria for thinking about resistance and social
change" (Escobar 1998).

The crucial question "Who controls the dominant discourse?" is easily
answered in relation to the Third World. If the dominant discourse embraces rationalism, scientism, and development, then it obviously has
evolved historically within the West and is controlled by the West. Global
hegemony, then, is not primarily a matter of economic differentials, the

structure of world capitalism, class interest, military power, or modes of production; rather, the globalization of the Western discourse ensures that development will follow a Western model and will be internalized by Third World states, by development agencies, and by many of the individuals who are victimized and maintained in subjection by it. This discourse is everywhere contested by local discourses that do not embrace Western ideology, but which have little defense against development institutions such as the World Bank, the IMF, the InterAmerican Development Agency, and various NGOs. Alternative discourses are marginalized or wiped out in the processes of development. If this is the case, then merely changing development goals and methods—adopting participatory strategies or sustainability, for example—will do little good; what needs to be reconceptualized is the discourse of development itself. According to some theorists, the very concept of development needs to be abandoned in its entirety and replaced not with some new metadiscourse but rather with alternatives decided by and adapted to the local community.

Foucaultian discourse analysis has been employed by both applied anthropologists and their academic critics. Practitioners of development anthropology use poststructuralist analysis to redirect attention to local knowledges and practices and to examine the underlying assumptions implicit within agency discourses. Those academic anthropologists who reject applied anthropology altogether, often with considerable vehemence, argue that the entire discourse of development must go (and with it, of course, the practice of development anthropology). In short, development must be abandoned altogether. According to Escobar (1995: vi–vii), who seeks to "unmake" development, "The voices calling for an end to development are becoming more numerous and audible." Ferguson (1997a: 170) describes development as "an unwanted ghost, or an uninvited relative" within the field of anthropology. For Wolfgang Sachs (1992: 1), "The time is ripe to write [development's] obituary." "Development," according to Gustavo Esteva (1992: 22), "has evaporated." In the more polemical of these writings, such as Escobar's influential *Encountering Development* (1995), *The Development Dictionary* (Sachs, ed. 1992), and Ferguson's "Anthropology and Its Evil Twin" (1997a), one might easily get the impression that there has never been a clean water project or a farm credit program that did not lead to untold misery.

Deconstructing Development Discourse

Discourse analysis starts with the deconstruction of the term *develop-ment*. Implicit within this seemingly innocuous word is the devaluation of

Third World countries as "underdeveloped," not according to any conceptual scheme of the people and cultures to whom it is applied, but rather according to standards based on the historically particular industrial economy of the West. Within this construction is an economic and materialistic view of life, and a number of implicit dichotomizations: better and worse, superiority and inferiority, power and subordination, active and passive. Age-old traditional knowledges, social relations, religious values, aesthetic sensibilities, and attitudes toward nature may be irrelevant to or openly opposed by such theories. Also inherent within the development discourse are classifications by which people are reduced, objectified, categorized, and problematized. Through labels for "target" populations—"peasant," "small farmer," "proletariat," and even "women"—individuals and communities are reduced to a single feature or trait—access to language, for instance, or inability to read and write (Escobar 1995: 110).

The approach of the developers has been largely a scientific one: The methodologies of quantitative empiricism and economic modeling are brought to bear on carefully defined "problems," such as poverty or population growth, which are usually subject to the technological solutions of Green Revolution agriculture or modern birth control. Science has been conceived as objective in its methodology and neutral in its judgments; in reality it is neither objective nor neutral. Science carries with it the hegemonic philosophy and power of its source. The ideology of Western "progress" toward industrialization and expanded consumer consumption is implicit even in such enlightened concepts as sustainability and participatory development. In contrast to the perspectives of many traditional cultural ecologies, science is designed to conquer and manipulate nature, rather than adapt to it. Claude Alvares (1996: 219), a journalist from India, laments: "But for us, [science] always was another culture's product, a recognizably foreign entity. We eventually came to see it as an epoch-specific ethnic (Western) and culture-specific (culturally entombed) project."

Local knowledge and discourse are historically derived over centuries or millennia, adapted to a local ecology, and embedded in the entire complex of social relations, religion, politics, and economics that comprise the community. In contrast, the development expert brings a knowledge system from the outside that is highly general. According to Michael Edwards (1993: 78), who has worked for a number of development agencies in Africa, Asia, and Latin America, "The practice of development teaches us that problems are usually specific in their complexity to a particular time and place. . . . [I]t is impossible to understand real-life problems unless we grasp the multitude of constraints, imperfections, and emotions which shape the actions of real people." Research tends to be guided by the professional concerns of the researcher rather than the needs of the people themselves, and planning may be made at a high level of the bureaucracy, quite remote from local realities.

Some anthropologists have turned their attention from the targeted peasants to the development institutions themselves. Escobar (1995: 118–153) describes the elaborate machinery concocted to solve the "problem" of malnutrition in Colombia. This effort was directed by the Food and Nutrition Policy Planning (FNPP) program, under the Inter-Agency Project for the Promotion of National Food and Nutrition Policies (PIA/PNAN), based in Santiago, Chile. It started at the level of the United Nations, joined with the World Bank, and in Colombia alone ultimately embraced no less than thirteen institutions. Within Colombia, the Plan Nacional de Alimentación y Nutrición (PAN) and the Programa de Desarrollo Rural Integrado (DRI) were established. Multiple studies were done to define the problem and later to assess the program's performance. A "systems approach" delineated target populations and divided the project into phases. There was a production component (technology development, credit, and organization and training), a social program component, and an infrastructure component. Between 1976 and 1981, PAN and DRI together spent more than a half billion dollars. Ultimately, the program sort of petered out, and despite numerous evaluative surveys, "A significant and overall impact evaluation of the Plan has not been done, and probably never will be" (Uribe 1986, quoted in Escobar 1995: 136). Escobar suggests that the alleviation of hunger might be beside the point; when discursively analyzed, such development programs really have other goals, such as producing a disciplined society, enriching the state, and depoliticizing poverty.

Critiquing the Poststructuralist Critique

The discourse-analytic approach brought a new perspective and a needed degree of self-reflexivity to the development enterprise. Many of its insights are valuable, but its long-term influence may depend on toning down the revolutionary overstatement, which sometimes erases the line between polemic and analysis.

The main problem, however, is not the stridency of the argument but the concept of "discourse" itself. In anthropology as a whole, the term "discourse" seems to have become as casually popular as "function" or "structure" once were and, as with these other terms, there seems to be little agreement as to meaning. Crewe and Harrison (1998: 17) point out that "the danger with such a broad view of discourse is that it is possible for all things to become labeled as discourse, which diminishes its use as an analytic tool." For those not entirely sold on postmodern epistemology, the primacy of discourse as an explanatory or analytical element of argument is problematic. From a slight shift in perspective, it is the discourse that needs to be explained. What brought about this particular discourse? A cultural materialist might have little difficulty with the analysis of the way that language and other symbol systems create boundaries to cognition and act as means of control, but he would probably see the particular discourse of development as arising from material conditions. Is the structure of international relations and the self-interest embodied in the logic of capitalist expansion irrelevant to the production of the discourse of development (unfortunately, these would normally be analyzed in the conceptual schemes of forbidden grand theory)?

The unity of the discourse of development is another major problem Escobar (1995: 39) considers development to be a relatively unitary "space in which only certain things could be said or even imagined." Hobart (1993: 12) distinguishes at least three different discourses of development: that of the professional developers, that of the local people who are the targets of development, and that of the national government. Cooper and Packard (1997: 10) note that different countries have conceptualized development in ways quite different from that of the West. However, even in general parlance, development has multiple meanings. So are there one, three, or myriad discourses of development? As Figure 4.1 shows, development theory has been so varied and so subject to change over time that it is very difficult to find some core discourse that encompasses all versions. Operationalizing a philosophical concept like discourse for social science usage may be more problematic than has been recognized.

A similar problem of clarity exists with the term "power." Perhaps Foucault's most influential contribution was to show how power is infused within discourse, how power and knowledge (or "power/knowledge") are inseparable. However, such subtle analysis might well overlook more conventional manifestations of guns-and-money power. The state still maintains a monopoly on the legitimate use of physical force, and hierarchies of wealth, caste, and class still hold quite overt power. Such power so far has not been particularly subject to discursive analysis. In much of Latin America, the single most important economic factor is who owns the land. This is *German!* a matter of historical aggrandizement, legal titles, government protection, and, all too often, hired guns; while perhaps subject to discourse analysis at some level, one must be careful not to trivialize or underrate these non- or peripherally discursive bases of coercion and constraint. We must also be careful that an ill-defined and all-embracing power does not become an

Figure 4.1
Theories of Development

Based on whether the
major perceived causes of underdevelopment
are within the country (internal focus)
or within the international sphere (international focus)

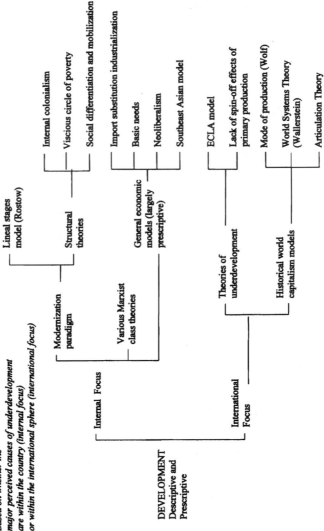

ephemeral spirit force that suffuses everything, like function in 1940s British theory or adaptation in 1970s American anthropology.

The pronounced antiscience bias within the poststructuralist viewpoint is also a problem, as it is in postmodernism in general. Hobart (1993: 9, 10) emphasizes the "extent to which [scientific] knowledge is a social activity" and points out that local knowledges in the Third World are "devalued or ignored in favor of western, scientific, technical and managerial knowledge." For Arturo Escobar (1995: 204), science—referred to as a "narrative"—is an aspect of Western hegemony that displaces local knowledge with no consideration for the complexity of culture within which local knowledge systems operate. For Claude Alvares (1992: 231), science should be understood "not as an instrument for expanding knowledge, but for colonizing and controlling the direction of knowledge, and consequently human behavior within a straight and narrow path conducive to the design of its project." One of the most important contributions of the postmodern perspective has been to reveal the degree to which science has been a controlling discourse of Western expansion and the degree to which it has displaced important local knowledges. It is a quantum jump, however, from this recognition to the assumption that scientific data and methodology should be abandoned.

Without treading too deeply into the swampy minefield of the science wars, which would require a book in itself, it might be argued that a conscious awareness of scientific discourse—of how scientific methodology by its very nature must classify and objectify and of how power is inherent in the scientific process—should greatly improve anthropological methodology and the interpretation of data derived from that methodology. Lawrence Kuzner, in *Reclaiming a Scientific Anthropology* (1997: 41), suggests that "practicing scientific anthropologists not try to do the job of the philosopher, but heed philosophers' arguments, look for potential pitfalls in scientific practice in these arguments, and then adjust methods accordingly so that they can better achieve their scientific goals." To suggest that because science is socially embedded (can anybody doubt it?) it should be rejected as a methodology is simply a non sequitur. Discourse analysis is every bit as socially embedded as science, as is any other methodology one can think of.

Finally, the postmodern claim that underdevelopment is a fiction of Western discourse needs to be challenged; the term also embraces something more substantial, more tangibly, empirically real. While never quite stated, among some anthropologists there seems to be an implicit supposition—not that different from that of the early modernization theorists—that non-Western cultures are somehow, if not pristine or traditional, at least coherent and organic. Communities are viewed as having their own discourses, folkways, cultures, whatever, and they are being unfairly problematized as in need of development. However, while dependency theory has proved disappointing in its predictive claims and has failed to provide a viable ideology for betterment of the human condition, its key idea and the historical facts upon which it was based remain convincing: Underdevelopment, at least in the sense in which it has been employed since the 1950s, is not and never was an innate condition; it was created. The expansion of the West, from the 16th century onward, introduced new modes of production, new forms of exploitation and oppression, and entirely new ways of thinking to the peoples of Latin America, Asia, and Africa. Neocolonial economic dependency, extremely rapid population growth, bloated militaries supplied by a vast international arms market, governments striving to provide attractive investment climates to huge transnational corporations, ethnic conflict caused by colonial favoritism of one ethnic group over another (as in Rwanda) or by state boundaries drawn by Europeans, vast migrations of displaced peoples both within and between countries, the rapid growth of marginalized diaspora communities—this is the true face of underdevelopment and there is nothing innate about it, nor does it have much to do with traditional culture (except to the extent that it is destructive of it). The presumption that underdevelopment is simply a linguistic construction imposed by the powerful on the Other is based on a further presumption of a more or less pristine Other. If underdevelopment is a condition that was created by Western expansion, then underdevelopment is quite real—its effects can be seen, felt, touched, experienced, quantified. To the extent that development is an attempt to overcome such underdevelopment, the concept should not be too easily dismissed.

Development Discourse in Lesotho

Postmodern theorists have often decried a "crisis of representation" brought about by an emerging consciousness of the difficulty, or impossibility, of portraying other cultures with neutrality and objectivity. This has been especially evident through the poststructuralist discourse analysis of development agencies, such as Arturo Escobar's study of the war on poverty in Colombia. James Ferguson (1994, 1997a) takes a similar but less didactic approach to the Thaba-Tseka Development Project that targeted Lesotho, a tiny landlocked country surrounded by South Africa. At least twenty-six different countries, from Australia to Switzerland, have been involved in the project, which in 1979 alone poured in $64 million in development assistance, $49 for every man, woman and child in Lesotho.

In order to justify such massive assistance, the World Bank concocted an image of Lesotho as a stereotypical subsistence peasant society, isolated from the market economy. It was faced with a growing population and declining land fertility that forced most of the adult males into migrant labor. All of this was untrue. The Lesotho economy has not been based on subsistence agriculture since the 1800s, when most of the good land was taken over by Dutch settlers. It was the colonial system that had forced the men into migrant labor. Far from being peasants recently displaced by population growth, 70% of household income was already derived from wages, and only 6% from domestic crops. The fact that Lesotho was resource poor was attributed by the World Bank to geography, not to the fact that South Africa had created the country out of wasteland that was not wanted by the whites. Actually, Lesotho, far from being the self-sufficient entity of the developers' dreams, was mainly a labor reserve for South African mining interests. What is missing from the development discourse is just about everything that is really important: the colonial history, the class situation, politics, and power relations. The people are treated as an undifferentiated mass of underdeveloped subsistence farmers. Little wonder that the project had either a negligible or negative effect.

Strongly influenced by Foucault's ideas on discourse and the permeation of power through nonpolitical institutions, Ferguson is more interested in the machinery of development than the "target" population. Avoiding the community focus of most applied anthropology projects, the international and state contexts are absolutely integral to the analysis, which also (in contrast to the poststructuralist bias against science) makes appropriate use of scientific methods and quantitative data. Though utilizing discourse analysis, Ferguson has no illusions about the primacy of discourse over material and structural factors.

Discourse and thought are "articulated . . . with other practices, but there is no reason to regard them as 'master practices,' overdetermining all others. . . . The whole mechanism [of development] is . . . a 'mushy mixture' of the discursive and the non-discursive. . . . Systems of discourse and systems of thought are thus bound up in a complex causal relationship with the stream of planned and unplanned events that constitutes the social world" (Ferguson 1994: 275–276).

The Anti-Politics Machine reveals how insightful this new approach can be, but only if the more constricted and ideological aspects of poststructuralist philosophy give way to an open and versatile pragmatism. If the latest antidevelopment arguments and discourse analyses are to be substantive enough to have any lasting impact, it will be necessary to tone down the development-is-dead rhetoric, to stop demonizing applied anthropology, to avoid treating Foucaultian philosophy as a self-contained and holistic viewpoint for the social sciences, and to reintegrate some of the ideas which poststructuralism has been too quick to discard.[7]

WHERE THE BUCK STOPS: WOMEN IN DEVELOPMENT

At the bottom, where the buck stops, one still finds women.

Jan Knippers Black[8]

The process is a familiar one and extremely widespread: Agricultural technology, such as Green Revolution crops or tractors, is introduced into a peasant region where women have traditionally been a mainstay of household labor in subsistence fields. As land becomes more valuable, it is concentrated into larger farms and turned over to cash cropping, which brings it entirely under male domain. If the land is retained by the household, women may end up working as unpaid labor for their husbands, with a corresponding disempowerment and less control over how household income is distributed. If the land is lost, except for a small plot, the men will seek wage labor elsewhere, leaving the women to eke out a few crops insufficient for family subsistence. Women may be pushed into wage labor in local factories or agricultural work, not as a replacement for cooking, raising children, cleaning, finding fuel, and the myriad other tasks demanded by the household, but *in addition to* them, thus greatly increasing the work load. Younger women may need to travel to export zones to work in assembly factories at wages and under conditions that would draw violent protest from men.

Development transforms women's labor in ways very different from those of men. Yet until the last few decades, gender was not even a consideration in development plans. It was assumed that the effects of development were the same for both sexes and that income would be distributed through the household the same way, whether it was earned by the husband or the wife. In reality, women often suffered disempowerment and added work from development projects, and money earned by men was much less likely to be distributed within the family than money earned by women. If women were considered at all, it was as a barrier to modernity that had to be overcome; men were perceived as the progressives who would bring development.

As a result of feminist analysis and the documentation of inequities, within the past thirty years discussion of gender relations has become a routine component of the development process.

Bearing the Brunt

Women still represent up to 80% of the labor force in subsaharan Africa, produce 70% of food crops, and represent 30% of heads of household in rural areas. In South Asia, women comprise from a third to half of the labor force. Despite such numbers, women are rarely able to obtain credit in their own names, have far less literacy than men, eat less, and earn only 60% of what men do in wage labor. They start working younger, usually at seven or eight years, in the home or in the fields, and almost always carry the "double shift" of running a household while working for wages or tending subsistence crops. In Zaire, women do 70% of the work. In the Philippines, women work sixty-one hours a week to men's forty-one. In Uganda, the ratio of women's work to men's is two to one (Brohman 1996: 280; Black 1999: 143–144).

In the processes of modernization, men continue to control the means of production—resources, technology, capital—and, to a great extent, they control an ideology of patriarchy that legitimizes female exclusion. Whether development is planned or unplanned, relative to men, women find themselves with only limited access to resources and a lack of control over their own labor and the products of their labor. Also, they often lack the mobility that might improve their condition because of their duties to the household. Where women are able to or forced to enter wage labor, they are routinely excluded from managerial positions or promotion, often being let go after only a few years.

Poor women, more than any other segment of Third World populations, have borne the brunt of structural adjustment policies as dictated by the IMF. These policies give first priority not to development but to paying interest on the national debt. The macroeconomic theory underlying neoliberal structural adjustments assumes that women's unpaid household and subsistence agricultural labor will be maintained whatever policies are enacted; as a result, cuts in services may greatly increase women's labor. Structural adjustment policies that require the reduction in government expenditures through cutting social services disproportionately hit women's jobs, which tend to be in the caregiving and services professions: nurses, social workers, educators. In Ukraine, for example, 80% of those who lost jobs in the first half of the 1990s were women (Black 1999:148). Many countries have been forced to eliminate subsidies on food prices, which usually hits the women's budgets harder than the men's.

Beyond the Decade of Women

Development is often subject to fads, which tend to peak in Warholian fifteen minutes of concentrated publicity before succumbing to a lower level of routinization. In the 1980s, for example, the Reagan administration shifted developmental focus from aid to the encouragement of private enterprise. "Development from below," "participatory development," "sustainable development" have all had their day, leaving a residue of long-term influence to be sure, but never quite living up to the public relations promise. In 1975, the United Nations declared a Decade of Women, which stimulated significant conferences in Mexico City, Copenhagen, and Nairobi. This in turn gave rise to a "Women in Development" approach.

However, the realities of funding did not correspond to the enthusiasm of the women involved. During the entire Decade of Women, only 3.5% of projects at various development levels, representing 0.2% of the UN budget, targeted women. By the 1980s, only $5 million of the UN's $700 million budget was specifically used for women's projects. Whereas most aid money was spent on large-scale hydroelectric dam projects or developing and export of infrastructure, women's projects tended to be small-scale, short-term, and something of an afterthought to more ambitious development schemes (Brohman 1996: 280). Women were often excluded from managerial positions in aid agencies. Women's projects had little interest for men in such agencies and were usually handed off to women in subordinate positions. Both men and women in agencies assumed that "gender" was just another word for "women" rather than, as contemporary feminist scholars insist, a relational term requiring an understanding of the interaction between male and female domains. While there have been attempts to attack the problem of marginalization by bringing consideration of women into normal policy discussions, there is still not much of a sense that gender considerations might apply to the aid agencies themselves, not just the targeted women "out there" (Crewe and Harrison 1998: 56).

The developmental approach has tended to be integrationist, that is, it has sought change and women's empowerment within existing social frameworks, rather than trying to change those frameworks. To the extent that women's subordination exists within deeply embedded structures of gender inequality, development will often exacerbate rather than solve the problem. Yet to change such structures would not only be beyond the abilities or inclinations of agencies, but would undoubtedly bring cries of cultural imperialism if such attempts were made.

As a result, much of the most effective change to benefit women has originated not from outside agencies but from community-based mobilization that might be assisted after the fact by aid agencies. While such popular movements may grow into regional or national organizations, they are typically focused on local everyday problems, such as domestic abuse, food prices, health care, schools, and environmental conditions. In India, such organizing by women has successfully blocked commercial logging, halted dam construction, and blocked military firing-range testing (Brohman 1996: 290–293).

Women's Empowerment in India

> Cooking and cooking I remain hungry. Twelve, twelve children have I borne but still no one to tell.
>
> Rajasthan song[9]

Development programs are often criticized for not being sufficiently participatory and for failing to take into account local discourses. However, even when these are central to the project, there can be quite significant problems. Maya Unnithan and Kavita Srivastava's (1997) forthright analysis of a "successful" women's empowerment program in India reveals how complex such social change can be.

The Women's Development Program (WDP) was established in Rajasthan, India's largest state, in 1984. The countryside is characterized by subsistence agriculture at low levels of productivity. Previous development programs aimed at women had been devoted to procuring sewing machines and smokeless stoves, goals that merely locked them into their social stereotypes. The WDP was designed almost entirely by women—academic feminists, aid workers, and anthropologists—toward the very general objective of empowerment. This would involve a sort of consciousness-raising that would alter women's individual self-image and foster bonds among village women that would make them active participants in family and community decision making. Development was defined as improving the quality of life through gaining control over economic resources and the ideologies that governed the women's lives.

As is true throughout rural India, in Rajasthan, women live within a strong patriarchal, kin-based, and semifeudal ideology. Women are defined largely in terms of their marital status and reproductive capability. There are strong restrictions on mobility and attire. They are secluded, often even within the family, where they are subordinate to their husband's kin and have little say in family decision making. Paradoxically, rural women are considered strong and outspoken by town dwellers. One of the basic assumptions of the WDP was that women did not necessarily internalize the patriarchal values of their culture; rather, subordination was a long-term strategy of survival. This could be built upon to provide women with a voice and with some control over their lives and communities.

The WDP, which originally included six of Rajasthan's twenty-six districts, was organized in four levels: state, district, "block," and village. The most important level was that of the village, which was represented by a *sathin*—a local woman who received a remuneration of US $8 a month for her part-time work. She would work with an urban *pracheta*, also a nonprofessional, and the relationship between the two would be crucial to success. The *pracheta*, who was responsible for ten *sathin* in her district, would in turn be trained by those in the levels above her. Training was not top-down but bottom-up: the *sathin* "trained" the *pracheta*, a process that involved nondirective discussions of daily life—marriage, births and deaths, caste, women's roles, and relationships within the family. Only later, with mutual understanding, would the potential for change emerge. There would be no timetables and no pressures to meet specific goals.

In her interactions with the *pracheta* and with village women, the *sathin* would employ songs, which were of great cultural significance. Songs, often gender-specific and sometimes improvisational, expressed the concerns and longings of daily life. In addition, discussion was stimulated by films and informal theater. *Sathin* and *pracheta* met with team members, lawyers, and governmental officials to learn the details of minimum wage law, available health programs, birth control campaigns, famine distributions programs and the like. One *sathin* was able to organize village women to pressure a factory to purify water emissions that were polluting a local river.

Despite its limited and purely qualitative goals, a number of problems arose, both with the villagers and within the WDP team itself. When a *sathin* attempted to interfere in the illegal marriage of the one-year-old daughter of a powerful man, he retaliated by having her gang-raped. When she reported the crime to the police, they did nothing, accusing her of being a prostitute. Through the support of WPD personnel, the rapists were brought to court and convicted. Other *sathin* were sufficiently intimidated that they demanded not only to be paid as full-time employees but also to be officially attached to the government, which would give them a degree of protection. This was refused, since it was against the basic philosophy of the program. Also, there was a tendency for the *sathin* to bond among themselves, rather than with the villagers. As a result, the *sathin* were disbanded in 1993, and the program planning and coordinating teams formed direct contacts with village groups instead of individuals.

Within the program personnel there was also conflict. The field anthropologists often felt that the feminist academics were ideological to the point of being impractical, refusing to make needed adjustments to local culture. Also, although every attempt was made to avoid hierarchy among WDP personnel, inevitably hierarchies were established based on education, language, and caste.

The program was considered sufficiently successful that, nine years after its inception, it was extended from the original six districts to fourteen. It is obvious, however, that success must be measured in small, qualitative increments.

CONCLUSIONS

Development shows little sign of disappearing from the vocabulary of foreign aid, economics, or anthropology. Far from being a unitary discourse, it would be hard to find a concept that has been subject to more rapid evolution or to more simultaneous meanings. In its broadest sense, as the betterment of humankind, it should be decided and implemented at the local level, since that is where humankind lives. One problem is that localities have very complex structures, so that the development of one sector may lead to the devolution of another; the empowerment of one group may mean the disempowerment of another. Even so, the emergence of grassroots, participatory development is a significant advance.

Globalization can both help and retard development. On the one hand, aid agencies have responded to increased grassroots demands, especially when local peoples can hook up with transnational pressure groups to make their needs felt. On the other hand, states are losing their ability to guide their own development as their efforts and money are redirected to neoliberal structural adjustments aimed mainly at paying off international debts, thus leaving development to be guided by Western agencies. Globalization tends to concentrate the power of multinational corporations that have no interest in development but which, by default, are in the position to steer it in the direction of maximizing corporate profits. The fluidity of the "local" as labor markets become globalized, and the high mobility of potential local leadership, may make it difficult to organize and to maintain continuity at the grassroots level.

The role of the anthropologist in the development process must be removed from the polemics to which it is too often subjected, and the chasm between academic and applied anthropology needs to bridged. Despite proclaimed differences of discourse, there seems to be a fairly wide consensus within the field that local knowledges need to be respected, that women need to be empowered, and that the real meaning of development, at least in its prescriptive form, is people having more options to decide their own futures.

Chapter 5

Constructing Identity

The movements, the attitudes, the glances of the other fixed me there, in a sense in which a chemical solution is fixed by a dye. I was indignant; I demanded an explanation. Nothing happened. I burst apart. Now the fragments have been put together again by another self.

Fanton Frantz[1]

Only when a people learns from its history and affirms its identity does it have the right to define its future.

Maya Indian poster from Guatemala[2]

The character of this displaced "homeward" journey . . . "ends" not in Ethiopia but with Garvey's statue in front of the St Ann Parish library in Jamaica: not with a traditional tribal chant but with the music of Burning Spear and Bob Marley's Redemption Song. This is our "long journey home."

Stuart Hall[3]

Stuart Hall, one of England's foremost scholars of culture, recalls a childhood and adolescence in Jamaica "in the shadow of the black diaspora." His own, his family's, and his community's blackness was all-pervasive—accepted, unquestioned, unreflected, felt only in its relationship to whites. No one ever talked of Africa. It was only in the 1970s that Africa was "rediscovered" through a simultaneously popular and highly intellectual process related to the *negritude* movement of Aimée Ceasire and Leopold Senghor.

An emotionally charged, historically deep, and intricately theorized racial and ethnic identity emerged fairly rapidly out of a rootless and virtually unconscious sense of blackness. As interpreted by Hall, his particularly Black Caribbean identity was at the center of three axes of similarity and difference, continuity and rupture that historically represented the triangular trade in slaves across the Atlantic: the *Présence Africaine*, the *Présence Européenne*, and the *Présence Americain*. The African presence in the Caribbean was no longer direct, but was still deeply embedded in a repressed and fractured spiritual life, and in arts, crafts, musical styles, rhythms, and language. Africa lives on, transformed, in Haitian voodoo, native pentecostalism, Rastafarianism, and Black saints. The European presence was also never found in a pure state but always fused, as in Black British filmmaking and certain avant-garde art styles, always evocative of centuries of violence, hostility, and aggression. The American presence was built on slavery and mixed with the extermination of entire native peoples, such as the Arawaks, emerging in a sort of "cut-and-mix culture" in which white and Indian blended with Black to produce Caribbean cuisines, religions, and styles of dress and design.

One way of understanding this phenomenon is to view identity as a collective true self buried beneath layers of superficial and artificial selves; this hidden essential self is the one that has historical continuity, shares common codes with others of similar descent, and, when discovered and consciously affirmed, reproduces one people. This is the idea underlying the pan-African *negritude* movement. Hall rejects this position. The creation of "a people"—whether defined as an "ethnicity," "a nation," or a "diasporic community"—is not a matter of archeologically unearthing layer after layer until the original layer is revealed; rather, it is a matter of imaginative and creative rediscovery, in which contemporary interpretations and needs fill in the gaps, re-create the past, and bridge the discontinuities with new mythologies. Identity is not an accomplished end point of a people's history, but a constant process of becoming. It is never complete, but always temporarily positioned within a particular context that needs to be imaginatively and adaptively interpreted (Hall 1990).

While most contemporary scholars would agree with Hall to the extent of rejecting primordialist theories of group identity, they would concur on little more. Identity has been one of the most problematic and contentious fields within recent anthropology. There is little accord about the definition of such terms as "ethnicity" and "nation"; about the nature of identity; about how identities are created, reproduced, and transformed; about whether the nation-state is threatened by an increasing profusion of politicized identities; or about the role that globalization plays (one point of agreement is that globalization does seem to create and solidify identities).

Just conceptualizing identity can be quite complex. The way that people understand themselves very seldom coincides with the way others perceive them. In the United States, whites (itself a highly ambiguous term) lump together all Native Americans within a generalized category called Indians. The term "Native American" is itself a recently popularized euphemism, and most of the people so designated continue to use the term "Indian" for themselves; one need only look at the names of their organizations: The American Indian Movement, National Indian Youth Council, National Congress of American Indians.[4] It is mostly liberal non-Indians, and a minority of politicized Indians, who use the term Native American.[5] This may seem paradoxical, especially considering that the term Indian is blatantly and undeniably the white oppressor's invention. (As Indians like to point out, Columbus was not just a little lost; he was about 10,000 miles off, making him the most lost person in history!) This is reminiscent of Edward Said's (1979) observation that many Western-created stereotypes about the Orient have been adopted by Orientals themselves. However, Indians only identify themselves as Indians when dealing with non-Indians. Among themselves they are Navaho, Iroquois, Klamath, or Menominee, and they identify other Indians according to tribal designations. Oops!—that word "tribal" is increasingly taboo in anthropology, having been replaced by "ethnic," and "nation." But many Indians prefer the term, partly because it is in common usage and partly because they identify "tribal" with a proud past. While the tribe tends to remain the primary focus of group identity, at a national powwow or when organizing for political rights that identification can dissolve into a more generalized pan-Indian identity. If that is not confusing enough, during World War II, a great many Indians became as dedicated and patriotic and self-sacrificing as any American; in other words, in a situation where the country was threatened, primary identification shifted to the nation-state (only to revert to the tribe when the threat was past). When the *Richmond Times Dispatch* (Petkofsky 1995) ran a near full-page poster of eight leaders of Virginia's remaining Indian tribes, all but two were wearing Plains Indian feathered headdresses; it is unclear whether these leaders have succumbed to the movie-based stereotype that all Indians are Sioux or simply have assumed what might be termed a tourist identity for political and commercial purposes.

Through the 1950s, identity was not a problem; the groups that anthropologists studied seemed bounded, circumscribed, easily and obviously delineated by language and culture. If identity was an issue, it was phrased in terms of "national character" or group personality. In Ruth Benedict's *Pat-*

terns of Culture (1989; orig. 1934), the author views culture as "personality writ large"; culture was conceived as a sort of straitjacket of identity into which each individual was confined. The structural-functionalists made it easy; they took the synchronic view, analyzing cultures as they would a still photograph, a slice out of time, unambiguously bounded, replete with structure, but devoid of history or wider context. Anybody within the photograph possessed the identity of the tribe portrayed.

The Manchester School, under Max Gluckman, made huge strides in recognizing the fluidity of boundaries, the centrality of conflict, the necessity of taking account of history and context, especially colonialism, and in documenting changes that occurred when people became urbanized. However, identity did not really come to the fore until the anthropological self-questioning of the late 1970s and 1980s, when postmodernism shifted attention away from supposedly objective structures and facts to the subjective experience of the people being studied. Rendering a voice to the subaltern and learning to decipher marginal discourses often meant, in practice, paying attention to the multitude of ways that people belong, or do not belong, to groups.

DEFINING "IDENTITY"

Part of the problem with defining "identity" is that the term applies to at least three completely different concepts: first, how the individual perceives himself; second, how the person is popularly perceived; and, third, how the individual is perceived by the social scientist.[6] The first is the most complex because the way that a person identifies herself at any given time depends on context; she is at one time a sister or daughter, another time a wife, another time a church member. In other words, self-identity changes from context to context and there are simultaneous overlapping identities. This can be simplified if we only consider identity in a social or cultural sense, rather than psychologically, as applying to group membership, either formal or informal. But, as is evident from the Indian example earlier, this still leaves a lot of overlapping, shifting, and situational identities in the same person. The second definition, how the individual is popularly seen, is quite different, less complicated. Society lives through its stereotypes, its overly generalized and monolithic classifications. Walking down Peachtree Street in Atlanta, a respected Zulu surgeon with a doctorate from Oxford is not, to those he passes, Doctor, Zulu, South African, or English; he is, plain and simple, Black. A refugee from Thailand is an Asian—or, if we are to put a really fine point on it, East Asian, despite the fact that she cannot speak a word of Korean and has no knowledge whatsoever of the culture of Java.

The third perspective, that of the social sciences, may attempt to consider the individual's self-definition, but not necessarily. In the past, and to a great extent in the present, there is the need to fit the individual into some sort of culture, which may be amorphous at best. When I first entered the field among the Aymara Indians of Peru, I assumed that "Aymara" referred to a culture. However, there was little sense among the people themselves of such identification. The people seemed to think of themselves as Aymara mainly in a linguistic sense. The term *Indio* was pejorative and was never used. They preferred to identify themselves as *campesinos*, which is basically a job description, roughly meaning "peasant" but with connotations of a sort of rural, slightly heroic fortitude vis-à-vis the effeteness of city people. Identifying themselves primarily as *campesinos*, they conjoined themselves with the much more populous Quechua, who spoke another language, had a much different history, and with whom there was a degree of rivalry. Rather than identify themselves culturally, they positioned themselves mainly against the *mistis* (a common but contemptuous term for mestizos) and the *cholos*, Aymara who had stopped being *campesinos* to become truck drivers and entrepreneurs (the term *cholo* can be positive, negative, or neutral depending on the tone of voice). Most had no sense of history, though when pressed they would trace themselves back to the Incas (who had actually conquered them). Of course, I wrote them up as a "culture."

DIMINISHING CULTURES, INCREASING IDENTITIES

Such cultures, that is, broad linguistic groups, are diminishing. There is an almost direct inverse relationship on a world scale between population growth and the demise of languages. As population pushes above 6 billion, languages, perhaps numbering 10,000 in the distant past, have shrunk to around 4,000; if the trend continues at the present pace, there will only be 2,000 languages at the turn of the next century.[7] This decrease in the types of cultures traditionally studied by anthropologists is more than compensated by the explosive emergence of ethnicities, nations, religious cults, local and international interest groups, transnational associations, clubs, political parties, virtual on-line networks, and every other conceivable form of sodality. Not all of these have much to do with identity; transnational ecological organizations, such as Greenpeace, and human rights organizations, such as Amnesty International, involve a vast range of individuals from any number of ethnic groups, ideologies, and nationalities without impinging on preexisting senses of personal identity. Ethnicity and nationalism, on the other hand, often elicit a primary sense of identity.

The multiple processes of globalization are creating a "global arena of potential identity formation" reflecting "the interaction between locally specific practices of selfhood and the dynamics of global positioning" (Friedman 1994: 117). What are these processes? A number have already been suggested: increased travel, the uprooting of peasant and tribal cultures through population growth, land exploitation by agrobusiness, mass media, the transnationalization of labor, and, in more general terms, the movement from traditional to modern or postmodern.

The increase in global interdependence affects the individual in a multitude of ways: his job, his relationships, his travel, his tastes, the very way he thinks. Jonathan Friedman (1994: 97–98) analyzes the ways that various peoples are integrated into the global, placing the emphasis on how society is reproduced over time. Using a dual subjective/objective model of interdependence, he suggests a continuum of global integration. At one end of the spectrum would be the nonmodern,[8] those who still maintain kinship as a primary form of social structure and for whom the local community provides the key set of relationships that are reproduced from generation to generation. For such societies, integration into the global system in any significant way would mean dissolution; the group would simply cease to exist as a culture. These would include those relatively isolated peoples in Amazonia, India, and New Guinea whose resources—lumber, gold, uranium—are in demand by the larger polity and whose leaders may be co-opted, but who, for the moment at least, can maintain traditional social and cultural systems. Next along the continuum are those more classic Third World societies of peasants, pastoralists, and villagers whose local production is more directly subsumed by larger global processes through cash cropping, specialization of production, trade, and circular-migrant labor. Once again, local strategies of social reproduction may be more or less intact, but influences from the wider world are constant and systemic. Finally, there are those whose traditional modes of social reproduction have been dissolved by integration into national or global systems so that their identities and social structures are closely tied to these systems. Yet for them, the integration is incomplete; they remain trapped on the margins, maintaining numerous elements of nonmodern culture, in shanty-towns, inner city slums, and migrant labor camps.

Consumerism can be a major component of identity. While Coca-Cola, Nike shoes, transistor radios, and tourist T-shirts are found around the world, the mode of apprehending these goods is distinctly local. Among the very poor, an imported manufactured product may emerge as a symbol of upper-class, elite culture because of its glamorous advertising and cost. This was one of the main issues that forced Nestlé to change its advertising policy for powdered milk in Third World countries; allegedly, children were dying because poor women with no access to safe water were associating modernity with the substitution of powdered milk for breast milk. What is important here is not some shallow, homogenized global Coca-Cola culture, but rather the association of self-identity with consumer goods. In David Rabe's trenchant satirical play *Sticks and Bones*, the Ozzie Nelson-clone father of an all too typical American family is forced by the Vietnam War to confront his entire world view. This results in a profound existential angst, a numbing terror that in questioning America he is losing his foundational identity, his sense of self. In response, and in order to prove that he exists, he compiles a long list of everything he owns, from his house and car to his ballpoint pens, mimeographs the list, and hands out copies to passersby on the street corner. While exaggerated, this is as good an image as any of the relationship between consumerism and identity in capitalist culture. In Third World countries, purchased goods may take on a significance not that different from brand-name jeans for mall-haunting teenagers in the United States.

LANDSCAPES AND IMAGINATION: ARJUN APPADURAI AND THE "WORLD OF FLOWS"

Critics have often bemoaned the lack of the postcolonial, native, or subaltern voice in anthropology, noting that the point of view has been distinctively white and Western. The processes of globalization have provided a partial solution by bringing increasing numbers of Latin American, Asian, and African social scientists to Western attention. Among those extensively cited in this book, for example, are Néstor García Canclini, Ana María Alonso, Meena Krishna, Stuart Hall, Aiwah Ong, Alejandro Portes, Alejandro Lugo, and Xiaoping Li.[9] Of course, such scholars are normally from the upper classes, speak fluent English even if they were educated in their home countries, teach at universities in the United States or England, and come from families where Western influences were profound. Thus, they may have as much difficulty speaking for the poor of their countries as do sociologists in the United States. Nevertheless, they bring to their writing a personal experience of transnational identity and dual or multiple cultures that provides a needed authority in the study of globalization.

One of the most important of these scholars is (East) Indian anthropologist Arjun Appadurai (1991, 1996, 2000), who analyzes the fractured nature of culture and the imagination. Objectively, globalization might be defined in terms of flows of capital, goods, and people, but for Appadurai it is in the imagination of individuals that its full impact is most acutely expe-

rienced. In opposition to preglobalization-era characterizations of rigidly
bounded cultures, he draws a metaphor from mathematics and computer
modeling to describe the globalized world as made up of fractals, geometric
patterns that are repeated at ever smaller scales to produce irregular and unpredictable shapes that are not subject to Euclidean geometric analysis. In
Appadurai's imagery, these patterns overlap, move, flow, and are transformed to create ever new and more complex patterns of interaction and
thought. For example, mass migration is normative in world history, but
when conjoined with the electronic media—television, radio, movies, and
the Internet—new patterns emerge. Whereas in the past, imagination was
the property of the artist, the shaman, the poet, and the scholar, imagination
is now part of everybody's everyday life. Mass media creates new scripts
for possible lives and possible futures. The limits of what can be conceived,
of what is possible, have been enormously extended. Whether viewed in the
private space of television or the public space of movies, the adventures of
James Bond or the sinking of the Titanic are absorbed into the general culture. A certain degree of cosmopolitanism is inevitable even for the peasant
or urban street vendor as news from thousands of miles away presents itself
as normative knowledge. This does not mean that media images are digested intact or that Asians watching *Dallas* reruns will see the same world
as Texans. As images are filtered through culture, situation, individual personality, and the anxieties and triumphs of migration, ever-new configurations arise. It is important to distinguish between "fantasy," which is
individual, and "imagination," which can be collective. Collectively, imagination can create solidarities, provoke resistance, provide a basis for organization and action. Films like *Rambo* give international terrorists a heroic
model. News images of the Palestinian *Intifada* and the Israeli response selectively unite Arabs on the one side, Jews on the other, throughout the
world.

The ease and cheapness with which media can convey information have
created a certain degree of democratization of ideas. While American movies and television continue to be widely distributed, the United States is now
just one node in a complex network of image making that spreads around
the world. Bollywood, the Indian film industry centered in Bombay, makes
more movies than any other country; Brazil has a thriving television industry producing *telenovelas* that are dubbed into multiple languages for pre-
sentation across the Third World; in Nigeria, a thriving mini-industry exists
of videos created by natives and circulated throughout the country.[10]
Whereas traditional culture placed limits on what could be thought, and
thus on the limits of life's possibilities, to different degrees media erases

those limits. Because people act on what they think, imagination has emerged as a form of social practice, a type of agency.

In a "world of flows," media comprises only one of multiple global influences on groups and individuals. Utilizing the trope of landscape, Appadurai proposes five relatively independent "-scapes" that dominate the individual's fractured world:

Ethnoscapes are the "landscapes of group identity," which used to be tightly connected to particular territories, communities, or cities. In the globalized world, groups are constantly on the move, redefining themselves. Thus the "ethno" in ethnography assumes a highly equivocal, nonlocalized, and slippery quality. Many people are permanently or temporarily deterritorialized: tourists, immigrants, refugees, exiles, and guestworkers. The homeland from which people are separated may be partially invented; it may exist largely in the imagination, as for many Black Americans the Africa of the African diaspora is more a place of the mind and the heart than an actual continent.

Technoscapes are those fields of evolving technology, providing jobs here, eliminating jobs there, crossing national borders with little regard for a country's ability to assimilate such novelties, filling the air with mostly useless information, filling the skies with jets that can carry anyone anywhere within mere hours. At the local level, technology can mean a tractor that multiplies a landlord's income while reducing his paid workforce by half, or it can mean the opportunity for employment in India's growing computer industry.

Mediascapes are largely image-centered. They provide imaginative visions of distant worlds and entirely different life trajectories, challenging gender relations and conventional values, creating groups, and propelling individuals to act in new ways.

Ideascapes are often, but not always, conveyed by media images. They can also be transported by word of mouth or letter or by a sort of cultural osmosis that recognizes no borders. The landscape of ideas, at least those ideas that people act upon, tends to be dominated by politics, by the ideologies of states, and the counterideologies of resistance against the state. The Zapatistas in Mexico put down their guns and take to the road in a cross-country media frenzy that brings their cause, or at least their colorful masked presence, not only to cheering Mexicans, but also to the world.

Financescapes are the rapid and mysterious flows of global capital that are almost impossible to follow, as billions of dollars of electronic currency move through computers at the speed of light. A small panic in Japan or Korea, set off by a rumor, can affect stock prices in New York, which impacts the livelihoods of Mexican pensioners who will never have any idea why their income dropped 20% this month.

These various landscapes—the building blocks of the imagined and multiple worlds that globalization has forced us to live in—are disjunctive, that is, they are to a degree autonomous, ebbing and flowing in different directions and at different rates, often in conflict. Media flows bring distant images of wealth, beauty, and happiness that cannot be realistically fulfilled; ideas about universal human rights generate demands that are repressed by state violence; a new computer assembly plant produces high-tech work for a select few, exacerbating national inequalities; ease and cheapness of transportation allow states to rid themselves of excess population, but the transnational networks created by migration threaten the state itself.

Appadurai is not without his critics. Jonathan Friedman (1994: 210–211) agrees that identities are constantly on the move, congealing into particular configurations in specific regional, national, or local contexts. However, what seem to be disjunctures among ethnoscapes, mediascapes, and financescapes actually have a deeper underlying unity, ultimately all being part of the same system. To put all the emphasis on fragmentation is to ignore that in the larger perspective the different parts are interrelated. It should be no surprise that India exports high-tech engineers to a Southern California that to some extent has been bought up by Japanese investors; it is all part of the same processes. What appears on the surface as disorganization, disjuncture, fragmentation, and postmodern chaos is really quite systematic if we take the time to understand the larger system. Appadurai might well respond, however, that he is not offering any grand narrative about world system dynamics; rather, he is trying to express the manner in which the globalized world is *experienced* as fragmentary.

Appadurai is more an essayist and philosopher of semiotics than a field anthropologist; in his writings, his observations are seldom supported by any evidence beyond the brief reference or anecdote. It is yet unclear to what extent he is generalizing to the world at large processes and patterns that mainly belong to an elite form of transnationalism. That is a question that will ultimately need to be answered by a multitude of focused empirical studies. Meanwhile, perhaps more than any other contemporary scholar of globalization, he seems to have struck a familiar chord with many anthropologists who have found his ideas to be useful in the analysis of their field research.

HYBRIDITY—ALL THE WAY DOWN

I am Mexican, but I am also Chicano and Latin American. On the border they call me "chilango" or "mexiquillo"; in the capital, "pocho" or

"norteño," and in Spain "sudaca." . . . My companion, Emily, is An-
glo-Italian, but she speaks Spanish with an Argentine accent.

Guillermo Gómez-Peña[11]

Among scholars of globalization, who agree among themselves on very little, there seems to be a general acknowledgment that the forces of homogeneity and heterogeneity, unity and diversity, sameness and difference are either fighting it out in the global arena or are symbiotically related. Or as Benjamin Barber (1995) puts it in the title of his popular book, it's *Jihad vs. McWorld* out there: religious and nationalist fundamentalism pitted against a rapaciously indifferent global neoliberal capitalism. One aspect of this Manichaean struggle is the tendency for people to become more culturally mixed at the same time that ethnic identities are being solidified.

In the past, cultural mixing was encompassed in such words as diffused, acculturated, bicultural, and syncretic. Today, one is more likely to encounter hybrid, creole, mestizaje, intercultural, transcultural, or intermixed. Creole, a term that is regularly employed in postcolonial studies of literature, has been generalized from linguistic fusions resulting in pidgin dialects, specifically within the French-influenced areas of the Caribbean. *Mestizaje* refers to the Iberian-Indian conjuncture in Latin America, from which mestizos were born.

Unfortunately, the dominant term in globalization studies is "hybrid," a trope borrowed from biology, referring to the offspring of dissimilar parents, either plants or animals. I say "unfortunately" for four reasons: First, animal hybrids tend to be sterile and that is not at all what this metaphorical usage is designed to impart (Cohen 1997: 131); second, only two parents are involved in producing the hybrid offspring, whereas humans can be the products of multiple cultures; third, hybrid has passive connotations, a hybrid being the predictable result of deliberate breeding, whereas the process of cultural intermixing is active, creative, and unpredictable; finally, hybridity denotes only fusion of traits, whereas the reality is that *compartmentalization* is also common in this process, that is, individuals can absorb bits and pieces of different cultures that can be selectively used in different settings. However, we seem to be stuck with the word, mainly because it has been thoroughly popularized in the title of a best-selling (and very good) book titled *Hybrid Cultures* by García Canclini (1995).

Traditional versus Modern: Conflict and Accommodation

Although most of the terms mentioned above suggest mixing among *any* cultures, the way that García Canclini and most anthropologists use the term hybrid is much more specific: It is the intermixture of cultures *at different levels of traditionalism and modernism*. This may seem surprising. The traditional/modern dichotomy is closely associated with modernization theory, a form of developmentalism that has been discredited. The underlying idea was that, as modernization commenced, a dual economy emerged, one progressive and expanding, one conservative and static. With a little planning, help from international sources, and a bit of luck, the modern economy would expand to encompass and ultimately wipe out the traditional economy. Because modernity was good and traditionalism bad, this process was supposed to be beneficial. Mostly, this process did not happen, and when it did a lot of people were left powerless and impoverished. As a result, the whole concept of dual economies and the traditional/modern dichotomy came under question. When deconstructed, traditional was revealed to be a derogatory term, implying primitive, backward, and parochial, whereas in reality the communities so designated need be none of these; they were often progressive and dynamic and usually were to some degree—often to a great degree—interactive with the so-called modern sector. That a once discarded "tradition" should be resurrected at the forefront of contemporary anthropology is ironic, but hardly surprising. The premature discarding of ideas is fairly normal. Today, there is a different, somewhat more complex and subtle understanding of what is meant by *modern*, and thus also a new understanding of *traditional*.

In anthropology, which has historically left the study of modern societies to sociologists, the very term modernity is as ambiguous and contested as globalization. We might speak, for example, of a philosophy of modernity upon which the idea of human rights is constructed—a breaking away from parochialism and a recognition of universal values built around respect for difference. In the jargon of neoliberal development, modernization may be the exact opposite of such modernity, since it aims at a homogenous state of capitalism, individualism, industrialism, secular rationality, and consumerism (Wilmsen 1996: 18–21). The idea of multiple modernities is prevalent in anthropology, however, removing the term from the singular techno-industrial trajectory usually associated with it.

For Jonathan Friedman (1994: 91–95), traditionalism and modernism are key poles in the space of cultural identity.[12] *Modernism* is defined in relation to the individual, as a "continuous process of accumulation of self," that is, a "dangerous" constant movement and growth that divorce the self from external meanings. "Modernist identity depends on expanding horizons, the possibility of individual and social development, mobility and liberation from the fixed and concrete structures of surviving non-capitalist forms: family, community, religion" (94). This requires an expanding modern sector within the global system that can support and encourage such growth. *Traditionalism* is represented by being situated within culture, within a set of rules and a totalistic cosmology of meaning. The traditional individual lives in a world of personal relations, dominated by structures of legitimate authority.

These rather specialized definitions of modernism and traditionalism seem somewhat remote from García Canclini's quite practical agenda, but they do bring out some crucial points. Traditionalism tends to be much more culturally embedded, with a high value on continuity; modernism is more individualist, atomizing, and supportive of change. Within traditional societies, family, kinship, and community are the primary relations, whereas in modern societies, individuals are involved in a multitude of often impersonal relations based on jobs, clubs, sports teams, and government agencies. Traditionalism is often associated with parochialism, subsistence agriculture, economic systems based on reciprocity, social division that is semiegalitarian or based on rank rather than class, and the structuring of society around religion.

A tradition-modern conception of hybridization has not proved very useful within the United States or Europe, where the dominant modes of cultural contact are better theorized in terms of assimilation and transnationalization (see Chapter 7). However, for García Canclini, a crucial and very practical problem facing Mexico, and by implication most of the Third World, is how to respect the rich traditional heritage while at the same time incorporating the positive aspects of modernization and democratization. In Africa, Asia, and Latin America, tradition is not something that only existed in the past; it is every bit as contemporary as jet planes or computers; people live it every day. Nor is it the same traditionalism that existed in the past, since all communities are constantly changing and adapting. It is quite legitimate to speak of modern traditionalism, that is, contemporary traditionalism in which people drive motorcycles rather than ride oxcarts and get their weather reports from the Internet, but still gain status through a religious cargo system and recognize kinship as their primary social structure.

Varieties of Hybridity

Focusing on artistic production, García Canclini (1995: 265) points to four "defining features or movements" of Latin American modernity: first, *emancipation*, which took place in the 19th century and was based on European Enlightenment ideals, the liberalization of politics, the secularization of culture, and the rationalization of social life, breaking the primary bonds of kin and community; second, *renovation* refers to the rapid growth of intermediate and higher education, artistic experiment, and the acceptance of modern technology; third, *democratization* is not so much a political change as a cultural one, as, in the second half of the 20th century, electronic communications media and nontraditional ecological, feminist, youth, and urban organizations spread the ethic and practice of popular participation at all levels; finally, economic *expansion* has offered more a promise than reality of modernization, since stagnation or even retrenchment has been the rule in Latin America.

It needs to be remembered that all cultures are *already* hybrid, so what we are witnessing today is one hybrid culture mixing with another. For example, a Mexican mestizo entering the United States will encounter an Anglo-Saxon culture that has been heavily influenced by numerous waves of migration, mainly from all over Europe. Actually, the Mexican may not encounter such a culture directly; his main contact point might be a neighborhood in Los Angeles where third generation Latins, many of whom do not speak Spanish, have established a Chicano subculture that is neither Mexican nor "American." "The pluralist perspective," observes García Canclini (1995: 264), "which accepts fragmentation and multiple combinations among tradition, modernity and postmodernity, is indispensable for considering the Latin American conjuncture." In other words, cultures are neither encountered nor merged as wholes; they are picked up piecemeal. Major aspects of modernity—such as individualism, secularism, or consumerism—may be flatly rejected, while other aspects are adopted effortlessly. The process of modernization is not unidirectional, from traditional to modern, as anthropological evolutionists might have it. A Nahuatl potter may follow traditional designs but use the most modern electrical equipment, while a thoroughly modern craftsman may prefer a foot-treadle potter's wheel. Mexico's greatest artists, such as Orozco and Rivera, turned to Indian or peasant subjects, colors, motifs, and design structures to produce art that was simultaneously traditional and modern. Indeed, in art, it is often difficult to differentiate the modern and the traditional.

There is a very old joke about a pragmatic American who meets an Eastern mystic and inquires about the nature of the universe. The mystic describes the Earth as being held on the shoulders of a giant. "But what," asks the Westerner, "is the giant standing on?" "He stands on a great elephant." "But what is the elephant standing on?" "A great turtle," replies the sage. "And what supports the turtle?" The wise man thinks it over a moment, and replies with disgust, "It's turtle all the way down!"

Hybridity can offer similar options. To the extent that it is a combination of the traditional and the modern, it can rest on a tension between polarities or it can be a catch-as-catch-can process of multiple small syncretisms. Or it may be a permanent and ongoing condition of all cultures—in Renato Rosaldo's (1995: xv) words, "hybridity all the way down."

THE HUNTING OF THE SNARK: THE SEARCH FOR THE ELUSIVE ETHNICITY

> When a reporter asked Abdul Wali Khan his primary identity, his response was that he had been Pakistani for thirty years, a Muslim for 1,400 years, and a Pathan for 5,000 years.
>
> Stanley Tambiah[13]

As far back as 1967, Morton Fried wrote, "If I had to select one word in the vocabulary as the single most egregious case of meaninglessness, I would have to pass over 'tribe' in favor of 'race'" (154). While I certainly do not bemoan the demise of "race" (which may, after all, be making a comeback), I would like to insert here a brief and not particularly sorrowful elegy for the late term "tribe." The real problem with tribe was that it was what might be called a "bridge" term. Anthropological taxonomists could fairly precisely define band, chiefdom, and state, but this left a huge gap between band and chiefdom in the evolutionary schemas of the time, based mainly on structural complexity. The vast majority of premodern societies fell within this gap, which included everything from Nuer semimigratory lineages—which were spread all over the place and had virtually no sense of solidarity—to tightly knit Tewa matrilineal moieties to mutually hostile Yanomamo *shabonos*. "Tribe" was a term that mainly meant *not* a band and *not* a chiefdom (Lewellen 1992: 21–35). Its ambiguity was hardly the sole reason that the term was dropped. A major problem is that tribe suggests an essential, primordial, changeless, original state, which is no longer acceptable; all groups are seen to be in constant flux.

However, the submersion of groups formerly designated as tribal within the very general term "ethnicity" joins both traditional and very modern, lumping together Englishmen in Buenos Aires with Trobriand Islanders, Serbians with the Asmat of coastal New Guinea. And, no matter how broadly it is defined, ethnicity will always be replete with anomalies and borderline cases (Erickson 1993: 18–35). Anthropology is stuck with a basic contradiction: It desperately needs more differentiations, but that would require taxonomies—pigeon-holing, positivist objectification, subjecting people to the demeaning and subordinating Foucaultian gaze. The Age of Classification is long past.

As a result, anthropologists have compressed group identity into two overlapping categories, *ethnicity* and to a lesser extent *nation*, each so broad that no widely agreed-on definition of either is possible. A great deal of time and energy—entire books, in fact—have been devoted to futilely trying to isolate the elements common to a multitude of incommensurables. John Comaroff (1996: 180) observes that any particular theory of identity politics can explain, at best, one third of the cases, leaving the rest to other theories. If absorbing "tribe" into ethnicity is not sufficiently expansive, Ronald Cohen (1978: 1) suggests that ethnicity has also subsumed "culture" and "cultural," making it one of the most general terms in the anthropological lexicon. In Lewis Carroll's *The Hunting of the Snark*, the ship captain comes up with a map of the middle of the ocean; it is completely blank. Our present map of ethnicity may be the opposite; it has just about *everything* on it. Indeed, ethnicity can collapse into a single word: class, biological race, economic status, gender, territory, language, descent, and historical memory. More concretely, it can include dress, craft styles, art, mythology, great battles, religion, and cuisine (Wilmsen 1996: 5–6). One solution to being stuck with undefinable terms at the very center of our discipline has traditionally been, after much agonizing, to declare the term to represent not a thing, but a "process" or a "relationship." This strategy has been applied, with varying degrees of success, not only to ethnicity and nation, but also to culture, Third World,[14] politics, and power. Another solution would be to take seriously what everybody already knows, namely, that words are arbitrary and seldom, if ever, really demarcate what they refer to. This is why science demands that terms be *operationalized*, that is, words must be precisely defined in testable terms *for the present research*. Good examples are "field" and "arena" as used in political anthropology; their general meaning has no specific referent whatsoever; they can only be concretized within the narrow confines of a particular study, a specific analysis. Unfortunately, when anthropology—or a significant part of it—shifted from aspiring to be a social science to being a poor-cousin subdivision of the humanities, operationalizing one's terms became a relic of anachronistic Positivism. The poetics of postmodern anthropology are not only fuzzy, they are supposed to be fuzzy.[15]

Defining Ethnicity (or Trying to)

The term "ethnic," from the Greek *ethnos* meaning heathen, has a long history, but the noun form "ethnicity" does not appear in the *Oxford English Dictionary* until 1972, where its usage is attributed to sociologist David Reisman in 1953. Ethnicity has been a major preoccupation of anthropology for about four decades. Whereas classical anthropology tended to focus on ostensibly closed and isolated tribal, peasant, and aboriginal societies, by the 1960s, most had been or were being structurally absorbed into the larger nation-state and many individuals were moving, either temporarily or permanently, to cities. Ethnicity came to refer to groups that lived in mutual contact, rather than in isolation, but were clearly different from each other. This is still, perhaps, the baseline agreed-upon characteristic. An ethnic group, then, becomes a relative concept, dependent on the perception of difference. Ethnicity collapses class distinctions within the ethnic group itself, so that rich Jews and poor Jews are all the same from a position outside the Jewish community. However, in terms of class, quite different ethnicities may be lumped together, as in certain parts of the United States Blacks, American Indians, and Chicanos occupy roughly the same level of the class hierarchy. Ethnicity is often relative to a particular territory, usually a country or region; Jamaicans would be considered as a single ethnic group in the Dominican Republic, but in the United States, they are Black, Caribbean, or Latin.

To the extent that ethnicity can be defined at all, it might be conceived as a self-conscious or projected group identity that emphasizes and naturalizes one or, usually, a number of specific attributes, such as skin color, language, religion, place of origin, ancestry, descent, or territory (Tambiah 1996 168–170). I use the phrase "self-conscious and/or projected" because ethnicity can refer to a self-defined group with some sort of collective identity, or it can be an ascription of the larger society, such as "Asians" in the United States, for which the people so designated have very little self-identification. Boundaries between groups are not necessarily territorial, unless the group is mostly confined to a ghetto or a certain part of the country; more likely boundaries are social, based upon perceived differences. Thus ethnicity is a matter of degree on two counts: first, the degree to which the people themselves have a sense of common identity, which can range from intense to none, and, second, the degree to which surrounding groups perceive them to be different. For the individual, ethnic identification may be situational: A member of Parliament representing Orissa state in India commented, "My first ambition is the glory of Mother India. I know in my heart of hearts that I am Indian first and an Indian last. But when you say you are a Bihari, I say I am an Oriya. When you say you are a Bengali, I say I am an Oriya. Otherwise, I am an Indian" (quoted in Tambiah 1996: 139).

Do majorities or dominant groups have ethnicity? This is a complex question. Some scholars would answer categorically in the negative. If ethnicity represents a relation of power, a group is only ethnic within a wider political field. Since dominant groups are in control and thus have the power to define who is ethnic and who is not, they are never ethnic themselves. In the United

States, for example, there is no White tribe or set of Caucasian Americans.[16] From this perspective, ethnic politics is, by definition, the politics of marginality (Wilmsen 1996: 4). In Foucaultian terms, whoever controls the dominant discourse determines who gets named and who does not. Since the dominant group considers itself universal or the essential group, the referent culture for all others, it is above ethnicity. In England, Englishness is not ethnic; however, where the English are not dominant, such as in Argentina or India, they become ethnic. Dominant groups, it should be emphasized, are not always in the majority; South Africa during apartheid is a prime example.

But there *do* seem to be politically dominant groups that are also ethnic. The Hutu and the Tutsi in Rwanda are an example; these two have alternated power ever since colonialism. Other examples of dominant ethnic groups might include the Ashkenazim in Israel, the Alawites in Syria, the Hashemite monarchy supported by Bedouins in Jordan, and in Egypt the Muslims over the Copts (Pieterse 1996: 33–35).

Primordialism versus Constructionism: Theorizing Ethnicity

The contrast between *primordialism* and *constructivism* is central to theorizing ethnicity. As far as I can tell, in the social sciences, primordialism is no longer considered valid by anyone. Therefore, there is not much real controversy here. Nevertheless, a certain convention has been established that all discussions of ethnicity *must* include a diatribe against primordialism . . . so here goes. Primordialism is the idea that ethnicity is based on some deeply inscribed, long-term group cohesion, with shared claims to blood, soil, language, and a mythologized history. When skin color, hair, height, and other physical features are taken into account, the implications are that ethnic groups have been genetic breeding populations in which culture has become conjoined to race.[17] Since the early 20th century, Western anthropologists have been in the foreground of refuting such racial nonsense; quite explicit in Franz Boas's historical particularism was the idea that culture had virtually nothing to do with race. However, Western anthropology has, until recently, closely related ethnicity to tribalism, for example, viewing tribal groups moving to cities as retaining the cultural characteristics of their rural identities. In the former Soviet Union, a particularly extreme form of primordialism, called "ethnos theory," emerged, conjoining ethnicity to Marxist evolutionism. Its practical goal was to help incorporate a multitude of non-Russian peoples into the nation-state (Banks 1996: 14–142).

At the opposite pole, *constructionism* views ethnicity not as the survival of an ancient tribalism, but as a collective identity that is created either by the dominant culture or the group itself, most likely as a reciprocal action of both. Fergus Bordewich's (1996: 60–79) description of the Lumbee of North Carolina offers a fairly extreme case:

> The Lumbees challenge almost every preconception of what Indians should be; they are an anthropological no-man's-land located beyond the conventional boundaries of race and political organization that traditionally define Indian's identity. They run the physical gamut from blond hair and blue eyes to the nearly Negroid. They have no chiefs or medicine men and no reservation. They have no memory of the tribe from which their ancestors may have come nor of the language they spoke nor of any religion older than the pious and passionate Baptist faith that, to a person, they today profess. Even their present name is a neologism, coined in the 1950s from the way old folks pronounced the name of the Lumber River. Yet for as long as any Lumbee can remember, they have possessed an unflagging conviction that they are simply and utterly Indian, a tenacious faith that is troubled only by the failure of most other Americans to recognize it. (63)

In 1936, the Bureau of Indian Affairs sent an anthropologist to try to determine if the Lumbees were physically Indian. Using the techniques—and prejudices—available at the time, the anthropologist carefully assessed lips, noses, earlobes, and hair, finally concluding that of the 108 studied, only three could claim at least one-half Indian blood. After this evidence was severely criticized, the Secretary of the Interior ended up rather arbitrarily proclaiming twenty-two Lumbees as sufficiently pure "Siouxans" (!). Finally, in 1956, the U.S. Senate voted to allow the Lumbees to call themselves Indians, though they were still not legally recognized. This was not much help, since at the time President Eisenhower was busy terminating much more established tribes, such as the Klamath of Oregon and the Menominee of Wisconsin. By the 1990s, the Lumbee Tribal Enrollment Office listed 41,000 members, which, if ever federally approved, will make it the ninth largest tribe in the nation.

As Table 5.1 shows, there are multiple versions of the constructionist perspective. The *instrumentalist* viewpoint would hold that ethnic groups emerge when some sort of collective identity would benefit them materially, such as by maintaining ownership of territory or controlling a particular resource. In the United States over the last decades, legislation regarding federal recognition of tribes, plus a number of financial, health, and educational benefits that attach to such recognition, has helped stimulate the renewal of tribes that earlier had faced disorganization or dissolution. The passage of the Indian Gaming Regulatory Act (IGRA) of 1980 recentered a number of tribes around reservation casinos, though few if any tribes appear to have actually come into existence because of the IGRA. Other groups that had sought federal recognition for a century or more were rewarded for their persistence by the new liberal attitudes toward multiculturalism (Bordewich 1996).

Table 5.1
Types of Ethnic Theory

Primordialism	Ethnicity is a primal condition, such as a "tribe" (or even "race"), into which one is born. A form of essentialism, in the sense that it involves an ongoing, relatively unchanging group identity.
Neo-Primordialism	Primordialism which has been conjoined to instrumentalism; in other words, the weakened or threatened tribal identity has been reinforced by some sort of group utility, such as control over trade routes, access to a valued resource, maintenance of territory, or a political need to present a united front against governmental infringement.
Constructionism	The dominant theoretical perspective today. Ethnicity is constructed situationally and in constant flux. Flatly rejects primordialism.
Instrumentalism	Groups are built up out of a cost-benefit analysis, in which some sort of objective interest or common goal, such as maintaining control of an economic niche, is the prime motive for group formation.
Cultural Constructionism	Shared symbols and practices, what have traditionally been called "culture," are the foundation for group cohesion and reproduction. Belonging gives a sense of meaning and community.
Political Constructionism	Elites within the nation-state fashion a dominant set of ideologies, artistic styles, linguistic usages, and the like, which become normative; ethnicities are created by exclusion and marginalization.
Radical Historicism	A Marxist approach in which social identities are created historically over long periods out of the division of labor, class struggle, and class consciousness. Focus is on material conditions and mode of production.
Relationalism	Identities are not "things" but relations, thus any attempt at a general definition of ethnicity is bound to fail. Ethnicity has its historical origins in inequality. It is manifested in the minutiae of daily life, especially in encounters between the ethnic group and the dominant power in the nation. Once established, ethnicity takes on a powerful feeling tone, so that the group seems primordial; thus the sustaining character of the group may become divorced from its origins, which will then be mythified.

Source: Roughly adapted from Comaroff 1996: 164–167. Comaroff includes neo-primordialism as the attachment of instrumentalism to primordialism, and lists "realist perspective" where I have put "instrumentalism." His own theory, which he does not give a name to, is what is called here "relationalism."

A classic instrumentalist ethnography is Abner Cohen's (1969) study of the "retribalization" of the Hausa of Nigeria, which focuses on a group that lived in the Sabo quarter of the city of Ibadan. Neither pastoralists nor peasants, the Hausa had established themselves as high-profit traders, moving cattle and kola nuts between north and south ecological zones. The Hausa were so scattered in multiple interconnecting networks over a vast region that maintaining the sense of cohesion necessary to preserve their trade was becoming severely threatened. There was not much "culture" left that they could rally around. Traditional chiefs found themselves devoid of authority, and the young were drifting away. Exacerbating Hausa disintegration, the central government enacted a policy of actively discouraging tribalism. In response, the leaders more or less consciously set out to reestablish tribal identity through a Moslem religious brotherhood called Tijaniyia. This highly puritanical religion involved intense community ritual and a strong religious hierarchy that replaced the authority of the declining chiefs. The efforts were successful. The Hausa were able to reaffirm their identity and reinforce their lucrative trade monopoly.

This study has been criticized for introducing primordialism into the argument. Yet I suspect that Cohen is more right than his critics. The rejection of even the slightest hint of primordialism (a term that is sufficiently pejorative as to be self-dismissing) is unfortunate. The Hausa were not constructed out of nothing; they have a long history and prehistory in the region as a language group, political force, and culture. The group that Cohen describes is an offshoot of a much larger group, but it is not something entirely new. Hausa retribalization is a continuation of processes that have been going on for a long, long time as they—superb adapters—constantly reinvent themselves. Cohen never claims any essential timelessness; quite the opposite. The simple recognition that most ethnic groups really do have depth in time, that no matter what their present invented, mythologized, or selective histories, there is really a "there" there, does not diminish their present-day creativity and agency. For the people themselves, primordialism is not a problem; it is a validation.

The materially instrumental aspects of ethnicity are foremost in many other cases, too. The Pacific Rim network of Hong Kong business families is based more on self-interest than a deep sense of shared culture (Ong 1992, 1993); indeed, this may be one of the world's more cosmopolitan and multicultural (or decultured) groups. Labor migration, in general, tends to follow networks that are at least partially kin-based, with the result that a fairly small and integrated group will be strongly represented in certain job markets. However, in most cases, especially when considering very broad and highly dispersed ethnicities, such as Kurds or Sri Lankan Tamils, either culture or political interest predominates over material interest. Ethnic Chinese in the United States range from very poor illegals to quite wealthy entrepreneurs, with little in common besides their country of origin. Where ethnicity does involve access to jobs, finance, high status, or political influence, it becomes a very real form of cultural capital, similar to education, recognized artistic talent, or certain skills.

Despite the ever-present element of individual volition, rational-choice theories may be of little use in explaining ethnic behavior. In most cases, ethnicity is an economic deficit that reduces access to good education, skilled jobs, and political power. Within a highly prejudiced society, clearly manifest ethnicity based on skin color, language, mode of dress, or behavior severely reduces the range of options available for assimilation. Becoming or remaining ethnic may never be perceived as a choice; other possibilities may just not be conceivable. In such cases, keeping an ascribed ethnicity may have more to do with following the path of least resistance or of staying within the comfortable circle of friends and family than with any well-thought-out choice among consciously perceived options.

In a country like Kuwait, where labor ethnicity is legally circumscribed and tightly controlled, assimilation is never a possibility. In most countries, however, cultural assimilation usually becomes easier the farther one is removed from the original migration; the first generation has few options, but the third or fourth generation may find assimilation relatively easy, in some cases inevitable, especially if the children are educated in public schools.

Modernization theory predicted increasing homogenization through this type of generational assimilation. However, just the opposite is occurring, largely due to global technology. As we will see in some detail in Chapter 7, the possibility of maintaining one's ethnic identity indefinitely is much greater today than it used to be. Quick flights back to the home country, cheap and instantaneous communication with family that stayed behind, business networks and money moving both ways, expatriate participation in home-country politics, and a constant flow of new blood from the old country all contribute to the production and reproduction of migrant ethnicity over long periods of time.

Becoming Ethnic

Ethnogenesis is the process by which a people becomes ethnic. Usually this involves both the wider society and the people themselves; prejudice and rejection may force a sense of marginality and self-consciousness that stimulates individuals to reflect on forgotten histories and unconscious cultures and organize around them. In Greenland, Inuit social structure has tra-

ditionally been kin-based and highly local with no real sense of
Eskimo-ness, of belonging to a wider group; however, marginalization in
European-dominated towns, plus the need to collectively negotiate for government benefits, has stimulated a pan-Inuit identity that never existed before (Erikson 1993: 128–130).

The development of ethnicity may be seen as part of the modernization
process. In multicultural countries like the United States, ethnicity is seldom entirely a matter of ghettoization; assimilation, or attempted assimilation, is always an option. Thus, ethnicity is to some extent a conscious,
individual decision. A great many African Americans, Native Americans,
and Latin Americans have assimilated into the dominant white culture and
broken ties with ethnic roots. However, prejudice, need for a sense of community, ideology, peer pressure and family pressure, or any number of personal factors may make ethnicization appealing. Increasingly, in the United
States, ethnicity, often of a faddish sort, is something that is actively sought
out by fully assimilated people. The phenomenon of the 150% Indian is familiar on many reservations; a Blackfoot who left the reservation at age 18
and worked in a factory until age 45 will retire and return to the reservation
where he will become the most active in reviving and participating in the
Sun Dance and other indigenous ritual activities. Fourth generation Italians
will boast of their ethnicity, celebrating their Italian heritage, and revel in in-
viting friends over for authentic Italian cuisine (it should be noted that the
founding migrant did not think of himself as Italian, but rather as Sicilian,
Neapolitan, or Calabrian) (Pieterse 1996: 31). Sometimes, particular ethnicities go in and out of fashion; when the miniseries *Roots* became the big-
gest hit in television history, African-Americans were accorded both intense
interest and a certain guilty respect for a time; the movie *Dances with
Wolves* accomplished much the same for Indians (my "North American Indians" class doubled its enrollment for two years after the film came out).

John Comaroff (1996) rejects both primordialist and constructionalist
interpretations of identity. Given the multitude of quite different groups embraced by the term "ethnicity," he argues, no characteristic or group of characteristics common to all of them can be found. As a result, treating
ethnicity as a thing, a noun that refers to a bounded set of groups, makes no
sense. Rather, ethnicity must refer to relationships. Since "the substance of
ethnicity and nationality cannot be defined or decided in the abstract . . .
there cannot be a theory of ethnicity or nationality per se, only a theory of
history capable of elucidating the empowered production of difference and
identity" (166). Ethnicity originates in inequality, but it is not just an imposition from the stronger group; rather, there is always "struggle,
contestation, and sometimes failure" as the two groups maneuver for opti-

mal power. Once constructed, ethnicity becomes objectified and assumes a character that seems natural, essential, inevitable. The original conditions that give form and substance to an ethnic group may give way to a seemingly incongruous sustaining culture; the processes of creation and the processes of reproduction may be quite different. Ultimately ethnicity will become routinized, acted out, more or less unconsciously, in the minutiae of daily life.

Ethnicity, Power, and the State

It is possible to view ethnicity largely in terms of culture and meaning, but a number of scholars see it primarily as a relation of power. According to Edwin Wilmsen (1996: 3), "however embellished by expressive signs or shielded in a cloud of symbolic values, the essence of ethnic existence lies in differential access to means of production and rights to share production returns." From this point of view, ethnicity is an aspect of class struggle, a means by which the dominant class maintains its power by pitting different groups against each other. Thus, there are always two, and usually more, ethnic groups designated within any given political field. Ethnicities form out of necessity in order to stake a claim against competing ethnicities. Ethnic terms, usually based on existing "tribal" names, condense localized identities into overarching generalized identities.

The actual practice of ethnicity is determined by relative position of power. During British rule in Botswana from 1909 to 1966, colonial officials developed a symbiotic relationship with regional mining interests centered in South Africa, encouraging an emergent Tswana ethnic group to support them. These Tswana did not represent the entire language group, but only an aristocratic faction; the British subordinated the rest of the Tswana as well as a host of Khoisan-speaking people, consigning them to foraging until needed for labor. All were collapsed into an undifferentiated ethnic category, the Basarwa. Basarwa developed into a racial classification that continued after decolonization, spreading to encompass other groups until it included almost all of the poor. The process may now be in retreat as local groups begin to reassert themselves under more specific designations (Wilmsen 1996: 6–8).

The tragedy in Rwanda can be traced to similar processes. In order to strengthen and organize their rule, the Belgian colonizers created three racial categories: the Tutsi, Hutu, and Twa. The latter were a tiny minority of marginal hunting-gathering peoples. The terms *Tutsi* and *Hutu* originally meant leader and follower, respectively, and applied to clan social position. Though the people shared a single language, the two groups were given separate histories that legitimized the difference. These ethnic histories were taught in the schools as scientific fact. Identity cards were issued that specified ethnicity. Tutsi, representing about 10% of the population, became elite administrators, while the Hutu laborers were denied higher education or positions in government. To prepare for independence, the Belgians began incorporating Hutu into administrative positions and did not oppose the uprising in 1959, which brought the Hutu to power. A campaign of persecution against the Tutsi created a flood of refugees into surrounding countries, where they formed a resistance movement. The genocide of 1994 was a continuation of ethnic strife, massacres, and revolution that dated back to the systematic creation of ethnicity by the colonizers.

A number of global forces are converging to generate the present wave of ethnic politics. In Eastern Europe and the former Soviet Union, the end of communist rule has collapsed a unity—forged of raw military might, police surveillance, and failed ideology—back into a myriad of passionate nationalisms. Throughout Africa, Asia, and the Middle East, governments sustained in power by allegiance-buying U.S. and Soviet arsenals and by covert CIA and KGB assistance have given way to fractured, incipient democracies and pseudodemocracies. With the dictators out of the way, long-simmering demands have surfaced, often coalescing in ethnic mobilization. Two decades of recession or poor economic performance in the Third World have exacerbated both international and national inequalities. Meanwhile, the establishment of diaspora communities as a normative adaptation within the host country has ensured substantial ongoing populations with neither the desire nor the need to assimilate.[18]

NATIONALISM: IMAGINED COMMUNITIES AND INVENTED HISTORIES

In one sense, nationalism may be the most powerful motivating force on earth: People will kill for money or power, but they will only enthusiastically die for ideology. The processes of globalization seem to have unleashed a plethora of such nationalisms, each, by definition, claiming its homeland as a natural right. While many of these make their claims peacefully (and ineffectually), a host of armed conflicts around the world result from more aggressive claims.

Although the modern state came into existence in the 16th century, what is today called nationalism may be no older than the late 18th century. Before that, European states consisted of enclaves made up of administrators, aristocrats, and clerics who presided over much larger populations of peasants that might grudgingly pay taxes but otherwise professed no allegiance to any but the monarch. For the common man, there was little mobility within such states; outside of a few small cities, different languages, dialects, and cultures were rigidly separated both socially and territorially. The sense that *all* people within a bounded territory should identify themselves with the state, as Germans, Frenchmen, or Englishmen, emerged gradually.

Benedict Anderson (1983) ties the rise of nationalism specifically to Gutenberg and the emergence of "print capitalism." Before moveable type, the Latin language, understood by only a few, was the language of writing, and this placed Truth in the hands of a highly exclusive elite. This elite controlled the ideology of the state, an ideology closely tied to religion in which men and cosmos shared the same hierarchies. Monarchs ruled by divine right and therefore could not be challenged. With the commodification and rapid spread of vernacular texts, ideas were no longer the sole possession of the elite. As one of the earliest forms of capitalist enterprise, publishing grew hand in hand with capitalism, spreading literacy as it went. Protestantism, which required that all believers be able to read the Bible, also promoted literacy.[19] Thus nationalism began with language, as print defined groups in terms of vernaculars: "From the start the nation was conceived in language, not in blood" (145). Anderson lists three other early influences: first, *the census*, which divided people into tribal and other groups; second, *the map*, which defined these groups in relation to territories; and third, *the museum*, which is conceived less as a building than as a general process by which regimes and peoples legitimized their unity by attaching themselves to the heroes and accomplishments of antiquity.

Thus, for Anderson, the nation is "an imagined political community . . . imagined because the members of even the smallest nation will never know most of their fellow-members, meet them, or even hear of them, yet in the mind's eye of each lives the image of their communion . . . a deep, horizontal comradeship" (6–7). Nations are also imagined in the sense that they do not really resurrect to consciousness some long dormant sodality; rather, unity is invented where none existed before. Their histories are highly selective, often mythological. It would be futile to try to distinguish nations according to their genuineness or falseness; rather, the concern of the researcher is to analyze the *style* by which they are invented and imagined. This suggests a couple of paradoxes: While the nationalist believes his passions are deep-rooted in history, the historian considers the nation to be modern invention and some specific nationalisms as only years old; also, whereas nations tend to be rigidly circumscribed in terms of population and territory, nationalism itself is universal—everybody has one.

Once the idea of nation-state developed in Europe, it was spread around the world by the processes of colonialism, though it never really took hold in any substantial way within the hearts and minds of the subject peoples. As a result, early theories of nationalism tended to be highly Eurocentric, assuming nationalism as an explicitly political ideology focused on the state. The ideology of the nation-state assumed that state territoriality was coterminous with a common culture or at least a dominant culture that established the norms of nationality. Even those who did not share the dominant culture were expected to make the state the primary loyalty, overriding local group identification (Banks 1996). In the United States, white English-based culture was the referent culture for new immigrants who were expected to assimilate in the national melting pot. In this sense, nationalism fits Ernest Gellner's (1983: 95) definition as "entry to, participation in, identification with, a literate high culture which is coextensive with an entire political unit and its total population."

Most anthropologists would assume a far different definition, one that makes room for many nationalisms that do not identify with the state. In fact, most Third World nationalisms began as virulently antistate opposition groups within colonial or postcolonial states. Ethnicity and nationalism often overlap: Both stress common ancestry, are constituted out of a sense of difference and thus in relation to other ethnicities or nations, and both often employ the language of kinship, such as fatherland or motherland. However, unlike ethnicity, nationalism involves either incorporation as a state, the goal of establishing such a state, or at the very minimum attaining a degree of sovereignty within a state. Once routinized, nationalism becomes second nature, a part of one's very being (Alonso 1994: 382). In this sense, nationalism may be considered a form of tribalism, involving intensely emotional and self-conscious identities.

In reality, of course, nationalism is a matter of degree, ranging from violent jingoism at one end of the spectrum to indifference at the other. For most, in normal day-to-day interactions, the local community or ethnic group is the focus of activity, and the nation may be conceived as amorphous and remote. It is only in times of war or perceived threat that us/them distinctions become absolute. Even at the height of the Cold War, Americans tended to think of the Russian people more as victims than enemies; the "them" that American nationalists dichotomized themselves against was either a disembodied, monolithic, and pervasive Communism or the government of the USSR, not the people.

Types of Nationalism

Two distinct types of nationalism can be delineated: state nationalism and ethnonationalism. The first is what Gellner describes above: the nation-state historically conceived in Europe and predicated on the identification of the nation with the political state. Originally, such nations were founded on the ideals of the French Revolution and the Enlightenment; they were based on the formal equality of all citizens and linked to the rise of industrial capitalism (Tambiah 1996: 124–127). The idea of such state-level nationalism, often quite removed from any origins in the Enlightenment, has spread around the world. Since mid-century, every successful revolution—Cuba, Algeria, the People's Republic of China, the Socialist Republic of Vietnam—has defined itself in national terms. Multicultural and multilinguistic India gained its independence through a Ghandian concept of collective nationhood, and politicians can still make claims, however unrealistic, on an overarching patriotism in India's conflict with Pakistan. Virtually all Third World leaders have attempted to unify their countries around such a concept of the nation-state. However, outside of Europe, only a few countries, such as Japan, have the ethnic homogeneity to approximate the nation-state ideal. In Africa, where the artificial state boundaries drawn by European powers enclosed multiple mutually hostile groups, governments were often formed along tribal lines; those excluded would hardly identify with a state that was viewed as an alien oppressor.

The second form of nationalism might be called ethnic nationalism or simply *ethnonationalism*, because it overlaps with or is coterminous with ethnicity. Unlike the nation-state concept, ethnonationalism has no common history, no center; it originated numerous times through the world, often in reaction *against* the attempts of a state to enforce a countrywide nationhood. Such nationalism comes in many forms, sometimes regional, as in Egyptian President Nasser's call for a united Arab peoples, sometimes diasporic, as in Zionism, and sometimes cultural.

Nation and State

The relationship between nation and state is a complex one. The political history of a number of countries, such as India, Sri Lanka, Guyana, and Nigeria, can be broken down into three phases. During the period of decolonization, either through peaceful or violent means, a rough unity was established. Then followed a period of highly optimistic, even strident, nation-building, focused on the creation of state sovereignty, national integration, and a national culture. Coalition governments brought together various groups that cooperated to create five-year plans funded by foreign aid. The Sandinistas who ruled Nicaragua during the 1980s, for example, attempted to unify a divided country by means of a populist form of corporatism, establishing state-sanctioned organizations of women, teachers, farmers, ranchers, and the like so that all interest groups were represented in the government. At the same time, they attempted to create *lo popular*, a common national political culture identified with Sandinista developmentalism. It failed, not only because of the U.S. proxy invasion that left the country impoverished, but also because hardened class divisions could not be overridden, and local groups increasingly found that their own goals were at odds with those of the state (Lewellen 1995: 144–145). Finally, as the state becomes increasingly exclusive, ostracized or marginalized ethnic groups begin to form oppositional nationalisms, demanding or negotiating for rights or sovereignty. The dissatisfactions that coalesce substate nationalism may involve what language should be the national language, how to overcome a hierarchical ranking of ethnic groups, and how to adjust horizontal ethnicities to vertical classes. Rapid modernization may stimulate mass migrations and population shifts, bringing formerly separated ethnicities into conflict, and increasing literacy may stimulate rising expectations that cannot be met (Tambiah 1996: 127–131).

While there is nothing new about ethnic violence, globalization seems to be exacerbating it. Such violence is rife within the Third World, Eastern Europe, and the former Soviet Union; on a world scale, only a few First World countries have been spared. Development is a highly uneven process, leaving numerous countries stagnating in the dust of poverty; as a result organized assaults on existing governments are virtually inevitable. Through the 1970s, governments were able to partially stave off serious strife with subsidized food and gasoline, bureaucracies, and state-run corporations that provided employment and other semiwelfare programs; all of these have been drastically cut or eliminated through IMF-mandated reforms. But perhaps equally important is political opportunity; imperfect as the worldwide spread of democratization in the 1990s might be, the end of extremely repressive dictatorships in many countries did succeed in releasing long pent-up forces.

Appadurai (1996: 154) traces nationalist conflict to the "distorted relations and the large-scale identities produced by modern nation-states and complicated large-scale diasporas." Especially virulent forms of violence occur, for example in the former Czechoslovakia, when hatred is turned against neighbors as paranoid nationalist ideologies expose the long-time "treachery" of intimates, people once trusted who are now unmasked and exposed; nothing—not even torture, rape, or mass murder—is too terrible in the vengeful retaliation against such imposters.

A "Traveling Identity": Creating a Tibetan Nation in Exile

If they have lost their homeland, Tibetans have, in a sense, gained a world.
Amy Mountcastle[20]

A "Traveling Identity": Creating a Tibetan Nation in Exile

If they have lost their homeland, Tibetans have, in a sense, gained a world. opology
Amy Mountcastle[20]

Few peoples so clearly demonstrate the convergence of ethnicity, nationalism, and a self-consciously and systematically constructed global identity as the Tibetans. Amy Mountcastle's (1997) analysis of this process provides one of the more detailed accounts of identity formation in the global arena.

In 1959, a full decade after the Chinese Communists invaded and occupied Tibet, 80,000 Tibetans followed the Fourteenth Dalai Lama into exile. A political and cultural headquarters of sorts was established in Dharamsala, India, now occupied by about 7,000 Tibetans and the home of the present Dalai Lama, who is the symbolic center for the Tibetan diaspora. The Dalai Lama is believed to be a *bodhisattva* who has the spiritual insight to attain nirvana but has chosen to remain and help others. He represents a long line of reincarnated Dalai Lamas who ruled Tibet, either nominally or actually, since the 17th century. Today, the present Dalai Lama is leader of more than 120,000 exiles who are dispersed throughout numerous countries, living in a liminal marginality devoid of political standing.

Despite its remote and notoriously inaccessible location high in the Himalayas, Tibet has a history of interaction with the West. It was perceived by the colonizing British Empire as a strategic buffer zone between India and Russia, and later became a bargaining chip in British negotiations with China. From the 1960s through the mid-1970s, the U.S. Central Intelligence Agency was deeply involved in a massive and bloody resistance movement against the occupying Chinese. Previously ignored by the U.S. populace, in the 1970s, Tibetan Buddhism became popular. Numerous Buddhist centers opened. Gradually the Tibetan exile emerged into public consciousness, gaining legitimization when the Dalai Lama received the Nobel Peace Prize in 1989. In 1996, a rock concert organized around Tibetan freedom drew an audience of 100,000. March 10 is commemorated around the world as Uprising Day, in recognition of what was, at the time, a relatively minor mob insurrection against the Chinese.

Tibet never really had a sense of nationalism until the early 20th century. The region was characterized by highly disparate peoples with no sense of unity. Only in 1911 did the Dalai Lama declare Tibet to be an independent state, and even then statehood was not widely recognized, either internally or externally. Right up until the Chinese invasion, there was no sense of common Tibetan peoplehood; the diverse groups were focused almost entirely on kin and clan. It was only in exile that Tibet really became a nation.

The goal of reclaiming the Tibetan homeland has always had an air of desperation about it, a sense of racing the clock, since within the country itself the invaders have set about systematically destroying indigenous culture while resettling hundreds of thousands of Chinese there. In order to gain sympathy and support, it was necessary to validate Tibet's claims to nationhood by establishing a common religion and a democratic government. Prior to 1959, what Tibetan government existed was an authoritarian theocracy. Buddhism, however, was composed of such a multiplicity of highly differentiated sects that no real pan-Buddhist identity existed. Only after the exile, and partially as a result of Western simplifying stereotypes, was Buddhism proclaimed a unifying religion. In 1963, a Tibetan constitution was created, formally establishing Tibet as "a unitary democratic state"; prior to the exile, it had been neither unitary, democratic, nor much of a state. Slowly the trappings of democracy emerged—democratic reforms, a legislative body, an administrative hierarchy, election procedures, and the education of the people into the principles of democratic government. While the Dalai Lama remains the central figure of authority, since 1960 he has attempted to reduce his own political influence. However, many Tibetans in exile have been reluctant to accept such reforms, which are in opposition to traditional Tibetan political culture.

The problem that the Dalai Lama and his government in exile faced was to appeal to three separate constituencies representing three different constructions of identity. First were the Tibetans themselves, both within Tibet and in exile—a highly diverse group that was mostly traditional and parochial in its outlook. Many of these feared that too many compromises for public relations purposes would destroy the very culture that ostensibly was being preserved. A second set of identities was needed for non-Tibetans, mainly Indians and other foreigners who actually had contact with the exiles. Because the goal was to get foreigners involved in the struggle, virtually all interactions were motivated by politics and prospects for gain. Toward this end, a unified traditional culture was created. This culture is exemplified by the Norbulingka Institute, described by Mountcastle (205) as a "Tibetan Disneyland," where non-Tibetans can purchase tourist crafts and take courses in the Tibetan language, Buddhist metaphysics, and traditional folkways.

The third locus of identity was the global arena; here Tibetan exiles had to establish themselves as a people belonging to the world, with a unique and valued identity. Human rights provided a niche for this identity and an obvious nexus for negotiating the polarities of East and West. The West was perceived—and it perceived itself—as rich and technologically proficient, but spiritually underdeveloped. Tibetans established a sort of patron-client relationship in which, in return for protection, they provided religious, ethical, and spiritual services, for example, in helping establish a Human Rights Desk in the United Nations.

Many Tibetans maneuver between all three identities, depending on the situation in which they find themselves, slipping easily between modern or traditional, fragmented or unified, democratic or authoritarian.

None of this is meant to be cynical or to suggest that Tibetans are in the process of somehow developing an "artificial" identity. Unless challenged, identity is to a great degree unconscious and invisible. In the face of disaster, identity becomes objectified, subject to conscious cost-benefit manipulation. Whether conscious or not, identity is always interacting, adapting—becoming. Tibetans have managed to create a "traveling identity" (331) that is independent of place, although imaginatively connected to an increasingly unrealizable homeland. Against all odds, a minuscule group on the world stage has established a position of respect and moral authority.

PART II

Globalization and Migration

I have been a stranger in a strange land.

Moses, Exodus 2:22

I can live anywhere in the world, but it must be near an airport.

Chinese investor based in San Francisco (Quoted in Ong 1993: 41)

Chapter 6

Migration: People on the Move

The changes in migration patterns are not merely matters of individual choice but rather reveal structural factors beyond the control of individuals.

James Mittleman[1]

Thus, in the United States as well as in Mexico, the place of putative community—whether regional or national—is becoming little more than a site in which transnationally organized circuits of capital, labor, and communications intersect with one another and with local ways of life.

Roger Rouse[2]

There is nothing new about long-term, long-distance migration. At the turn of the 21st century, an estimated 100 million people live outside of their countries of original citizenship.[3] While this figure is impressive, it is less than 2% of the world's population, which means that, at any given time, 98% are staying home, or at least within their own national borders (Hammar and Tamas 1997: 1). Percentage-wise this is not historically unusual, nor is it exceptionally significant in regard to world structural change. Archeologists tell us that our prehistoric ancestors migrated out of Africa, spreading through Asia and Europe, crossing oceans to the Americas and Australia. History is replete with mass movements, often based in military action, such as Alexander's conquests, Rome's policy of colonization, the spread of Islam, and the migratory conquests of Genghis Khan and his followers. After 1500, with the Industrial Revolution and the emergence of Europe as a world colonizing power, we see a relatively different emphasis of mass migration, based more on labor needs than on conquest. As many as 8 million slaves were transported from Africa to the New World and to Southeast Asia, decimating entire regions and plunging tribes and kingdoms into war. Between 1815 and 1914 alone, mass migrations included 60 million Europeans, 10 million Russians, 12 million Chinese, and a million and a half Indians (Mittelman 2000: 59). The United States is, of course, largely an immigrant nation, with more than 20 million legal migrants entering the country between 1900 and 1930 alone (Staring 2000: 204). Although impressive in sheer numbers, migration today does not usually involve the great structural changes of past diasporas: the settlement of continents, the decimation of whole populations through the spread of disease, such as was the case with Native Americans, or the depopulation of entire regions as with African slavery and the Irish potato famine. We need to keep this in mind when postulating migration as a key aspect of globalization.

This said, 100 million people is a lot, and that figure does not include the even greater numbers of migrants who travel within state borders. Displacements caused by World War II and its ripple effects were as large as the greatest migrations of the past, and migration has continued at a high rate. It is a truism that transnational migration today, like internal migration, follows patterns of unequal development, as people move in search of economic betterment. This truism, however, can be easily overstated; employment is *one* of many factors involved (Wilson 1994). We must also consider differences in fertility patterns, mortality rates, living conditions in different countries, age structure, and networks that extend from country to country (Castles 2000: 46). If movement from developed to underdeveloped were the primary variable, then we would expect First World countries to be more inundated than they are. On the receiving end, state policy and public attitudes play a significant role; Western Europe relied heavily on foreign labor in the three decades following World War II, but reaction against migrants set in by the mid-1970s with the result that highly restrictive laws closed the borders. This did not stop undocumented aliens from entering Europe any more than similar policies in the United States stopped Mexican *braceros*; indeed, illegal migration may have more than made up for the clampdown on legal immigration. The total volume of South to North migration has increased since 1965 at a rate of 2% per year (Vertovec and Cohen 1999: xiv–xv).

Nevertheless, most international First World migration is from one developed country to another, and by far most Third World migrants travel *within* the Third World. For example, more than 90% of South Asian migrants travel to oil-producing nations, mainly in the Middle East, that actively recruit labor (Hammar and Tamas 1997: 3, 6). The country with the highest percentage of international migrants is the United Arab Emirates, with more than 90%, followed by Kuwait with more than 70% (UNDESIPA 2001). Overall, the greatest number of cross-border migrants, about 35 million at the turn of the 21st century, is in subsaharan Africa. About 20% of the world's migrants are involuntary, having been displaced by war, famine, or other disasters (Mittelman 2000: 59; Castles 1998: 180).

MIGRATION AND GLOBALIZATION

Migrations in the current age of globalization exhibit different patterns from earlier migrations. For one thing, there seems to be a much greater diversification of types, motives, and networks. Often the same individual will shift from one type of migration to another over a single lifetime or even within a few years (Shuval 2000: 45). To some extent, migration today is more extensive and less intensive—that is, while routine distances may often be longer, proportionally the numbers of people involved in South to North migration, especially legal migration, may be fewer than at times in the past; in the United States, for example, migrants accounted for 15% of the total population in the early part of the 20th century, but only 10% today (Staring 2000: 204–205).[4] Although illegals continue to flow across porous borders in great numbers, with less need for what might be called railroad labor, the United States, Europe, Australia, and Japan have turned to encouraging elite migration, seeking highly educated people with specialized high-tech skills. Meanwhile, illegal migration tends to be focused either on seasonal agriculture or on the informal sector in cities: gypsy cab drivers, maids, nannies, prostitutes. The collapse of the Soviet Union and the resulting loosening of constraints on travel brought 450 million potential migrants into the global pool, while at the same time creating a number of new ethnically ambiguous states that encourage movement in or out on the basis of religious or nationalist aspirations. As the Southeast Asian "tiger" countries approach full employment, there are new demands for imported factory labor at the same time that specialized workers may need to seek jobs outside, thus resulting in extremely complex migration patterns throughout the region (Van Hear 1998: 2–3, 24–37).

The time it takes to get from one place to another, especially over long distances, has decreased enormously during the last century, or even half century, with a concomitant reduction in cost. Combined with cheap and instantaneous global communications, this suggests a major change in the nature of elite migration, which may no longer be felt by the migrant as

[handwritten margin note: U.S. wants skilled legal immigrants and unskilled illegals]

between two vastly distant poles but as a continuum separated only by quick access to e-mail or a few hours on a jet plane. The huge growth in multinational corporations has created the need for a new breed of deterritorialized transient executive or highly specialized labor migrant that travels from country to country, from Singapore to New York or from Johannesburg to Moscow, as a routine part of the business week. A key aspect of postfordism within the First World has been the shift of factory production to a handful of Newly Developing Countries, such as Mexico, Brazil, and South Korea, with resulting internal migrations to urban centers and free-trade zones; this has several effects, such as bringing great numbers of women into the migration stream and reducing factory labor as a motive for South-to-North migration. Although well-paying industrial jobs are limited in the Third World, their very existence, along with advertising, modern shopping centers laden with purchasable goods, and word-of-mouth from friends and relatives abroad, has raised consumption standards and life expectations, increasing the draw of migration to more developed regions (Portes 2000).

Despite all this rushing about, the vast majority of people stay home. This simple fact, sometimes referred to as the immobility paradox, contradicts purely economic theories. Most people do *not* take advantage of migration possibilities even when these might appear from an outsider's standpoint to be indisputably beneficial. Indeed, migration patterns seldom conform to what might be predicted from an economic Rational Man model of decision making. Although an abstraction, Rational Man is an individual, but, as we will see, individuals do not normally make migration decisions. As much as statisticians would like a simple or predictable relationship between poverty and migration, no such relationship exists (except, perhaps, that the poorest are often the *least* likely to migrate). Another economic assumption has been that economic development that provides increased opportunities should reduce out-migration; mostly it does not (it may increase it). Finally, if purely economic motives stimulated migration, countries at the same economic level should have similar rates of emigration and immigration; actually, rates vary markedly among countries at the same economic levels (Malmberg 1997; Bjerén 1997).

Benefits and Deficits

Promoters of neoliberal globalization as an ideology point to the numerous benefits of migration: a flexible global job market that provides opportunities outside the country of origin, repatriated wages that can become a substantial part of a poor country's national income, realignment of populations with a concomitant reduction of economic and ecological pressures, and the transfer of skills from more developed to less developed regions (World Bank 2000). The economic assumption of comparative advantage underlies population equilibrium theories that hold that labor moves from regions that lack capital but have large labor forces to more developed regions that need labor.

While such benefits are real, the overall picture is more bleak, as economic and other developmental inequalities between rich and poor countries continue to widen at a rapid pace (World Bank 2001b: 51). Despite antimigrant prejudices and policies, wealthy countries profit greatly from the existence of a "disposable labor force" (Mittelman 2000: 67) that can be hired or fired at will, that will work for minimum wages, and that need not receive pensions or health insurance or, on the state's part, education or social security. When nearly all of the costs of reproduction of the labor force are borne by the home country, remittances may cover only a fraction of actual expense (Lawrence 2000). In the United States, undocumented immigrants are excluded from welfare or educational benefits and may be effectively confined to ghetto enclaves, a situation that is also true in some countries of Europe for legal migrants. A third of all immigrants in Western Europe are Muslim, which has given rise to fears of Islamic resurgence in some countries resulting in increasingly frequent attacks by skinheads and others seeking an outlet for frustrations (Mittelman 2000: 71). Immigrants, wherever, often suffer high levels of poverty, maltreatment, instability, insecurity, and stress.

Given the realities of unemployment and underemployment in the Third World, such considerations may seem academic to the migrant himself and to the authorities in the sending country. In the 1980s, a Thai migrant could earn abroad almost five times what he could earn in Thailand; by traveling to the Middle East, Filipinos could earn six times what they could in the Philippines, and Sri Lankans could bring in anywhere from five to fifteen times home country wages (Stahl and Arnold 1986: 900). Remittances are often considerable: In 1992, wages returned to Pakistan totaled U.S. $1.5 billion (down from almost $3 billion in 1973), about 3% of the country's total gross domestic product (World Bank 2001a). In 2000, $6 billion was returned to Mexico by migrants, placing remittances in the top four sources of national income (World News 2001). However, such remittances are usually spent on family needs and consumer purchases, with relatively little investment that would promote national development; studies in Pakistan showed that 62% was spent on consumption, 22% on real estate, and only 13% on investment, mostly in savings and local commercial activities (Stahl and Arnold 1986).

First World policies that encourage elite immigration contribute to a severe problem of brain drain, which has had a devastating effect on development in many poor countries, such as India or Indonesia, where not only are the talents of the best and brightest lost to the United States and Europe, but the quite considerable costs of upbringing and education are borne by the natal country. On the receiving end, migrants from developing countries help fill professional vacancies, often resulting in greater racial and ethnic disharmony. Although women also enter the transnational migration stream, comprising the larger percentage in certain regions such as the Caribbean, men are still predominant overall. In areas of Africa and Asia, male populations in some regions have been decimated, leaving wives in dependency status on their husbands' relatives; in India, symptoms of this "Dubai syndrome" include headaches, sleeplessness, seizures, and chest pains (Mittelman 2000: 66).

Classifying and Analyzing Migration

Migration tends to be so complex—individually, structurally, socially, politically—that generalizations must be tentative. However, it is possible to examine mass migrations within a common conceptual framework by examining: *extensity* (how far?), *intensity* (how many?), *velocity* (how long to get from place to place and how long the stay?), *impact* on both host and sending countries, *infrastructures* of transportation and communication, and *institutions* that direct and maintain labor markets and migratory flows (Held, et al. 1999: 283). *Social class* needs also to be considered (who goes?—the poor and uneducated or the elite?).

Another method of analysis focuses more on the causal, motivational aspects of migration. First, what are the *root causes?*—that is, the underlying factors such as a long history of colonial, postcolonial ties between certain countries or close contiguity between countries of unequal development such as Mexico and the United States or Turkey and Germany. Second, what are the *proximate causes?*—perhaps an economic downturn, ecological devastation, or long-term political turmoil. Third, we need to consider immediate *precipitating causes*, such as the loss of a job, having a family farm taken over by an agribusiness, warfare, or flood. Finally, *intervening factors* that constrain, facilitate, or accelerate migration must be specified—migration networks, available transportation, supportive organizations, and the like (Van Hear 1998).

Often such causes and factors are difficult to separate out; generally migration involves long-standing links stemming from colonization, trade, cultural ties, or established networks. It has become a commonplace that households, not individuals, make migration decisions, but this has come under fire as ethnocentric, essentializing a cross-cultural concept of household. Actually, each culture has its own norm of household composition, and this norm may or may not concord with reality (in the United States, for example, the cultural norm is the two-parent household, but the reality is a multiplicity of forms). Also, not only the household but the wider kinship group and community may be involved (Bjerén 1997: 223). What seems clear is that migration is seldom the decision of the individual alone. Sometimes, out of years or even generations of such group decisions, a culture of immigration emerges in which such travel is normal and expected, so seeking out immediate precipitating factors may be difficult or futile (Castles 2000: 46).

Any attempt to classify migration runs into many types and subtypes, all with multiple exceptions and much overlap (Table 6.1). The apparently obvious classification into global, regional, and transnational is a case in point. While it is possible to easily differentiate internal (within border) migration from transnational (cross-border) migration, what might be the criteria for distinguishing a global migration from a transnational or regional one? The motivating forces for travel, such as employment, can be the same whether one is traveling from Yemen to Kuwait or from Thailand to the United States; both might take about the same amount of time, and both might involve similar networks. Money-costs, relative to the migrant's income, may not be that different for a peasant moving from one African nation to an adjacent country versus a professional engineer flying from Singapore to England. Nor, within a globalized economy, is it easy to disengage global forces from transnational forces. It is often possible to differentiate migration types by motivation: forced, voluntary, political, social, or economic. However, motivations are seldom only those of the individual migrant and are usually multiple and complex.

Mobility patterns do offer the possibility of classification if we follow the migrant over a long enough period of time (Malmberg 1997). We can differentiate permanent international migration from temporary migration and short-term migration from long-term, but it would be necessary to divide each into multiple subtypes. Permanent migration might involve never returning to the home country, or it might involve often returning and maintaining strong family and friendship networks in the old country. Temporary migration might be a once-in-a-lifetime thing, or it might be a yearly routine. *Step-migration*, in which either the individual or a kin network migrates in increments, stopping for years at each place, may ultimately become permanent migration. *Migratory chains*, or "network-mediated chain migrations," occur when someone opens a path of internal

Table 6.1
A Brief Glossary of Migration

Internal Migrant	One who travels, usually for employment and often from rural to urban areas, for long periods within the country of citizenship.
International Migrant	A person who leaves his country of citizenship, often multiple times and to different countries, and returns without making a significant long-term social investment in the country or countries of destination.
Immigrant	One who leaves his country of citizenship to live permanently, or for a long term, in another country. Refers to the country of settlement. ("Emigrant" suggests the point of view of the home country.)
Transnational Immigrant	One who maintains multiple contacts—social, cultural, political, economic—with both the country of origin and the host country. This may involve the constant construction and reconstruction of a "nation" or diaspora community that transcends borders.
Diaspora	Dispersal from a homeland to multiple countries. Often implies forced dispersal. Sometimes extended to include groups from general regions, rather than a specific location, such as the African diaspora or the Caribbean diaspora. Usually suggests some sort of emotional relation to the homeland.
Refugee	One who is forcibly dispersed through war or political repression, and, by extension, famine, earthquake, etc. A refugee may be "internal" (within the country) or international.
Step-migration	When a community or kin group migrates in stages, usually from rural to urban, with individuals from each generation moving farther from the place of origin and establishing network links to the new location.
Migratory Chain	The formation of a complex network as individuals constantly carry the network forward, often to multiple locations, so that any migrant can follow the network at different times and to different end points.
Circular Migration	Migration away from and back to the home community. Often quite routinized, as in some forms of agricultural labor migration.

or cross-border migration that will be followed by other family, community, or tribal members, creating a network that increases in complexity over time. Typically, these start with an individual; in some countries military recruitment or conscription will take a young man away from a traditional community, and when he settles elsewhere he will provide the first link. As later migrants follow, the chain will evolve into a network, perhaps with multiple end points, and become self-sustaining. This may ultimately result in a "culture of migration," in which travel is expected as a rite of passage for young men or women. Such a culture may create a virtual "migration industry" of smugglers, agents, organizations, and lawyers (Castles 2000: 46; Wilson 1994).

THE ANTHROPOLOGY OF MIGRATION

Migration was not a major area of research for anthropology until the late 1950s, when the conscripted, tightly bounded tribes, communities, and cultures described by structural-functionalists began to give way to more fluid conceptions. Early studies tended to focus on the movement of peasants into cities, creating a model of stage migration, in which each generation would move to a more populous area, ultimately ending up in big city shantytowns. This work, focusing on adaptive strategies, classified different types of migration and laid the groundwork for emphasizing social networks rather than individuals.[5] It was only from the early 1980s that international migration began to assume a dominant place in anthropology. However, as Gunilla Bjerén (1997: 220) observes, the "contentious, fragmented, and contradictory character of development and the dependence of migration on it are partial reasons why anthropology offers no grand theories of migration and development, despite the large number of empirical studies focusing on migration and development in the discipline."

Studies of migration might be classified roughly as classic, modern, and emergent. During anthropology's *classic* period, through the 1960s, the dominant models of migration were largely based on push and pull factors that either drove rural peoples out of the countryside or attracted them to cities. Once in the city or in another country, migrants would assimilate into the dominant culture, perhaps over a generation or two. The *modern* period is characterized by neo-Marxist models that focus on structural inequalities that siphon people from less developed to more developed regions in search of jobs. The recent period may be characterized as still *emergent:* Models focus less on general theories and more on the specifics of particular migrations. Migration is viewed as extremely complex, as are the motives and experiences of those who move. In contrast to "assimilation" and "cost-benefit," the new vocabulary of migration is one of transnationalism, diaspora, multiculturalism, citizenship acquisition, social movements, and refugees (Heisler 1992).

Since the earliest studies, anthropological approaches to migration have been closely tied to economic development theory, because, almost invariably, movement was from a less to a more developed region. Because urban areas are the focal points of development, much of internal migration theory was tied to the rural base at one end and the city at the other. Anthropological research on international migration tended to follow the same underdeveloped-to-developed trajectory, but not necessarily with the urban focus, as in the much-studied Mexican migration of agricultural workers to the United States.[6]

Migration and Modernization Theory

As interpreted by Michael Kearney (1986), migration theory in anthropology has accompanied development theory through three key phases: modernization, dependency, and articulation. As we have seen in Chapter 3, modernization theory, which was closely conjoined to the structural functionalism that dominated anthropology until the mid-1960s, was based on a dualist model that contrasted traditional and modern and maintained the belief in a unilineal evolution toward a better world through industrialization, technological development, education, entrepreneurial values, and democracy. Migration would accelerate these beneficial processes as rural people, already enmeshed in what Robert Redfield (1941) termed a folk-urban continuum, moved to the cities where their repatriated wages would be used for development of the countryside. They would assimilate modern values: individualism, the desire for education, entrepreneurialism, and a taste for innovation and change. Returning migrants would bring these values back to the rural areas, along with their savings, thus breaking down the stultifying fatalistic traditionalism that kept peasants mired in their primitive ways. The flow of modernization was one-way, from urban to rural. Implicit in the modernization paradigm is an economistic Rational Man model, with its emphasis on individuals calculating the costs and benefits of various options. Motives for migration were reduced to pull and push factors: the enticements of urban jobs and bright lights versus rural overpopulation, land scarcity, and unemployment.

Unfortunately for the theory, already by the mid-1960s it was becoming evident that moving to the cities did not necessarily lead to the psychological transformation of the migrant, and it certainly did not result in development of the hinterland. "Peasants in cities" became a more or less permanent status as migrants were marginalized, isolated from the modern sector within slums, shantytowns, and self-contained informal economies. Decision making turned out to be made by families and kin networks, not individuals, and external constraints often were so limiting that actions might be funneled in a single or just a few directions. For example, for the large majority of Aymara Indians of highland Peru, who lived almost entirely on subsistence agriculture until after midcentury, about the only truly accessible avenue of entrance into the money economy was through seasonal migrant labor in the commercial rice fields hundreds of miles away on the coast (Lewellen 1978). Whether in Africa, Asia, or Latin America, particular communities tended to migrate to particular sites and participate in particular occupations, even when economically preferential options might appear to be available. Social and cultural strictures—such as gender roles, kin and friendship relations, and concepts of appropriate work—played a larger part than individual decision making in determining who would leave and where they would go. The individualist approach, with its focus on psychological factors, simply did not work at the level of general theory.

Migration and Dependency Theory

Dependency theory brought a new and virtually opposite orientation to the study of migrants. Andre Gunder Frank (1967) and others reversed the focus of interest from development to *under*development, the latter conceived not as some primal condition to be outgrown by modernization, but as something created and maintained by the processes of modernization. The modern/traditional, urban/rural dichotomies were replaced by a unified system of domination and dependency. Far from migration diffusing modernization from the cities to the countryside, the new theorists saw the hinterland as being drained of its labor and raw materials through the process of internal colonialism. What the rural areas received was just enough to reproduce and exacerbate conditions of poverty that would maintain a sufficient supply of surplus labor to hold down urban wages.

Early, purely structural versions of dependency theory came to incorporate historical depth, relating dependency to core/periphery relationships established over hundreds of years of colonialism and imperialism (Brettell 2000: 103–104). The level of analysis was radically elevated from the individual or household to the state or international system. The state might be considered an appropriate level of analysis, since states contained comprador elites, such as European-educated managers of local subsidiaries of multinational corporations, that represented the core within the peripheral country. However, dependency theory was most comfortable analyzing terms of trade, the spin-off effects of industrial versus primary production, and other relationships among core and periphery nations. This was a major problem for anthropologists who got little help at the community level from such a bird's-eye perspective. The anthropologist living for a year or two in a market town or a peasant community might be sympathetic to dependency theory, but would see little of it in day-to-day activities. Just as satellite photography may not be the appropriate tool for gathering data on the ratio of corn to beans sold by market women, so dependency theory did not provide much of practical use to the anthropological field-worker. The situation was hardly helped by the next stage in the evolution of theory, namely Wallerstein's world systems theory, which raised the level of analysis to a single *world* division of labor. Dependency and world systems theories had the effect of robbing anthropologists of their previous certainties without replacing them with much of value that was directly usable, except perhaps the negative value that individualistic, dichotomistic approaches were not viable.

Migration and Articulation Theory

The major postdependency migration-and-development perspective would be articulation theory (Kearney 1986: 341–345). Originally formulated by Marxist anthropologists in the early 1980s, this perspective starts with the recognition that precapitalist or simply noncapitalist modes of production continue to exist alongside capitalism. While global capitalism necessarily impinges on these alternative systems, forcing them to alter their structures and make multiple accommodations in unpredictable directions, they do not necessarily become capitalist; in fact, such systems may even be strengthened. Influence is not one-way; local systems must, of course, bear the brunt of whatever adaptation is necessary or desirable, but at the same time capitalism must also make adjustments. It is this articulation between the two systems—say, between capitalism and traditional African economies (Meillassoux 1981) or Chinese communism (Li 1996)—that provides the analytical focus of this perspective. In describing how the two systems communicate and interact, articulationists must define the relationships between various elements of the migrant system, especially the many dimensions involved in the movement between capitalist and noncapitalist economic spheres.

This orientation rejects the idea that there is a unitary world system; the periphery is more independent and dynamic than dependency theory would allow. This shift from the high-level determinism of dependency and world systems theory puts the ball squarely back into the anthropologist's court; it is the community and household that anchors the migrant, whether at home or away. The recognition that migrants participate in two spheres of production—a capitalist wage labor sphere and a noncapitalist sphere, such as subsistence agriculture—is crucial. Both are reinforced and reproduced, with no logical or historical desiderata that capitalism wipe out alternative modes.

While both modernization and dependency theories tended to treat modes of production as historical sequences, the articulation orientation takes a more horizontal perspective, either allowing for or insisting on simultaneous economies acting in rough symbiosis. A circular migrant, with one foot in wage labor and the other in subsistence agriculture, is more flexible and, in some ways, more secure than an individual committed to only one or the other. Without denying the exploitative aspects of a capitalist system that demands a massive pool of surplus labor, the articulation perspective legitimizes the circular migrant as a permanent rather than transitory category. No matter how far they travel, such migrants never entirely leave the base of family, household, community, and culture. For the field anthropologist, articulation theory returns the focus of analysis to the level of the group that is actually studied. It also recognizes a basic fact, rediscovered by many anthropologists but antithetical to early modernization viewpoints: In most cases, as we have seen, returning migrants do *not* bring back money for transformative investment, *nor* do they bring back transformative skills (most skills learned in either industrial or agricultural labor have little or no relevance at home). Another important contribution of this perspective is its emphasis on the labor of women, who may be employed as wage laborers, but at the same time must toil as unpaid workers outside the capitalist sphere, that is, within the household, small-scale marketing, and subsistence agriculture.

MIGRATION THEORY AND GLOBALIZATION

The internal dynamic and logic of international migration streams are set by the coordinates of gender, reproduction, and the search for livelihood, and played out in a whirlpool of thresholds and loopholes, opportunities and booby traps rigged and structured by forces beyond the reach and maybe beyond the vision of the individual migrant.

Gunilla Bjerén[7]

As long as migration was tied to development and to theories drawn from economics, it tended to have a Marxian materialist bias, emphasizing the movements of labor and resources, and a strong focus on *internal* migration. Several factors tended to break down these linkages during the 1990s. Certainly, one of the most important was the emergence of postmodernism, which refocused attention on the symbolic, linguistic, and constructed aspects of society. A vehement discourse-analytic critique tended to delegitimize the very concept of development, while a "Writing Culture" school called into question the objectivity and self-confident representations of much ethnography. Reflexivity, subjectivities, alterity, agency, and discourse became the key terms of a major refocusing away from grand theory, especially materialist theory, and onto the experiences, expectations, and identities of the migrants. Paradoxically perhaps, globalization had a positive effect on anthropological positioning. With its focus on the global-local nexus and on culture, transformation, and the ways that time and space are experienced, globalization brought migration theory back down to earth from the empyrean heights of dependency and world systems theory, while at the same time shifting the focus away from in-country rural urban movements to cross-border research.[8]

Transnationalism

Transnationalism emerged less as a theory than as a set of ideas and conceptual tools of analysis. Such dichotomizations as beginning point/end point, push/pull, rural/urban, traditional/modern had been in a state of exhaustion and decline for some time; now they were finally abandoned altogether in favor of a continuum of space and time and of overlapping processes. With the increasing rapidity and ease of transportation and communications, place of resettlement, homeland, and everything in-between became points in a social field. The bounded community of traditional ethnographic fieldwork gave way to multiple, shifting, and interpenetrating spaces, perhaps most notably articulated in Arjun Appadurai's (1991, 1996) differentiation of *ethnoscapes, mediascapes, technoscapes, financescapes,* and *ideascapes* (see Chapter 5). Space was no longer an objective given, but something that was constructed in the process of migration. The communities, societies, cultures, and peoples of traditional anthropology were, for some, replaced by "imagined communities" (Anderson 1983) that were created in the act of migration. This required a new or revamped vocabulary for describing the fluid and undefined interaction zones characteristic of contemporary migrants: border theory, transculturation, transnationalization, creolization, hybridity, diaspora and diasporic communities, to name just a few. This shift was, to some degree, from a materialist economistic focus on labor to a more subjective, experiential mode of analysis: "What we are describing is, first and foremost, the movement of peoples, not labor, even if, more often than not, labor has been key to their movements" (Held, et al. 1999: 283). Taking cues from both Pierre Bourdieu (1977) and Michel Foucault (1973, 1995), power came to be understood as a key component of all social interactions; this power took on more complex and subtle forms than in conventional political analysis, embedded as it was in "discourse" (Foucault) or "field" and "habitus" (Bourdieu).

Both the commonalities and controversies of this new perspective were articulated in a 1995 conference on the anthropology of migration (Szanton Blanc, Basch, and Schiller 1995). The greatest conflict was over the role of the nation-state: whether its power or even its existence was in decline; the locus of power within the state and its effect on both legal and illegal immigrants; and whether the concepts of nation and state should be separated. However, some significant elements of a new analytical framework emerged. First, any comparison of migrations required historical depth in order to differentiate the present form, based on global capitalism, from past forms. Second, the idea of space needed to be rethought, including the ways that space is symbolically manipulated and contested. Third, regimes of power, both within and outside of governments, must be clarified and related to the abilities of people to determine their own fates and control their own identities. Finally, identity politics emerging from migration needs to be analyzed in relation to the restructuring of the global economy and other transnational processes.

Migration studies, perhaps more than any other aspect of the anthropology of globalization, have been a matrix for the introduction and elaboration of new concepts of space and identity.

Testing Migration Theories in Jalisco, Mexico

In Los Arboles, a relatively well-off *rancho* (roughly "community") in Jalisco, Mexico, three-quarters of the 152 male heads of household repeatedly migrate to the United States for work. Many of the residents are from surrounding *ranchos*, pushed off of share-cropped land by the mechanization of agriculture. Landlessness, or ownership of only a few hectares, plus a lack of permanent jobs in the area stimulate a high degree of transnational labor migration. This situation provided Tamar Diana Wilson (1994) with the data to test three standard theories of migration.

The first theory, the immigration market model, views potential migrants as economic cost-benefit analysts who rationally measure the advantages and disadvantages of various countries and regions in terms of wealth maximization. Because this theory focuses on legal, documented immigrants, the selection process on the part of the target state is also important; education and particular skills will be advantaged. Migrants will be positively selected when high income earners in the home country also receive high incomes in the new country and negatively selected when low earners at home also receive low wages abroad. Thus, the crucial element is the amount of human capital that the migrant can bring to the table; those with the greatest abilities both can and do migrate.

When applied to Los Arboles, Wilson finds many problems with this model. It is not evident at all that the most able actually migrate. In Third World countries, even the most intelligent and ambitious may lack the opportunities to develop skills, and if one does, those skills most likely will not transfer across borders (or even within the country). Because this model focuses on the individual, it ignores the household, kin, and social networks that are actually the decision makers. Migrants will tend to follow established networks, only rarely venturing into areas where they will not have ready sources of information and a fall-back of group support. On the receiving end, pay will not be determined by the value of the work so much as by the degree of unionization, minimum wage legislation, and available and effective legal remedies for underpayment.

The second explanation, the stage migration model, postulates that migrants tend to travel short distances at first, perhaps to local towns, then farther, gradually moving toward and into the larger metropolitan industrial areas. As the earliest migrants move on, they leave a labor vacuum behind for new migrants to fill. This model dates back to studies in the late 19th century in the British Isles and has been applied extensively to peasants in Latin America, where a number of factors, such as poor labor conditions and seasonal work, encourage this type of temporary migration. This model has been largely dismissed as overly simplistic, failing to account for the variety and complexity of migrations. However, those moving into Los Arboles from poorer surrounding communities, then migrating outward in search of better conditions, do suggest just such a stage migration pattern, at least until they hook up with more developed networks.

The more useful theory of chain migration, which Wilson elaborates as "network mediated chain migration," views *relationships with previous migrants* as the primary variable. Complex networks provide information and support all along the line. Through such self-reproducing and self-expanding networks, the migrant learns where the best jobs are, how to get there, where to find housing, and how to get around in the new environment. Earlier migrants will arrange transportation and provide temporary housing while the new migrant gets established. Earlier theories assumed that the chain would link only two points. More recent research refutes this bipolar model; there may be many destinations available as the network begins to look more like a spider web than a chain. Some of these networks are quite extensive; one study of migrants in a single *pueblo* in Mexico found no less than 110 destinations in the United States. Nor is what is considered the home community a stable concept; networks have multiple homes.

Migrants from Los Arboles reveal a "foraging pattern" of migration. They do not necessarily return to the same place each time they cross the border into the United States; one year an individual may follow the network to any of a number of sites in California and the next year may end up in Milwaukee, another nodal point of the network. The network itself grows through marriage, friendships, and *compadrazgo* (fictive kinship) relations, so it includes many people who are not from Los Arboles. Available destinations shift over time, opening new regions or cities while closing off others. Reasons for such shifts may have to do with job markets, but may be less predictable and even somewhat arbitrary, as new links are formed for reasons more personal than purely economic. Access to the network becomes a sort of cultural capital, perhaps the single most important capital that the migrant possesses.

GENDER AND MIGRATION

In India, where "pollution" is a primary determinant of caste and where women have traditionally been forbidden to speak with unrelated men, the profession of nursing is often considered "dirty"; yet nursing has emerged as a major path of upward mobility and independence for women. Given the low status, low pay, and dismal working conditions in Indian hospitals, many Christian nurses from the state of Kerala have migrated to the United States.

One effect of such migration is to reverse gender roles; because women move first, they become the breadwinners for husbands that follow. The husbands, who may have to relinquish high-status jobs in India for unemployment or low-status work in the United States, often find themselves taking care of children and doing other domestic tasks, unthinkable for married men in India. Deeply embedded Kerala cultural values are not left back in India, but follow the couple to the United States, constantly reinforced by trips and communications back "home." To the extent that the dirty nurse status is culturally retained, it reflects on the husband's already diminished sense of self-worth. In compensation, men often turn to religion; sympathetic Christian churches in transmigrant communities have readjusted their official positions to accommodate men who must seek authority and approval outside their homes. However, the multiplication of religious offices has resulted in their devaluation, so the actual value may be minimal (George 2000).

This brief example reveals three important points: First, gender must be considered in analyzing the migratory experience; second, the issue of gender can be extremely complex; and, third, the term "gender" does not mean women (as it once did) but rather the relationship between men and women.

Until the 1970s, anthropological studies of migration tended to focus on internal movements, those within state borders. Research was mostly carried out by men who took an objectivist, functionalist approach that generalized all migrants, without considering gender. When gender was taken into account, it was to focus on marriage laws and alliances; women were viewed as appurtenances to men—as wives or daughters who either stayed at home or followed the family. The man was the sole or primary breadwinner and thus the obvious focus of attention. To a limited extent, this point of view was justified; most labor migrants at that time were men (Breger and Hill 1998: 2; Clifford 1994: 313).

Recent changes have brought about increasing research on the way that migration is gendered: more and more women are migrating, often independently of men, and more women anthropologists are studying migration. It is now recognized that women comprise the larger part of some migration streams. Women migrate in many different ways, as dependent wives, daughters, and mothers, to be sure, but also as workers and heads of households.

The wage work available to women is usually quite different from that available to men. Most work is in poorly paid jobs abandoned by citizens of the host country as too low-status, too boring, or too seasonal. Industrial enclaves created by globalization throughout the Third World are a primary source of in-country employment; the *maquilas* along the United States–Mexico border are the best known, but similar free-trade zones exist in numerous countries. Cross-border opportunities for women's migratory labor mainly follows a South-to-North trajectory, though not always. The oil boom in the Gulf states during the 1970s and 1980s coincided with a severe economic downturn in Sri Lanka. In desperation, more than a million young women accepted jobs as maids in Kuwait, Bahrain, Qatar, the United Arab Emirates, Oman, and Saudi Arabia, often leaving children and unemployed husbands behind. Back home, men were culturally restricted from crossing gender lines, so responsibility for children and for domestic care fell to female kin (Bjerén 1997: 241–242).

The most common job for women is in domestic service, followed by health services and garment manufacturing. Employers prefer women because they are believed to accept lower pay (morally justified on the erroneous assumption that they are not primary breadwinners), work longer hours at more boring and routine tasks, and are more subject to authoritarian oversight without protest and without unionization. To some extent, such feminization of labor can be seen as liberating, in the sense that it can set women free of onerous patriarchies at home, but more often than not the tradeoff is weighted heavily in favor of exploitation by the employer (Mittleman 2000: 66).

Motivation for women's migration may not fit neatly into any set of categories. Pregnant Bangladeshi women may be sent to London to give birth; this provides legal residence rights for the child, who will then return home to be brought up in the proper social identity and religion. Similar transnational strategies have developed for women from Somalia who are also sent to London to give birth. The process is designed to establish a base in a high income country while at the same time maintaining both physical and cultural links to the home country. In such cases, children with residencies or citizenship in both countries become an important bridge that maintains links between home and resettled kin (Bjerén 1997: 231).

Global Sex

The tendency for capitalism to turn everything into commodities certainly applies to the sex trade. The proverbial oldest profession commodified the female body long before capitalism came along, but globalization has tended to enormously increase prostitution and, to some degree, to change its very character. In the past, prostitution was mainly a local matter, though the movement of women across borders and over long distances probably dates back to the earliest slave trades. According to Dennis Altman, in *Global Sex* (2001),[9] what is different today is that it is not only the women who are crossing borders, but, more than ever before, the customers. Sex tourism has become an international industry of staggering proportions, often controlled by transnational mafias. Bangkok, Thailand, got into the sex business in a big way during the Indochina war, when 700,000 American GIs were briefly stationed there for R & R, rest and relaxation. Today, the city has achieved the dubious distinction as the archetypal global brothel. However, Bangkok is hardly unique. A single brothel in the port city of Narayanganj, Bangladesh, is said to have 16,000 workers. The International Labor Organization estimates that there are several million women workers in the sex trade in Indonesia, Malaysia, the Philippines, and Thailand. Although sex is the foundation of the political economies of only a few cities, usually those near military bases, it is an important part of a number of large cities in the Third World, especially those that are growing with great rapidity, luring uprooted, transient, and desperate people.

The influx of neoliberal capitalism and the relaxation of border restrictions have greatly increased the sex trade in communist and formerly communist countries. The economic and political crises in Russia brought about a national and international criminalization of the economy, as syndicated crime moved in to fill economic and power vacuums. Inevitably, a huge prostitution industry emerged throughout Russia, Ukraine, and Belarus, much of it transnational in nature. The government of Ukraine estimates that 400,000 women have migrated west in various forms of prostitution. Similarly, but at a lesser scale, Cuba and China have seen a rise in commercial sex due to increases in tourism, relaxation of government intrusion in the economy, and reduced border restrictions. A flood of mainland Chinese women, known as *dalumei*, have joined the sex trade in Taiwan.

In the past, prostitution was treated within both the media and social sciences as a moral issue, rather than as a business. However, while there continues to be a great deal of sexual slavery or pseudoslavery, and many girls are sold by parents into the profession as children, the large majority of prostitutes "choose" the profession as a survival strategy. Actually, there may be little option given the poverty from which prostitutes usually emerge. Nevertheless, the women, and often men, prefer to view themselves as professionals, and this is increasingly the way that social science is looking at them. As a form of labor, "sex work"—a term increasingly preferred over "prostitution"—is subject to the economic and social analysis similar to that accorded other professions.

As a profession rather than a hidden shame, the sex trade has been more free to organize for better working conditions, health benefits, and more money. The first sex-worker organization seems to have been COYOTE (Call Off Your Old Tired Ethics) established in San Francisco in 1973. In 1995, sex workers in the Sonagachi area of Calcutta organized the Durber Mahila Samanwaya Committee, claiming to represent 40,000 female, male, and transsexual sex-workers. Such organization is less possible where syndicated crime controls the sex industry.

Marriage Across Borders

The romantic notion that love knows no boundaries is statistically untrue; the vast majority of people marry not only within their own culture and race, but also within their own level of class and education. Nevertheless, cross-cultural marriage obviously has a long history. What globalization has done is increase the amount of intercultural connections and, thus, the possibilities for people from different countries to meet, as tourism, international labor movements, war, and ecological disasters bring diverse people together. Also, the emergence of transnationalism as a way of life for a great many immigrants has changed the nature of cross-cultural marriage; assimilation within the country's dominant culture need no longer be necessary.

In some ways, the Western concept of marriage is an ethnocentric one. There are at least four different meanings of the term, probably more: First, marriage can be an institution based on state recognition of a legal bond and on the legitimacy of children; second, it can refer to people routinely living together to comprise a household; third, it can be ceremonial, with the bond being formed mainly to create an alliance between groups, as was traditional for the marriage of children who might never see each other again among the Nyar of India; finally, it may be a psychological and emotional bond between individuals, even without the recognition of the state, as would be the case with homosexual couples in many countries. Or it might be a combination of more than one of these forms. It should be evident, however, that the Western concept of marriage based on romantic love may or may not have anything to do with it. As a curmudgeonly professor of mine used to say: "Everybody believes in romantic love, but most cultures aren't dumb enough to base anything as important as marriage on such lunacy." Many cultures view marriage primarily as establishing or maintaining alliances between families or wider groups and/or as involving a primary responsibility for producing children for the lineage. In many cases, marriage can occur between people who have never met, as when the household or kin group arranges the marriage or in the case of mail-order brides. In the Philippines, as well as many other poor countries, marriages arranged via catalogue or on the Internet are seen as a means by which women, and by extension their families, can establish themselves in the United States or Europe. Mostly, these involve older men with much younger women. Often virtual sexual slavery, with the attendant violence, is the result, but many such marriages turn out to be egalitarian and happy.

Cross-cultural marriage is, by definition, between two people of different ethnic groups. Beyond this, little generalization is possible. The cultural distance between the two partners may be extreme, as, say, between an Amazonian Indian and a college-educated Canadian. Or the distance can be relatively close as between a Chicana and an Anglo man, both equally fluent in English. In researching cross-cultural marriage, it is easiest to emphasize *difference*, especially since anthropology defines itself as the study of difference, while ignoring what might be quite a number of similarities (Breger and Hill 1998). A Peruvian woman and a WASP man who meet while attending Harvard will both be from the upper classes, will be highly cosmopolitan in outlook, may share the same interests in literature and movies, and may treasure cultural differences rather than see them as a burden. The exoticization of the other can lead to romantic fantasies. Women factory workers in the newly industrialized areas of China idealize Hong Kong businessmen as the perfect husbands; handsome and well-off, the men will take them away from the drudgery of their lives, while increasing their network capital, that is, expanding their networks across the channel (Ong 1999: 155–156).

On the other hand, migration to another country does not necessarily mean that a person wants to meet those of other cultures; it is usually not the first generation in the new country that marries out; with increased transnationalism even second and third generations may retain their cultural endogamy, as has been true, for example, for Miami Cubans. In cases where there is a relatively intact diaspora community, there will exist a tightly bounded conceptual image of the ideal woman, as well as sharply defined gender roles and concepts of male and female honor. These will act as strong constraints on outmarriage. Both women and men may travel back to the home country in search of spouses, or marriages in the new setting may be arranged by home-country kin.

Women's motives for marrying "out" were the focus of a study done in England of twenty cross-cultural marriages representing twelve different countries. Most of the subjects had known each other for an average of three years and had university educations, so the sample can hardly be judged typical, but some of the issues that emerged are most likely fairly universal to cross-cultural marriages. Prior to marriage, the foreign women felt marginalized, excluded, isolated, and unhappy. Many were alienated by parents who made little attempt to assimilate, but at the same time lacked any support from a cultural community. The women were often cosmopolitan in their values and outlook, which tended to cause dissention and to distance them from their families. Three of the women in the sample, all from the Mideast, felt that marrying was a way to escape the restrictive gender roles of their own cultures (Khatib-Chahidi, Hill, and Paton 1998).

American and British Wives, Indian Husbands

Another study focused on thirty North American and British women raised in upper-class nuclear families who married Indian men from extended patrilineal households; half of these were living in England or Canada and half in India. In all cases, the women resided with their husbands' families. Differences in values and expectations led to considerable stress. The Western women were brought up to be independent; they lived in families where residence after marriage was separate, in-laws had no authority, and contact between generations more likely followed the maternal than paternal line. The patrilineal household of the husband, however, was run by his mother, and the wife was in a subordinate relationship to her. This wife/mother-in-law relationship was the primary one, not the relationship between wife and husband. One husband broke off the honeymoon to return to London because his mother had a minor throat problem; it never occurred to him that his wife expected priority.

Privacy, highly valued in the West, was viewed as secrecy among the Indian family; a closed door was interpreted as an act of hostility. The wives felt overwhelmed by the constant presence of family and found it was almost impossible to be alone for any length of time with their husbands who, in any case, could not understand that there might be a problem. Women found it extremely difficult, even within the family, to make friends on a one-to-one basis because of the constant presence of groups. Needed emotional support based on private confidences was impossible since the family itself was the main source of stress. Family harmony was held to outweigh any desire to assert individual wants or needs.

Children added to the stress. Whereas in the West, the mother-child bond was expected to be intense, in the Indian families, children were cared for by a number of women. Independence was not encouraged for children; teen-age girls would be reprimanded if they expressed any social or political ideas at odds with those of their Indian elders.

Many of the women remained unhappy, feeling that their integrity and sense of self were constantly eroded by the deferential role they were expected to play within the family (Joshi and Krishna 1998).

CONCLUSIONS

The globalization perspective has completely transformed the ways that anthropologists look at migration and brought this once-marginal subject area to the forefront of globalization research. The clear-cut dichotomies of the past, such as rural-urban trajectories and push-pull models of motivation, have given way to much more fluid, complex, and amorphous conceptualizations. In the next few chapters, we will examine in some detail three specific topics of anthropological interest: transnationalism, diaspora, and refugees.

Chapter 7

Transnationalism: Living Across Borders

Transnational family networks are the underbelly of the global penetration of capitalism.
Linda Basch, Nina Glick Schiller, and Cristina Szanton Blanc[1]

You who are thirsty to return home, when you return you do not have to stay forever and give up residence elsewhere. . . . What we want is for you to be able to return home whenever you want and for you to be able to return where you are working now whenever you like. I am not asking you to return permanently and forsake the other place completely.
Jean-Bertrand Aristide, former President of Haiti[2]

In Haiti in 1804, freed Blacks and mulattos joined with slaves against Napoleonic France to achieve the Caribbean's first successful revolution for independence. The largely Black nation remained something of a pariah throughout the 19th century, isolated politically, though penetrated economically by international capitalism. Only in the 20th century did a semblance of a middle class emerge, referred to by the color term *milat* ("light skinned"). Although it comprised only 2% or 3% of the population, this class was itself quite stratified, with its wealthier members looking to Europe, mainly France, for culture and their children's educations. This dominant class, concentrated in the capital of Port-au-Prince but including elite families in the smaller towns, lived off whatever surplus could be extracted from the masses of poor peasants. The peasantry, which worked small subsistence plots with some market sales, spoke *Kreyol*, a mixture of French and various African idioms, and had a distinctive culture that grew out of the slavery period.

Throughout the 20th century, increasing foreign investment in large-scale agriculture led not to development but to mass dislocations. Peasants were thrown off their land and forced to work for minuscule wages as agricultural migrants on the sugar, rice, and cotton plantations. To protect its political and economic interests, the United States invaded in 1915, remaining for nineteen years. Among the long-term effects of this occupation was the introduction of U.S. racial concepts, which reinforced an already-existing near-caste system based on degrees of blackness. Some of the earliest Haitian migrants to the United States date to the turmoil of a 1918 to 1920 rebellion. Also, during the American occupation, there emerged a new layer of the middle class made up of skilled artisans, shopkeepers, teachers, and bureaucrats. It was through appeal to this class, as well as through a Black nationalist rhetoric that played to the growing need for a Haitian sense of identity, that Francois "Papa Doc" Duvalier came to power in 1957. Violent repression—felt most acutely through the actions of the semisecret police, the *tonton makout*—and the resulting downturn in the always fragile economy stimulated a new wave of migration to the United States. In 1971, Duvalier *pere* died and his son Jean-Claude ("Baby Doc") declared himself president-for-life. To the north, an increasing number of Haitian migrants rallied to work toward the goal of convincing the U.S. government to withdraw its support for the Duvalier dictatorship.

At first, migrants had little contact with Haiti except for occasional communications with the family left behind. Many remained in the United States only by overstaying tourist visas, since return home might mean torture, imprisonment, or death if the individual had been politically active against the dictatorship. Meanwhile, in the two decades after 1960, the global restructuring of capital led to new investment in export agribusiness, enriching a few, displacing many. Haiti's economic dependency on the United States increased, along with a burgeoning health and social service sector that was financed and staffed with both official and nongovernmental assistance from the United States. By the 1980s, about 10% of Haiti's 6.6 million citizens were living abroad. Remittances alone accounted for $100 million a year, equivalent to Haiti's entire foreign aid. Most immigrants settled in Miami, bringing their tightly stratified class system with them. A thriving Little Haiti emerged, but wealthy Duvalierists lived apart in expensive enclaves. These latter sent back sons schooled in the United States to assume technocratic and managerial jobs in Haiti.

In 1986, when Jean-Claude was forced to flee the country for asylum in France, an upsurge of nationalism precipitated increasing political activism, both within Haiti and among overseas expatriates, ultimately resulting in the landslide election of Jean-Bertrand Aristide as president. His election witnessed the first sustained popular participation of the masses in politics since the revolution of 1804, but it was short lived; Aristide was overthrown in a military coup a mere eight months after taking office. The political and economic crisis that followed stimulated yet another wave of emigration, most of it illegal, as thousands took to boats, many only to be turned back by the U.S. Coast Guard.

By this time, Haitian migrants had a significant presence not only in Miami but also in New York, Boston, and Philadelphia, as well as France and Canada. A great many of these immigrants have been intensely transnational. Family came to mean less a close group related by blood or marriage than a network of multiple households, tied together by a complex allocation of labor and resources. Money flowed both ways, as Haiti-based families sent to the United States their children, who were viewed as a primary means of maintaining, elaborating, and reproducing networks. Such networks were designed to maximize survival in more than one country, hedging against Haiti's volatile economy and against the unpredictable racial politics of the United States, where the immigration authorities might be pro-Haitian one day and anti-Haitian the next, and where Cuban boat people would be welcomed with open arms while the equally or more impoverished and repressed Haitian boat people would be excluded. Among the multiple functions of these networks were the education of children, care of the elderly, the establishment of small businesses both at home and in the host countries, and the acquisition of land in Haiti.

Differential perceptions and expectations often create hostility between those in the United States and those at home. Many Haitian immigrants have moved into white collar and professional jobs as secretaries, bank clerks, doctors, and engineers, but most remain in low-paying menial jobs. From the point of view of those residing in Haiti, and by Haitian standards, all U.S. migrants are wealthy and are thus expected to provide extensive remittances and other material benefits for those back home. Workers living in New York are much more acutely aware of the cost of living in a U.S. city, and often resent the demands from home.

In the past, Haitians tended to accept the traditional notion that all people, including themselves, were citizens of bounded nation-states. However, the 1990 reelection of Aristide, with 67% of the vote, despite competition from eleven other parties, mobilized emigrants within the *Lavalas* ("Deluge") movement. This movement, with its slogan "*Lavalas* for Home," united Haitians both within the country and abroad. President Aristide, reelected to serve from 1994 to 1996, declared those living abroad to be *Dizyèm Departman-an*, that is, the "Tenth Department," virtually a new state in addition to the nine geographical regions of Haiti. Such official recognition suggests both the influence and political power of Haiti's widely deterritorialized population and the desire by the government to maintain a Haitian homeland for its dispersed people (Basch, et al. 1994: 145–222; Richman 1992).

FROM ASSIMILATION TO TRANSNATIONALISM

Haiti's Tenth Department is an example of the phenomenon of *transnationalism*, and its evolution reveals how intricately this concept interweaves history, politics, economy, social structure, and identity. Until recently, the dominant paradigm of migration has been one of assimilation. Permanent immigrants would gradually, perhaps over two or three generations, adopt the language, values, and culture of the host country. This was especially true in the United States, where the ideology of assimilation was well embedded within the educational system itself; the axiom of the melting pot dominated history and civics texts.[3] In anthropology, it was recognized that, despite the United States' multiple voices, there existed a common referent culture, consisting of a "mainstream cultural value orientation" (Spindler 1990: 37) or set of "core values" (Hsu 1972), to which immigrants aspired. These premises were founded on a prior assumption, namely, that the nation-state was the natural focus of citizen loyalty and self-identity. In retrospect, it is clear that the situation was never quite so cut-and-dried, but there was sufficient truth that the assimilation paradigm was an unquestioned given of both the social sciences and popular culture. Gradually, a section of academia controversially redefined the United States as a multicultural society made up of ethnic groups. But even here, ethnics were assumed to be True Americans, well assimilated, or on their way to assimilation, within the boundaries of citizenship.

While most of the notions utilized to define postmodern society have borrowed from the humanities, the idea of transnationalism emerged first in political science and economics, where it referred to official international bodies, nongovernmental organizations, and multinational corporations. The idea of transnational cultures developed largely out of anthropological field work. The assimilationist and even the multiculturalist models no longer fit the emerging data. Throughout the 1990s, via a series of books and articles, the theory of transnationalism was developed by a trio of anthropologists who published jointly but researched separately with Caribbean and Philippine immigrants to the United States: Nina Glick Schiller, Linda Basch, and Cristina Szanton Blanc.[4] The idea of transnationalism has been so fruitful that it has become a standard, along with the term "transmigrant," within the more general field of migration studies.

Multinational People and Deterritorialized Nations

A transnational migrant is one who maintains active, ongoing interconnections in both the home and host countries and perhaps with communities in other countries as well. These relationships may be economic, social, cultural, or political; as often as not, they are all of these at once. Even though the migrant may take up permanent residence and achieve legal citizenship within the host country, this does not imply a break with the home society. Indeed, immigrants may retain the term "home" for the country of origin even into a second or third generation of legal citizenship in the new country. It is evident that transnationalism is thus a concept admitting of degrees; it may be intense—with constant phone calls, money transfers, back-and-forth travel, and participation in home politics and businesses—or relatively restrained, involving only occasional contacts. Ethnological study of transmigrants has only been going on for less than two decades so it is not yet clear if transnationalism will be reproduced over many generations; there is, however, good reason to believe that it will become an enduring alternative, competing with, but not replacing, assimilation.

Living across borders, transnational migrants break down the identification of nation and state and give rise to the paradoxical concept of deterritorialized state or, more accurately, deterritorialized space. This postmodern concept of space can be quite complex. It is basically *social space*, that is, it is defined in terms of social networks rather than in relation to political or geographical boundaries. Even the concept of community, as normally conceived in anthropology, must be reconsidered; communities have traditionally been thought of as having definable boundaries that separate inside and outside (Rouse 1991: 12). Migrant communities may have very ambiguous and quite fluid boundaries; a Hong Kong transnational community might extend to many cities along the Pacific Rim, in both Asia and the Americas. While defined in terms of social networks, these networks usually follow economic linkages, lines of capital, that unite the group within an interweaving of trade, finance, and remittances. Highly dispersed populations may construct themselves as deterritorialized nation-states with a common leadership, as is the case with scattered Tibetans who look toward the Dalai Lama as their moral guide, spokesperson, and symbol of unity.

Understanding deterritorialization of this kind requires an acknowledgment of the relatively shallow historical depth of the nation-state idea, which, as we have seen, only emerged after the 15th century with the rise of modern Europe and its colonial and imperialist expansion. In the sense of multiple and divided loyalties, say between feudal lord, regional king, and distant Pope, a form of transnationalism has a history that long precedes the political construction of states. However, contemporary transnationalism within the context of globalization is deeper and more layered than its precursors. Jonathan Crush and David McDonald (2000: 8–12) list five characteristics of transnationalism as it applies specifically to present-day South Africa. First, "lives are lived across borders" with a high intensity of ongoing social and economic interactions made possible by cheap and rapid travel and by instantaneous communication. Second, transnationalism is a fairly recent effect of the flexible job market made possible by the internationalization of capitalist production and finance. Third, transnationalism creates a novel type of migrant identity, a hybrid combination of both home and host, requiring that researchers develop new methods and new concepts to examine identity. Fourth, over time transnationalism becomes increasingly independent of its original conditions, as migrants gain knowledge and acquire cultural capital, and social networks are reformulated and expanded. Finally, transnationals develop new modes of resistance—diaspora communities, interstate institutions, support networks, and political power—to defend against their minority status in the host country and against asymmetries in the global marketplace.

Creating and Maintaining Transnational Networks

Within the United States and Europe, a number of specific factors are at work to promote transnationalism among recent migrants. Racism—which pushes migrants of color to the bottom of the status pyramid no matter what their occupations, wealth, or family status in the home country—creates both a social and economic insecurity that renders retention of even the most long-distance ties highly beneficial. Most Third World countries from which immigrants come are entrenched in the process of nation building, and both political leaders and opposition groups may look to their emigrants for financial aid and organizational support. Emigrants have been highly active participants in political struggles in Haiti, Grenada, the Philippines, and China. Often immigrants hold a relatively safe and privileged position for active opposition, which does not exist in the homeland; they can organize, criticize, and publicize without the immediate threat of imprisonment or death. When this is coupled with the need to develop a power base in the United States against subaltern status—not to mention the need for home-country political aspirants to seek voting support wherever they can get it—political participation in both countries may be highly advisable (Glick Schiller, et al. 1995: 50–58). Such politically active transnationalism can be seen as a strategy for maximizing social and economic potential by keeping one foot in each of two countries.

Transnationalism has created numerous economic opportunities for immigrants. Transnational communities of economic scale tend to form in global cities, and this creates an internal market for restaurants, food stores, and other ethnic-specific businesses. Although most of these are mom-and-pop (more likely extended-family) operations, there are also opportunities for larger-scale businesses, such as international labor contractors and air cargo companies. The need for culture-specific imports creates a niche of opportunity for capitalists who understand the language and culture and possess appropriate international connections. One of the primary opportunities that has emerged within transnational communities is in the field of travel and communication; agencies must be set up to handle the back and forth movement from home and host countries. Such companies send remittances, create and deliver videos and home-made cassettes, and move goods. One Filipino-American started a bulk air shipment business; within ten years he had offices in New York, Manila, and six other Philippine cities, and a fleet of couriers to pick up and deliver door-to-door (Glick Schiller, et al. 1995: 56). Using host-country money to invest in the home country is a particularly rewarding strategy, since American dollars or German deutsche marks usually convert quite profitably across Third World borders. Investments in property in the home country have multiple benefits: Kin or family can take care of the place while having a nice house to live in, thus increasing the status and influence of the investor, while at the same time a future home for retirement is ensured. Not all enterprise is legal; the high rates of Asian and Latin illegal immigration into the United States support a profitable network of agents and transporters.

Voluntary organizations are often crucial to the transmigrant. Such organizations extend economic and social networks, afford a base for political action, provide information, and give personal support. For example, the St. Vincent Education and Cultural Club, representing immigrants from the Caribbean island of St. Vincent living in New York City, is quite self-consciously transnational. In addition to sponsoring an annual cultural fair in Brooklyn, which usually attracts more than 1,000 people, it holds panel discussions and disseminates a newsletter in both countries. On the one hand, the club helps enculturate Vencentians into the New York economic and social system through seminars on education, real estate investment, and economic advancement, and, on the other hand, it maintains island identity by bringing speakers, artists, recording stars, and plays from St. Vincent, and featuring home events in the newsletter (Glick Schiller, et al. 1995: 95–96).

The widespread and growing existence of transnationalism, apparently as a permanent lifestyle, calls into question the anthropological concept of community. Boundaries—if the term can even be used—are ill-defined and constantly changing. In many ways, such communities do not exist as objective realities, but only relative to the individual or the family. The deliberate, systematic attempt to create a more coherent community can be seen in the efforts of the Caribbean Action Lobby, headed and largely staffed by Trinidadians, which has been trying—unsuccessfully so far—to develop a pan-Caribbean consciousness (Glick Schiller, et al. 1995: 119–120). The idea of borderless nations also calls into question the state as the primary locus of identity, giving support to the concept of the deterritorialized nation-state.

A CHINESE TRANSMIGRANT ELITE IN SAN FRANCISCO

Migrant studies, like ethnographies in general, tend to focus on underclasses or, at most, on the middle class. Aihwa Ong's (1992, 1993) study of a Hong Kong business elite settled in the San Francisco area reveals not only the intricacies of multinational networks based largely on investment, but also some of the barriers that even the most wealthy face in striving for cultural legitimization in a new country.

Hong Kong, which is the third largest financial center in the world after New York and London, has produced a complex network of interrelated Chinese communities throughout the globe, but especially in certain cities around the Pacific Rim. Several thousand of the most wealthy comprise about 10% of the exclusive San Francisco Bay–view community of Peninsula Peak (a pseudonym), where every home costs more than a million dollars.

Since its founding by the British in 1829, Hong Kong has been a transit point for Chinese immigration, ranging from impoverished laborers to merchants. The process of elite migration accelerated over the last decades because of a vigorous business environment, with high profits in need of reinvestment, and by the British turnover to China on July 1, 1997. Entrepreneurial families that made their wealth in textiles and electronics for export increasingly sought long-term overseas investments in real estate and service industries where profits were higher. Success requires, first, gaining transnational skills and assuming a sort of global culture adaptive to far-flung local environments, and, second, maintaining a strong focus on the family—in other words, simultaneous individualism and communitarianism. Toward the first goal, boys were educated in Hong Kong at prestigious British prep schools and sent abroad for college, basically an education for emigration. But the family remained central. Often young men and women on student visas would provide the first link in a family network that would, over the years, grow to considerable proportions and, through friendships and intermarriage, combine with other families creating an intricate weave of Hong Kong Chinese influence and finance. A pregnant woman might follow her family network to a Western country where the child would be born with a foreign passport.

Once on U.S. soil, the Hong Kong migrant was confronted with a culture that reduced even the most ambitious and wealthy entrepreneur to the status of ethnic Asian-American, a generic group, which not long ago was perceived as comprising coolies, laundry workers, and Yellow Peril. More recently, the stereotype has tended more toward techno-intellectuals who displace "real" Americans at the best universities, a concept that might induce even more resentment. Thus, the wealthy Hong Kong expatriate was faced with the problem of gaining "symbolic capital" (Bourdieu 1980), specifically those material goods, values, attitudes, and linguistic skills that are accepted as upper class in the United States. Some of this symbolic capital has become integral to a transnational capitalist class that crosscuts multiple nationalities; a Mercedes-Benz or an original Renoir can mean more or less the same in many different countries. However, much remains particular to the locale, and rich Chinese encountered numerous barriers to breaching the walls of the upper-crust culture of the California Anglo (a once-Mexican term that has gained usage among non-Latin immigrants and Native Americans). This has stimulated strategies of both exclusion and inclusion. On the one hand, many have isolated themselves within exclusive Hong Kong Chinese communities, networks, and clubs. As one migrant put it: "If the established SF power doesn't invite us to their [opera] balls, we have our own balls. They don't want to do business with us, we do business among ourselves. If they don't let us into Pacific Heights, we create our own Chinatown" (Calandra and Matier 1989[5]).

Some sought to buy acceptance through such tactics as supporting art museums or contributing to politicians. The latter would have the dual advantage of gaining cultural legitimization through government appointments while at the same time establishing business and financial networks that crossed ethnic boundaries. None of this worked quite as hoped in providing social acceptance equivalent to the aspirant's wealth. In fact, the effect was often the opposite. Less wealthy Asians resented being politically represented by individuals so far removed from their own communities, while Anglos were suspicious of Chinese influence and of the closed and secret financial networks through which Hong Kong families often operate. Since the influx of Hong Kong money and migrants on a large scale is relatively recent, Ong (1992: 141) predicts that "their economic importance will bring about new alignments with Anglo elites and will significantly condition American class, cultural, and racial formations in the coming 'Pacific century.'"

THE FUTURE OF TRANSNATIONALISM

Transnationalism seems to be one of the more fertile concepts that has emerged within the anthropology of globalization. Examples of firmly established transnationalism are legion: Jews in France, Palestinians in Jordan, Turks in Bulgaria, Mexicans in the United States, Tamils in Norway, Ugandans in India, Chinese in Malaysia. . . . Despite its faltering economy and high unemployment rate, postapartheid South Africa has become a magnet for transmigrants from all over subsaharan Africa. South African employers in construction, mining, services, and agriculture often prefer a foreign labor force that can be hired at sub-subsistence wages and with no benefits (Crush and McDonald 2000). There can be little doubt that increasing technological development and economic globalization will increase transnational cultural patterns.

The implied assumption in much anthropological writing is that transnationalism has *replaced* assimilation; indeed, one seldom encounters the term "assimilation" any more except in the negative sense that it has been superseded. This is probably incorrect. We do not have comparative statistics to show how many new and old immigrants would continue to fit into the assimilationist model as compared with those who fit the transnational model. While it is true that developments in communications technology and transportation encourage transnationalism, the high labor-mobility patterns in industrialized countries do not always favor the type of enclave environment that fosters the maintenance of transnationalism over long periods of time. Nor do single-language common-format public school systems encourage cultural maintenance and the reproduction of transnational cultures, no matter how sympathetic host governments may be to multiculturalism.

If the neoliberal phase of globalization dates only from about 1990, there has not yet been time to determine if the current manifestations of transnationalism can or will reproduce themselves over multiple generations. One can safely predict that, for certain groups, it most probably will, especially those groups for which the homeland assumes a deeply emotional diasporic symbolism. However, there will also continue to be a very large number of migrants who do assimilate, either as a conscious decision or gradually over generations. Assimilation and transnationalization should not be considered mutually exclusive models simply because anthropology as a discipline prefers to study one rather than another at a given time. Both models are matters of degree and undoubtedly blend into each other at the margins. While it is true that assimilation can no longer be supported as the only game in town, it is most certainly still being played.

Chapter 8

Diaspora: Yearning for Home

[Diaspora is] more than a voguish synonym for peregrination or nomadism. Life itself is at stake in a way the word suggests flight or coerced rather than freely chosen experiences of displacement. Slavery, pogroms, indenture, genocide and other unnamable terrors have all figured in the constitution of diasporas and the reproduction of diaspora-consciousness.

Paul Gilroy[1]

Sittu is still in Germany, and trying to find a way to go to Canada. Raj is thinking about going to Holland, but nothing is decided yet. I think Sitha will be going to Norway.

Mohan, a Tamil refugee, in a letter to his fiancée[2]

The claim that the Jewish Diaspora was precipitated by Roman General Titus's crushing of the Judean revolt and the destruction of the second temple in A.D. 70 is something of a myth perpetuated by early Christians who wanted to prove God's punishment for Jewish connivance in Jesus' crucifixion. The guilt theme is picked up in the medieval legend of the wandering Jew's restless peregrination until the Day of Judgment for having mocked Jesus on the cross. Actually, the Jewish Diaspora—often spelled with the capital "D" that sets it off as the archetype of a certain kind of forced dispersion—has been enormously complex, taking place over thousands of years and branching from myriad locations (Cohen 1997: 6–7). What unites Jews from countries as dispersed as the Sudan, Russia, Argentina, and Japan is not so much religion, which tends to be highly differentiated, but a common sense of history and homeland. The Jewish homeland, however, is an ambiguous concept. A small minority of the world's Jews actually live in Israel, and even before Israel's founding, relatively few considered themselves Zionists, in the sense that they actually planned to pull up roots and move to Palestine. Much Jewish dispersion was *not* forced; it followed kinship networks or the promise of better economic potential. Some Jews are transnationals, in the sense that they maintain ongoing cultural, political, and economic relations with friends and family in a country of origin, but most are fully assimilated citizens of the countries in which they live.

Given such a range of variation, it is difficult to sustain the claim that Judaism represents an "ideal type" of diaspora (Safran 1991), although, on the other hand, this very complexity and heterogeneity may be more typical than not. "Diaspora" has emerged as one of numerous terms that reject "old localizing strategies" inherent in such words as community, culture, region, tribe, center, and periphery (Clifford 1994: 303; Gilroy 1991: 294). The difficulty of definition is inevitable for any term that must encompass the African slave trade, the outmigration of the Irish during the mid-19th century potato famine, the dispersal of Armenians after the 1915–1916 genocide, and the emigration of two-thirds of Palestinians after 1948.

The term "diaspora" is based on the Greek *speiro*, meaning "to sow" and the preposition *dia*, "over." For early Greeks, the term represented the general ideas of migration and colonization (Shuval 2000: 42). Later, it came to refer more specifically to Hellenistic Jews scattered among gentiles. From the 17th century on, theologians gave the word more specifically religious connotations, applying it to other persecuted religious groups that had been dispersed, such as French Huguenots and Armenians (Tedlock 1996: 341).

DEFINING DIASPORA

Currently, there is considerable controversy about how "diaspora" should be defined in an era of globalization. Definitions can be quite specific. William Safran (1991: 83–84) lists a number of characteristics: First, ancestors were dispersed from an original center to two or more foreign regions; second, there is a collective memory or myth of an ancestral homeland that is regarded as the true and ideal home; third, the people are not accepted and are alienated within their countries of settlement; and fourth, they are committed to the restoration of their homeland if it has ceased to exist or to its maintenance if it continues to exist. For Gérard Chaliand and Jean Pierre Rageau (1995: xiii–xvii) diaspora is defined by forced dispersion of a religious or ethnic group precipitated by some sort of disaster, a

forced exodus

collective memory of this dispersion, and the will to transmit a heritage and preserve an identity from generation to generation. Whether a group becomes a diaspora will only be determined by time, that is, by long-term generational survival of the heritage. This latter requirement would deny diaspora status to contemporary peoples such as Tibetans and the Sri Lankan Tamils, who might be considered diasporas in the making.

At the other end of the scale from such criteria-based definitions are very general approaches; diasporas may be seen simply as any ethnic minority that retains group cohesion and sentimental links to a homeland (Shuval 2000: 3). Postmodernists, as might be expected, reject any type of essentialism, that is, any definition with reference to one or two necessary characteristics, preferring a broader, more encompassing view that would include various refugees, guest workers, immigrants, racial minorities, and overseas communities (Clifford 1994).

One common theme is the idea of collective identity formed around a homeland that has a sentimental, emotive meaning to the people. This, however, also has its problems; many Jews do not view Israel as a homeland in any but a historical sense. And what is one to make of the Black diaspora, which, for most, has no specific homeland, only a sort of generalized Africa? Diasporas may have multiple centers, such as may be found among Jamaicans, Haitians, Dominicans, and many others living in New York or Miami; they consider their particular islands home while adopting a pan-Caribbean identity based on Negritude, a common racial discrimination in the United States, and a distant African heritage. Even African Americans, descendants of slaves, may feel that they have never really been assimilated, that even after many generations the immigrant ideal never really worked for them. In such cases, a certain diaspora consciousness may emerge among long-time citizens who construct themselves in diasporic terms, perhaps by taking on the religion, dress, and culture of North African Islam (Kepel 1997).

Diaspora should not be considered an absolute, an objective thing that exists in some permanent or semipermanent form. Even long-term diasporas are almost constantly in a state of flux. For example, prior to the rise of Nazism, many Jews had settled comfortably in Europe, established themselves as valuable citizens of Italy, Germany, Austria, and Poland. Few were Zionists even after repression increased in the 1930s. After World War II, however, the idea of homeland became of central importance for the survivors. For Cuban and Haitian migrants to the United States, the degree of diaspora consciousness may depend on fluctuating U.S. policy toward the home country.

Another common theme is forced expulsion. This, however, would deny diaspora status to Chinese and Indian dispersals that grew mainly out of voluntary labor migration. A recognition of how the term is actually *used* in the social sciences would accentuate forced exit and affective homeland consciousness without making these absolute constituents. Minimal characteristics, which would differentiate diaspora from migration in general, might include dispersion from some center to two or more territories, an enduring but not necessarily permanent resettlement abroad, and a sense of common cultural identity among the scattered populations (Van Hear 1998: 6).[3]

Putting It All Together

Without essentializing any single attribute beyond some idea of homeland, a number of characteristics can be delineated. Any given diaspora will hold some combination of these. The homeland from which the people are dispersed may be a specific country or a generalized region, and it may exist today or only in the past. In any case, attitudes toward the homeland are usually imbued with highly selective history, perhaps part true and part myth, and a record of worthy achievements. It is the homeland, rather than simply economic interest or kinship networks, that forms the basis for long-term group identity, that sets this people off from other ethnic groups, and that helps form a transnational "imagined community" among people that have never met. Often there is a troubled relationship with the host country, which may derogate the group to lower-class status and subject them to routine discrimination (Cohen 1997: 26).

It has been suggested that rather than try to define a diaspora according to essential features, it would be more profitable to look at what diasporas are *not* and what they are defined *against*. They stand against the nation-state, for example, refusing full loyalty or complete assimilation. If they have nationalist aspirations, these aims are focused on the homeland and are not expressed toward the host country; thus they would not tend to be separatist, although persecution might bring about temporary separatist sentiments (Clifford 1994). While diasporas do not always begin with brutal forced migration, this is a common theme and part of the fundamental history-mythology that provides the emotional basis of diasporic cohesion.

Types of Diasporas

The postmodern bias against classification is partially based on the legitimate notion that globalization tends to break down categories; boundaries dissolve and once-differentiated types overlap, flow into each other, are transformed by contact into new forms, and take on unanticipated meanings in new contexts. As we have seen, globalization tends simultaneously toward homogenization and differentiation, often within the same person or group. With this disclaimer in mind, it is possible to list a number of types of diaspora with a focus on the motives for leaving the home country or region (Table 8.1). In layman's parlance, perhaps the most common form is the *victim* diaspora, which is based on forced exile. Refugee situations are often diasporic in nature, as in the large-scale migrations of Salvadorans, Guatemalan Mayans, and Nicaraguans in the 1980s. Ecological disaster may also force migration, as with the repeated droughts in the northeastern countries of subsaharan Africa. During the mid- to late-19th century, tens of thousands of Chinese and Indians dispersed throughout the world seeking jobs; such *labor* diasporas may be the most common form today. *Trade* diasporas were the products of merchants seeking resources, manufacturing centers, and markets; both the Chinese and Lebanese have been involved in extensive trade diasporas, and it is often difficult to separate colonial expansion from trade migration. The colonial period gave rise to a number of *imperial* diasporas among the colonists themselves, as English, French, Dutch, and German administrators spread throughout Asia and Africa, often creating continuous settlements that exist today. Whether *homeland* should be considered a type is questionable, since many scholars believe this is a defining quality of diasporas; however, for some subgroups within larger diasporas, such as Zionists or activist Tibetans, return to a homeland becomes a consuming passion, subordinating all other considerations (Castles 1998). The peoples of the Caribbean and the Gypsies would fit marginally into several of these categories, but neatly into none; thus, these might be considered *cultural* diasporas, in the sense that people seem to be following networks for myriad reasons with an emphasis on adamantly maintaining their cultural distinctiveness (Clifford 1994).

DIASPORA IN AN AGE OF GLOBALIZATION

Because diasporas, whether narrowly or broadly defined, probably date back well into prehistory, there is no obvious link to the current phase of globalization. However, many aspects of globalization certainly encourage diasporic emigration and help maintain the unity of widespread diaspora communities. The collapse of the Soviet Union, perhaps the single event that more than any other brought about an integrated world capitalism, thrust 450 million people, comprising multiple nations and ethnic groups, into the pool of possible migrants. The creation of fifteen new states within the former Soviet Union split ethnic groups and created state divisions that could be conceived of as homelands to some residents, alien places to others. The rapid developments in global communications and travel also contribute to the emergence and reproduction of diaspora communities. Not all

Table 8.1
Robin Cohen's Types of Diaspora

Type	Main Character	Examples
Victim	Dispersal because of extreme repression, forced exile, or natural disaster, which becomes a key aspect of collective memory, identity, and ideology.	Jews, Palestinians, Irish, Africans (slavery), Armenians
Labor	Large-scale outmigration for work, intended originally perhaps for short term, but resulting in permanent settlement in the host country. Often "transitional" in the sense that the attachment to the homeland may be lost over generations.	Indian and Chinese indentured workers, Italians to U.S. and Argentina, Turks to Europe after WWII
Trade	Formation of merchant communities, often accompanying but also often independent of colonial expansion.	Chinese (throughout Asia, often encouraged by European colonial powers); Lebanese (U.S. and South America)
Imperial	Expansion by colonial and imperialist powers via settlers, administrators, military personnel, missionaries, capitalists, and so forth. Often transitional.	British, Spanish, Portuguese, Dutch, German, French during colonial period
Homeland	The homeland is part of the definition of all diasporas. For some, however, return to a real or (usually) mythologized and reimagined homeland becomes the dominant force of diaspora.	Zionists, Sikhs (dispersed throughout the world, mainly after the end of British colonization of India; continue to demand an independent homeland)
Cultural	A postmodern conception based partially on theories of postcolonialism and James Clifford's (1994) idea of "travelling cultures"—i.e., that the idea of homelands as nation-states must be abandoned in favor of multiple reference points, such as gender, race, institutional location, and so forth.	Caribbean (actually Afro-Caribbean, a cross-border culture spread to U.S., U.K., the Netherlands)

Note: Since even the definition of "diaspora" is controversial, any typology must be doubly problematic. Some diasporas would be comprised of characteristics of *all* of these types, though perhaps with one predominant.

Source: Cohen 1997 (except the last).

diaspora communities are transnational, but many are, and the easy ability to maintain personal, cultural, and economic connections over long distances may be important to the maintenance of diasporic identity. Globalization encourages reactionary or adaptive ethnic, religious, and nationalist cohesion; it also encourages the reactionary racism and bias against migrants that negatively maintains the boundaries of immigrant communities from without. Finally, the increasing awareness and intergovernmental recognition of human rights has provided a moral platform for diasporic peoples to claim recognition, compassion, and political validation (Van Hear 1998: 2–3).

Both the politics of home and host countries may encourage diaspora. In Europe, the United States, the newly industrializing countries of Southeast Asia, and the oil-rich countries of the Middle East, the spread of flexible capitalism has created a market for a shifting labor force that can be cheaply imported, routinely surveilled, and expelled without having to pay the costs of raising the worker to adulthood, or of education, health services, and old age support. On the other side of the coin, the need to fill highly specialized technological and academic positions encourages elite diasporas. Because of dependency on remittances, lack of jobs at home, and the need to get rid of excess population, home countries are increasingly amenable to diaspora; Haiti, India, and Indonesia provide official encouragement of transnationalism by setting up offices to assist emigrants and homecomers (Sheffer 1995).

While the massive displacements of two world wars are a thing of the past, internal conflicts challenging weakened states have burgeoned. At the turn of the 21st century, there were only two ongoing cross-border shooting wars being fought: India-Pakistan and Eritrea-Ethiopia. However, outbreaks of ethnic, religious, or nationalist violence, often on a large scale—as in Rwanda, Israel, Afghanistan, and the former Czechoslovakia—create massive refugee populations that, if not quickly solved, can turn into long-term, highly dispersed diasporas.

THEORIZING DIASPORA

Perhaps the first theoretical problem facing diaspora researchers is determining the nature of this particular form of migration. As we have seen, definitions may be narrow, encompassing only a handful of historical mass movements, as would be the case if forced expulsion from a specified home country were the defining criteria. Or definitions can be so broad as to include nearly any migration that maintains some degree of cultural cohesion. Once a definition has been decided, there is the complex issue of how to compare and differentiate diasporas. Postmodernists tend to lean toward either refusing a definition altogether or emphasizing the need for self-reflexivity, that is, the recognition that any definition is constructed by the researcher and thus imposes an objectifying gaze or discourse onto people who are, in reality, quite individual.

Fighting over definitions can be a futile enterprise if some deeper issue is not at stake. As long as diaspora is conceived as an objective, measurable movement of people, the particular researcher has every right to define the specific field within which his subjects operate. However, perhaps the most agreed on aspect of diaspora is the *emotional* relationship to some sort of homeland, however conceived. As soon as affective aspects are admitted as central, questions of identity become important. Should diaspora be conceived as similar to the Marxist notion of class wherein people are part of, say, the bourgeoisie even if an illusion of national equality (as in the United States) ensures that they have little or no class consciousness? Or is some sort of willful diaspora consciousness necessary for the very existence of diaspora? If so, how is this developed and how reproduced in the next generation? How long before migration becomes diaspora? What are the conditions within the host country and the global system that promote or retard this diaspora consciousness? [4]

Politically, diasporas can be quite active. Tibetans have enlisted politicians, human rights groups, the United Nations, and several movie stars in their fight to reclaim their homeland. At the opposite end of the spectrum of political activeness are illegals, who must remain unnoticed if they are to avoid deportation. In reality, the full range from activism to apathy will be found within almost any diaspora, which brings analysis down to the level of the individual or the small subgroup.

Any diaspora will involve at least three major sets of political actors in complex interaction: the diaspora people, the host country or countries, and the homeland, any two of which can be analyzed in relation to the third (Shuval 2000). As we have seen, much Haitian organizing during the Duvalier family dictatorship was directed not at Papa Doc or Baby Doc, but at U.S. policy toward Haiti. Similarly, the Cuban community has been extremely active in maintaining the U.S. embargo against their homeland (although many believe that the embargo merely prolongs the Castro dictatorship). Homelands might do everything, including assassinations on foreign soil or imprisonment of returnees, to prevent the return of exiles, or governments can become so dependent on remittances, foreign education, and foreign business linkages via diaspora that there is either official or unofficial encouragement both to leave and to stay away.

Within the triad of diaspora-homeland-host are a multiplicity of other relationships. A micro-to-macro approach would include the individual, the household, migrant networks and institutions, the supportive or restrictive laws of the host country and its political climate, and finally the field of globalization itself with its trade, financial flows, and historical and current relations between countries (Van Hear 1998: 14–16).

DIASPORA AND ADAPTATION

In the short run, diasporas, like any form of migration, tend to be traumatic. In the long run, however, diasporas can become quite settled and routinized. One question that often arises is why people *do not* return to their homelands even though this may be both possible and culturally encouraged. In many cases, diasporic peoples have become wealthy or upwardly mobile within their host countries; while return may be a sustaining dream, the actuality is hardly worth the cost. Diaspora has many positive aspects quite independent of actual return. Overall, intergenerational diasporas tend to place high value on education and knowledge and to have strong occupational profiles. In many cases, such as the Chinese in Malaysia or Singapore, diaspora networks have been able to establish lucrative business niches within the national economy. Diaspora provides a more intense sense of identity and often of purpose in life than may be the case for the typical citizen. To the extent that diaspora establishes a common identity, an exciting and heroic history, strong transnational networks, and political cohesion, diaspora can offer a secure foundational culture, even when the homeland seems distant or unreachable (Cohen 1997).

DIASPORA WITHOUT COHESION: TAMILS IN NORWAY

The stereotyped image of the diasporic community as a close-knit, intimate society reproducing the homeland culture in a new setting may sometimes be accurate, but it is certainly not the case among the Tamils of Sri Lanka (formerly Ceylon) who comprise one of the lesser known contemporary mass migrations. About 700,000 refugees, one-third of the entire prewar Tamil population, have resettled on every continent, with the largest contingents in Canada, England, Germany, and Switzerland. Øivind Fuglerud's *Life on the Outside* (1999), a study of about 7,000 Tamils living in Norway, provides an in-depth perspective on "long distance nationalism."

Like so many other diasporas, the Tamil dispersion grew out of a situation of systematized terror. During hundreds of years of Portuguese, Dutch, and English colonization, the Tamils—actually four linguistically related peoples living along the eastern coast and in the north of Sri Lanka—maintained many of the traditions of their Dravidian kin in southern India, only miles north across the Palk Strait. After decolonization, a series of policies favoring the Sinhalese majority led to a Tamil liberation movement and the establishment of a multitude of political parties and armed revolutionary groups. From the late 1970s on, violence on both sides continued to escalate until by the 1990s military clashes, mass-murders of civilians, torture, and disappearances became virtually normative. While the northern state of Jaffna established itself as a Tamil enclave, the contested border zone was transformed into "a scene of absurd theatrical violence" (44) where each side vied to outdo the other in bloody excess. The Sinhalese military randomly bombed the Jaffna Peninsula, but made no attempt to actually invade. Internally, the Liberation Tigers of Tamil Eelam (LTTE) systematically destroyed its rivals through intimidation, assassination, terror, and a network of informants, until it was the only political-military organization left. The LTTE no longer represented the aspirations of the Tamil people, who were terrified into silence and looked at the secretive organization with fear and awe.

Migration is hardly new for the Tamils. British colonialism provided the opportunity for lucrative and relatively specialized foreign jobs in railroading and mining. However, a major difference from previous Tamil migrations, aside from its sheer scale, is that today almost all migrants are from a single generation, as men and women of fighting age are given priority by their families to leave Sri Lanka. The absence of close extended family networks in Norway creates a situation of relative isolation for the individual migrant. Complex networks are necessary, of course, but these are often impersonal, formed with distant cousins and friends of friends. Adding to this isolation is the need for constant deception, or as one informant put it, "Lying is our only security" (78). Lying to authorities is essential. While Norway belatedly and reluctantly accepted international law regarding resettlement, that law states that asylum should be granted in the first country of refuge. Since Tamils usually reach Norway only after passing through multiple countries, at extreme cost to their families, deceiving authorities through made-up biographies is essential. Many migrants originally came as students and were forced to manipulate the system in order to gain more permanent status as refugees. Nor can the migrant let his guard down among his own people, who are split among those who are for and those opposed to the LTTE, which has established itself in every migrant country; informants for both sides are everywhere.

In a country where the social and economic differences between Norwegian and Tamil are greater than between Black and white in the United States, assimilation is perceived as undesirable and unlikely. The Norway beyond the Tamil community appears hostile and threatening. Legal proceedings leading to political asylum begin with an antagonistic police interrogation that almost always requires judicious and believably consistent misinformation. In all interactions with the state, Tamils see themselves as depersonalized, degraded, and stereotyped, reduced to "cases" and to "problems" to be solved. This psychological marginalization is a key part of the process of disembedding them from their own culture and forcing them to define themselves in negations: *not* Norwegian, *not* white, *not* employed. Aside from the requirements of jobs and of legal interactions with the state bureaucracy, Tamils keep to themselves.

It is not only culture that is reproduced in the new setting, but also the cultural conflicts that follow the émigrés. Once established, or even before leaving the homeland, the refugee must choose between two opposed models of ideology and identity: the traditional and the revolutionary.

The traditional model looks back to the colonial period, a period in which British administrators not only recognized but fully exploited the caste system, providing education in English and middle-class jobs, both at home and abroad, as teachers, postmasters, and railroad managers. In this sense, and in the fact that more of the older generation than the younger in Jaffna speak English, such traditionalism was not antithetical to modernization. However, intricate hierarchies based on family, caste, seniority, and gender provided a well-defined and relatively closed system of values that offered security and identity while minimizing individualism. Much of this was based upon earlier migrations for employment; thus, tradition maintained the values and expectations of those better days: family networks, required remittances, close kinship ties, and caste distinctions. However, contemporary conditions of refugee migration are very different from those of labor migration. Asylum seekers face long periods of unemployment. Constant movement in search of work renders the establishment of stable kinship networks impossible. Hierarchies break down when the only face-to-face relationships one might have are those of common language, age, and job.

For the mostly young Tamil men in Norway, the dominant means of linking to the traditional life of Sri Lanka is not religion, which is of no great importance to many, but marriage. Marriage with a woman in the homeland, selected by the distant family and often sight unseen, is preferable for many reasons. Because of war and selective migration, women outnumber men in Jaffna seven to one, whereas the situation is reversed in Norway. Men want women from the home country, uncontaminated by the migrant experience, that is, women who are traditionally "feminine": chaste, shy, passive, obedient. Cross-cousin marriage is preferred, both in terms of selection by the family and as a romantic ideal. Brides bring with them not only large dowries, but also land rights and, equally important, valuable connections of kinship. The elaborate marriage itself might take place in a third country, such as Singapore. Marriage, more than anything else, creates, reaffirms, and maintains ties to the homeland and to Tamil culture.

In contrast to the traditional model is the revolutionary model singularly represented by the LTTE. Most of the members of the organization are in their 20s or younger, so hierarchy by seniority is roundly rejected. Caste, sometimes interpreted through selective historical analysis as a foreign institution introduced by Western conquest, is repudiated in favor of a social structure based on military models. The ideal of equality applies not only across caste and age, but also across genders. Many women have taken up arms against the Sinhalese, forming the Women's Front. In place of the *thali*— a pendant that traditional married women wear to represent the taming of their female power and their obedience to their husbands—LTTE women, like their male counterparts, wear a necklace hiding a cyanide capsule to be used in case of capture. Dowry is viewed as an anachronistic representation of women's enslavement.

While it might be assumed, and to a certain extent is true, that the traditional model represents the past while the revolutionary model looks toward an idealized future, ideologies are not so simple. Although the LTTE does reject traditional hierarchies of caste, seniority, and gender, it also seeks historical/mythical legitimization deep in the past, in the militant kingdoms of Dravidian ancestors in Sri Lanka and India during the period between 300 B.C. and A.D. 300. It also eulogizes and even exaggerates traditional respect for motherhood; a Mother goddess represents the homeland, and the mothers of the 60,000 martyrs of the civil war are idolized.

Caught between the expectations of family and the realities of life in Norway, and between the demands of two opposed ideologies, the Tamil migrant is compelled to choose. Individual choice forces individuation, so whatever decisions are made are inevitably transformative for those brought up within a closed, communitarian system of values. The individual choices would most likely be mixed—a bit of tradition here, a bit of revolution there—forming a bell curve with the fanatical revolutionary at one end and the devoted son and caste member at the other.

Fuglerud's ethnography calls into question some key anthropological stereotypes. It is not only that boundaries are amorphous and permeable, but this diaspora seems to lack much unity beyond a common homeland. The culture of the Tamil refugee, rather than being a uniting force, is fraught with tension, antagonism, and suspicion. Even when culture is defined as configurations of shared meanings, the differences between traditional and LTTE ideology gape wide. This may be more typical of diasporas than not. Cohesion can no more be assumed in exile than it can at home.

Chapter 9

Refugees: The Anthropology of Forced Migration

From the 1950s to the 1970s, as in the 1980s and 1990s, the movement of people (and the control of the movement of peoples) has been inescapably global, and the political, social, and ethical responsibility for it must therefore also be global.

Liisa Malkki[1]

Habari ya mihangaiko? (How are your anxieties?)
Common greeting of Burundi refugees in Tanzania[2]

The 20th century might deservedly be called the Age of Refugees; it is estimated that there have been 140 million people uprooted by war and the threat of political violence this century. In 1994 alone, there were 23 million refugees. Yet the systematic anthropological study of refugees is relatively recent.

The term "refugee" originally referred to French Protestants who fled religious oppression at the end of the 17th century. Present usage dates to people displaced during World War I. Although the League of Nations took responsibility for protecting and assisting refugees, following World War II, refugees were reclassified as a military problem and placed under the jurisdiction of the Displaced Persons Branch of the Supreme Headquarters Allied Expeditionary Force. Accordingly, the basic structure of refugee settlement was modeled after a military camp of tents or barracks. Principal elements of international refugee law and policy emerged from this postwar period, including perception of the refugee camp as a center where power could be focused and individuals would disappear into the mass, collectively susceptible to a host of interventions. In 1951, the United Nations High Commissioner for Refugees (UNHCR) was established. Especially since the late 1970s, a vast network of governmental and nongovernmental organizations has emerged to provide humanitarian aid, resettlement assistance, and protection.[3]

From 1945 to about 1990, most refugees were produced by the processes of decolonization and postcolonial state-making, which often involved bloody conflicts against die-hard colonial powers or among ethnic groups contesting for power in the new state, and the proxy wars fought by the United States and the Soviet Union in the Third World. Today, the vast majority of refugees are from developing countries, and about 90% will remain there, either repatriated or settled in the first country of asylum. Nevertheless, refugees are a global, not a Third World, issue. The rapid and enormous increases in refugees—there were about ten times as many in 1995 as twenty years earlier[4]—stimulated reactive legislation in many First World countries, which placed strong legal limits on asylum and financial limits on aid. Although the UNHCR has had to deal with 80% more refugees in 1989 than nine years earlier, its budget only rose by 15%. Overwhelmed, Japan severely restricted refugee aid to those from Indochina. Although 3 million refugees were resettled in First World countries in the 1990s, this was a small percentage of the actual number (Campbell, et al. 1993: 157).

THE ANTHROPOLOGICAL VIEW

As long as anthropology was associated with well-delineated cultures, refugees were off the anthropological map. By and large, they were liminal conglomerates of people, sometimes living in tent cities, with little that could be called social structure and with their cultures on hold. The recent breakdown of such limitations has brought refugees to the forefront of anthropology. In 1988, the Committee on Refugees and Immigrants (CORI) was established within the General Anthropology Division of the American Anthropological Association.[5] The newness of refugee studies as a subdiscipline within anthropology has meant that no broad theoretical perspective has solidified, although new directions are in evidence. The concepts of boundaries and communities are being rethought, as in anthropology in general, with an emphasis on process over structure, fluidity over stability.

The very definition of "refugee" is contested. The basic dictionary definition of the term embraces people fleeing war or persecution for political or religious reasons. The UNHCR (1988) defines refugees as those who have a "well-founded fear" of persecution in their home countries. However, environmental refugees—people escaping famine, flood, or earthquake—may be subject to the same processes as political refugees. Also, it is not always easy, in fact it can be quite difficult, to differentiate refugees from those who cross borders for economic reasons or to escape cultural oppression, such as traditional sexual mutilation practices or violent patriarchies. While subtle distinctions may be meaningless to the person affected, they can have enormous consequences in the way refugees are treated by aid organizations and immigration authorities.

ANTHROPOLOGICAL APPROACHES

In contrast to the participant observation of relatively stable communities or networks, refugees challenge anthropologists to research and understand rapid and sometimes chaotic social change. Thus, refugees require a reconceptualization of fieldwork. The year or two in a single community will obviously not do for people on the move, nor will even multisite or "traveling" fieldwork be of much use in understanding the dynamics of a camp that may be disbanded in a few weeks or a month. For permanently resettled refugees, decade- or more long longitudinal studies already employed for transnationals may be the most useful (Krulfeld 1993; Donnelly and Hopkins 1993). Also, as we have seen in relation to development anthropology, change agencies themselves may legitimately become the targets of anthropological theorizing. For the moment, a multitude of specific anthropological studies of specific groups of refugees reveal not so much a few ideal patterns as the wide range of possibilities. What such studies do demonstrate is the negation of tried-and-true concepts such as adaptation and acculturation as too simplistic. Given the multiple very-different refugee populations, the myriad causative factors, and the range of refugee experiences, generalized psychological interpretations may seem superficial.

Basically, there are three anthropological approaches that might be categorized as analytic, organizational, and interventionist (Harrell-Bond and Vourtira 1996: 1077[6]). While the *analytic* approach might require some specialized fieldwork techniques, it is basically classical anthropology, that is, face-to-face observation of and interviews with the people themselves, emphasizing adaptive strategies, social structures, values, and beliefs. The *organizational* approach is more focused on issues of policy and the structures and workings of agencies. From this perspective, the researcher is interested in the values and stereotypes held by aid workers, the interactions between immigration authorities and the refugees, and the ways that policy is established and enforced. Because the anthropologist places herself in a position between the refugee and the agencies, she is able to act as culture broker for both. Finally, the *interventionist* approach, which might or might not embrace the other two, is fundamentally the approach of applied anthropology, that is, anthropologists working for aid agencies toward the goal of helping refugees.

THE TRAGIC WORLD OF THE REFUGEE

Refugees can no longer be understood merely as people who once had a static traditional culture that has been temporarily disrupted. The environments of refugees were usually unstable for a long time before the period of dislocation, and cross-border refugees may have already undergone a period of in-country displacement. Refugees must constantly re-create and re-define themselves—legally, culturally, and materially—as their settings change. They are called on to create new structures in unfamiliar settings fairly quickly, submit to the authoritarian humanitarianism of camps overseen by bureaucrats, or adapt to asylum countries where they may be resented or hated.

Burundi Hutu in Tanzania

The range of refugee experience, even within the same wave of displacement, can be great. This is exemplified in two separate studies of Hutu refugees who fled the Tutsi massacres in Burundi and who, by the early 1990s, had been living in Tanzania for more than ten years. The first example looks at culture and identity in a camp, the second at a very small group of young Hutu tailors literally hiding in the urban capital of Tanzania.

Liisa Malkki's (1995; 1996) study of a large refugee camp reveals both the need to create history and identity, and the process of doing so. The intense animosity between Tutsi and Hutu that climaxed with the Rwanda genocide of 1994 is regional to the Great Lakes area of west central Africa, rather than contained within any particular country. In Burundi, violent conflict during the 1970s and 1980s sent tens of thousands of Hutu into exile in surrounding countries. The refugees in the Mischamo Camp in Tanzania viewed themselves as the rightful founders and heirs of the Burundi nation. Refugee status was perceived as "a vital, positive dimension of their collective identity in exile" (377), which would augment their historical vindication. Only by passing through this period of suffering, they believed, could they return to claim their country. Attempts to escape such hardship through attaining wealth or through assimilation in Tanzania were discouraged, since success in the present would tend to root them in the here and now; they saw exile not as an end point of their history but as part of the process of becoming, of creating history. That history derived from a collective process of construction and reconstruction by which they legitimized themselves as a unified people (which, in actuality, the Hutu never were). In their foundation myths, the original Hutu nation lived in harmony with the hunting-gathering Twa. The hated Tutsi were held to be "Hamites" or "Nilote" invaders from the north who had gained oppressive domination through trickery. Much historical construction derived from the minutely detailed remembering and documentation of mass killings of Hutu by the Tutsi army and Tutsi civilians.

By no means do all African refugees live in camps; about one-third live in urban areas, often illegally. Marc Sommers's (1993) study of a small group of Burundi Hutu refugees living in the Tanzanian capital of Dar es Salaam reveals another side of refugee life, one characterized not by collective historical legitimization, but rather by constant fear. After two decades in exile, many young men, some born in the camps, seek to escape the hopelessness and powerlessness of their confinement. Many are also crushed by a sense of shame and disgust at their identification as refugees; in Swahili the word for refugees, *mkimbizi* (literally "a person who runs"), is a designation connoting cowardice. The capital city, referred to in slang as Bongoland (Bongo means "brains"), offers one of very few alternatives to the camps. To escape from the camps, however, is to assume the constant insecurity of possible arrest or betrayal. Host nations of Africa do not want refugees in cities where they cannot be observed and controlled.

Sommers's study focused on about 25 young Hutu tailors living clandestinely in one of Dar es Salaam's overflowing, garbage-strewn slums. With or without the exit permit required to leave the camps, they followed networks to the city, attaching themselves as apprentices to already established kin. As tailors, they could eke out a meager living by repairing clothes and making pants and dresses (only the senior tailors could make jackets), working as much as twelve hours a day, six days a week, sleeping in a group room in the back of the shop, and almost never leaving except to attend a trusted church on Sundays. Although sometimes it was necessary to leave the sanctity of the shop, they had to remain invisible; thus, large areas of the city where they might be noticed—the downtown commercial area, the government area, embassy row—were strictly off limits.

The threat came from several sources. If found by police, the young men would be returned to the refugee camp. Worse, they might be discovered and beaten by their Tanzanian neighbors, who believed, or were perceived to believe, that the refugees would gain citizenship and become economically and socially dominant. Nor could they trust other refugees. Far from unified, the Burundi Hutu were divided into two mutually hostile "tribes": the Imbo from the Lake Tanganyika coastal regions, and the highland Banyaruguru. Despite their fear of each other, they had to work, eat, and sleep together in the capital. Betrayal was always possible. There was also a constant fear that someone might be a spy for the Tutsi-led government of Burundi.

What Sommers describes is a routinized paranoia, partially based on a realistic assessment of the social environment and partially based on deep cultural hatreds and suspicions.

ASSISTING REFUGEES

The UNHCR, which works with a complex network of refugee organizations, bases its activities on the 1951 United Nations Convention Relating to the Status of Refugees and the 1967 Protocol on refugees. While its focus is on those fleeing war or persecution across borders, it also has the option of providing assistance to "non-Convention" refugees, such as internally displaced flood victims. The UNHCR works through formal agreements with the host state and, if repatriation is possible, the home country. Its efforts are concentrated on three solutions to refugee problems: first and foremost, voluntary repatriation; second, integration in the country of first asylum; finally, if neither of these are possible, resettlement in another country of asylum. Fundamental to the process is the right of non-*refoulment*, or the right not to be forcibly returned to the country from which the refugee escaped.

The "country of first asylum" is the country that first provides legal refugee status. This can be a problem. For obvious reasons, the large majority of refugees will initially arrive in a country that borders on that from which they are escaping. In most cases, this country will itself be impoverished. Some of the largest refugee movements have occurred in the countries surrounding Rwanda and in the Horn of Africa, which includes Somalia, Ethiopia, and Eritrea, among the poorest and least stable countries in the world. Refugees escaping Afghanistan may first find themselves in Tajikistan, Uzbekistan, Pakistan, or Iran. Sometimes there may exist a same-culture community that will accept the refugees; in Djibouti, for example, there was an established Somali community that could integrate some of the refugees from Somalia in 1988. In ideal cases, the refugees will settle in, building diaspora communities or assimilating into the larger culture, as have done Palestinians in Jordan and Vietnamese in the United States. In most cases, however, refugees will receive a cold reception, assuming they are not turned back at the border. The principle of non-*refoulment* is often simply defined away. During the 1980s, refugees from extremely brutal U.S.-supported regimes in El Salvador and Guatemala were routinely rejected on the grounds that they were economic migrants rather than refugees. In Hong Kong, Vietnamese boat people were forcibly returned on the same grounds.

The international rule of first-country asylum declares that if the refugee has received protection in any country other than his own, that country retains responsibility until the refugee is voluntarily repatriated. One effect of this is for countries to refuse entry in the first place. The United States spends hundreds of millions of dollars each year safeguarding its southern border, whether intercepting Haitians on boats or arresting Mexican and Central American migrants trying to cross the Rio Grande. Indonesia turns back boats from Vietnam on the South China Sea. If the refugee is at first interned or accepted in a country that then finds itself overwhelmed or otherwise rejects the refugee, or if the refugee decides to push on, no third country is responsible by international law to take him. Since European and North American countries have few borders with Third World nations, they are less likely to be obligated with first asylum, and they often use third-country law to reject refugees.

The rule of "leave to remain," which is recognized by many countries, permits immigration authorities to deny formal asylum while granting temporary sanctuary. While this absolves receiving countries of any long-term commitment, the refugee is left in limbo without full rights. Often the refugee loses his use of travel documents, especially if his passport must be renewed at the embassy of the country from which he is escaping. Finding employment may be extremely difficult since his status is up in the air and he may be legally deported at any time.

The primary goal of the UNHCR is repatriation, which ostensibly must be noncompulsory. This goal derives originally from the return of refugees after World War II, when previously authoritarian home governments had been transformed into democracies. Today, the situation is far more complex. Many of the countries from which refugees escape remain dangerous for returnees indefinitely. Courts often find it difficult to clearly differentiate economic migrants from refugees (Campbell, et al. 1993). Pressure to repatriate may lead to overzealous or ill-advised action on the part of assistance agencies. After the 1994 genocide in Rwanda, the policy was to repatriate Hutu refugees from surrounding countries as soon as possible. The people themselves, over a million of them in several different countries, had little voice in the matter. The position of the UNHCR was that remnants of the overthrown Rwanda Army were trying to force the refugees to stay in the camps. Actually, the refugees had very legitimate concerns. There were many examples of returnees being killed. Often their property had already been taken over. In addition, 60,000 Hutus were arrested on the flimsiest of

evidence for participation in the slaughter; once arrested, their only pros-
pect was to await trial for years, or indefinitely, in prisons so packed it was
impossible to lie down (Malkki 1996).

HOW REFUGEES ARE VIEWED

The popular perception of the refugee is almost always a visual one, captured in dramatic photographs and grainy documentary films: the child with
the bloated belly, fleshless arms, and knobby joints of advanced kwashior-
kor (acute protein deficiency); the teeming tent camp of myriad dehuman-
ized humanity; the hopeless faces lined up at the food truck. In *Life*
magazine, the Rwanda genocide and refugee crisis was portrayed only in
several pages of grim photographs of death and terror. There is a dark and
powerful romanticism to such photos. Like Gustav Doré's etchings of
Dante's Hell, the stark hopelessness cannot help but touch the heart. The
complexities of the refugee situation are lost.

The refugee is usually photographed or videotaped for the news just after
the escape, as she carries her baby on her back through a thicket of border
soldiers to safety. The longer-term life of the refugee is seldom a subject.
Compassion fatigue ensures that a year or ten years after displacement, the
resettled refugee in New York or London may be viewed as a criminal—in
fact, if she is in the country without permission she will *be* a criminal—or as
a threat to the jobs of true Americans or Englishmen. Resentment and restrictive laws often replace sympathy when the pathetic subjects of the earlier dramatic photographs become next-door neighbors.

Anthropologists studying aid agencies have found that stereotypes and
deindividualization are endemic among those in refugee work. It may be inevitable that large assistance organizations tend to objectify, simplify, and
universalize the people under their care. The larger the mass of humanity,
the less the individual can stake a claim to attention. A number of assumptions may be made that limit conceptualization, creating an "ideal" refugee,
a figure who is dehistoricized and apolitical, the universal victim. A primary element of this ideal model, validated in the UNHCR mandate to repatriate as quickly as possible, is that the country of origin represents a home,
a place of normality. Another common misconception is that the entire refugee group represents some unified culture that can be reconstituted once the
refugees are returned home. Such stereotyping may be inevitable when
large masses of people must be dealt with rapidly and with inadequate staff-
ing and resources, often under tense political conditions. The camp, almost
like the colonial *repartimiento* in Latin America, is a place where refugees
can be concentrated, controlled, made dependent, and depoliticized (actu-

ally, camps may create the continuous association required for radical politicizing and factioning) (Malkki 1995, 1996).

THEORIZING REFUGEES

The exponential increase in refugees, from just over 2 million in 1975 to 23 million in 1994, overlaps two crucial periods of warfare: the last decade and a half of the Cold War and the rapid globalization of the 1990s. The term Cold War best applies to the United States and its Western European allies on one side and the USSR and its Eastern European allies on the other. They were prevented from direct confrontation by policies of mutually ensured nuclear destruction. Elsewhere, the Cold War could get quite hot, as the two superpowers supplied, trained, financed, sometimes created, and otherwise intervened in numerous wars, both small and large, in the Third World. From 1975 throughout the 1980s conflicts in Cambodia, Afghanistan, Angola, Ethiopia, Nicaragua, El Salvador, and Guatemala, among others, were direct byproducts of the communist/anticommunist confrontation. At the start of the Gulf War, President George Bush touted a New World Order that would bring cooperation among nations to replace the ideological conflicts of the Cold War; this may have been more prescient than is usually credited, not because conflict diminished but because it changed its nature.

Yahya Sadowski (1998) argues that today's ethnic conflicts are no more than long-simmering antagonisms, unaffected by the processes of globalization (defined as consumerism, the spread of democratic institutions, and capitalist enterprise). This ignores some of the more subtle aspects of globalization. It is true that the increase in refugees since 1990 is not an "explosion" but a rapid and steady movement in the direction it was already going. However, there are significant changes in the nature of refugee-creating conflict, which result not from East/West meddling, but from a general crisis of contested nationalisms. In North Asia and Eastern Europe, the *pax sovietica* imposed by sheer force of arms collapsed in a series of major and minor wars, most notably in the former Czechoslovakia; organized nationalism was not the cause of this collapse, but rather a result of it. Throughout the Third World, countries that were always ethnically divided but held together by Soviet and U.S. military support and covert intervention—Zaire and Indonesia are prime examples—fell into factional fighting.[7] To the extent that conflicts have involved a decline in the centralized, forcibly unifying powers of the nation-state, such wars are a direct result of the processes of globalization (Griffith 1998).

Despite withdrawal or reduction of direct military aid by the Cold War superpowers, a huge international arms market, dominated by the United

States, provides weapons to just about anyone who can pay for them. Many wars, however, are demilitarized with much of the violence being done not by armies but by militias, gangs, or mobs equipped with small arms or machetes and pitchforks, as was the case in Rwanda and more recently in Indonesia. As the global economy exacerbates inequalities and structural adjustment policies create class conflict, ethnicities or even regional peasantries are coalesced into ideological nationalisms. The Zapatistas of central Mexico, for example, view the North American Free Trade Agreement as a direct and primary cause of their distress. Increasingly, antagonisms among multiple nationalisms within the same country seem to have replaced, or at least found a place alongside, revolution and state-to-state conflict. The clearly vertical genocide of, say, Iraq against the Kurds is increasingly being replaced by the horizontal, neighbor-against-neighbor genocide that is so visible in Kosovo and Albania, Rwanda and Indonesia.

It has been suggested that the refugee experience can be modeled as a series of stages starting with the perception of a threat, decision to escape, flight, reaching the safety of a camp and settling in, resettlement in a new home, and adjustment and acculturation (Keller 1975). Malkki (1995: 508) rejects such stage analysis, with its implicit functionalism, that is, the idea that there is some stable, normalized, sedentary society from which the refugee is displaced and to which he will return. The situation that refugees find themselves in is seldom the result of some single traumatic incident, but rather has a long history of complex interactions involving colonialism, forced migrations, past wars, and oppressive government policies. By the time people become refugees, they have already been long a part of a constellation of social and political processes, many of which may no longer be visible. Before people escaped the war in Eritrea, they usually had experienced years of military occupation, repression, constant violence or the threat of violence, food shortages, impoverishment, collapse of the health care system, curfews, and the conscription and possible deaths of household men. By the time they ended up in camps in the Sudan or made their way to Canada, "traditional culture" had already been transformed many times over (Matsuoka and Sorenson 1999: 227).

Another theoretical tack has been to treat refugees in classic economic-rationalist mini-max fashion, that is, to analyze how they minimize adversity and maximize benefits. In reality, options may be very limited and erroneously perceived. It is difficult to factor in fear and panic. David Griffith (1998: 415–416) laments: "Failing to see the chaotic and irrational attributes of many human behaviors, especially in situations of extreme duress, anthropologists persist in searching for rational reasons for the behaviors of people for whom rationality is often a luxury. By contrast, in war and refugee flight, as in conditions of severe natural disaster, such conditions as irrationality, disturbance, and a lack of patterned behavior provide a certain flexibility." Treating refugees in camps as though they are a temporarily transported society that will return to normalcy when the situation is abated ignores the crucial element of chaos.

Victor Turner's (1974) analysis of the symbolism of *liminality* in ritual may be applicable here. As with the neophyte within a rite of passage, the refugee has left behind any claim to status or birthright; he has become invisible among an undifferentiated mass, divested of all social position, set aside in group seclusion out of the way of the larger society, reduced to, at best, a peripheral and marginal status. For initiates, this liminal state is a place of *communitas*, a spontaneous social bonding that is all the stronger because of the shared difficulties and forced equality (Griffith 1998: 504). On the other hand, while a refugee camp is indeed a liminal place, it may be more so from the perspective of agency personnel and outsiders than the refugees themselves. A refugee camp, instead of creating social bonding, may pit individuals and families against each other for restricted resources, create factioning rather than unity, and give way to rigid mafia-like hierarchies rather than equality.

The range of variation will be as vast as the range of conflicts, cultures, and types of settlement. People do carry their cultures and values into exile, and there is usually a degree of self-selection, of choice, in the matter. Depending on the circumstances, many or most people confronted with the same circumstances will stay behind to face out the crisis; it may be that their escape is blocked, or they have no resources to leave, or they do not perceive the danger as acute, or they believe their kin or neighbors will protect them, or they feel that they must remain with their land and possessions at any cost. The decision to abandon everything is not taken lightly.

GENDERING REFUGEES

Although refugees are often represented in the media by sympathetic photos of women and children, and women often make up the majorities of refugee populations, until recently the social science approach was to treat refugees as an undifferentiated mass, in which gender was not a relevant issue. In reality, the experience of forced migration can be very different for women and men. In situations of warfare, women are subject to rape and other violence. Often men are absent—dead, missing, or fighting with one of the opposition forces—so it is up to the women to protect the children and aged and hold together whatever can be salvaged of the household.

Elizabeth Colson's (1999) long-term study of the forced internal migration of the Tonga in Zambia reveals many of the processes that severely engender refugee streams. In 1956, 55,000 Tonga inhabitants of the fertile Gwembe Valley were moved to new settlements because of the construction of the Kariba Dam, which was completed in 1958. Prior to that time, rough terrain and lack of roads had isolated the people from commercial production, so farming tended to be largely devoted to subsistence and was small-scale. Many men migrated for jobs, but women stayed home. Traditionally, women managed the stock and fields and cared for the children. Few women ever traveled more than ten miles from their homes. Women owned their own land, which was passed on hereditarily in the female line, and they also received fields to work from their husbands. As a result, women were expected to feed their families from their own granaries, utilizing their husbands' granaries only when theirs were exhausted. Husbands thus controlled the surplus grain, which was employed along with wives' labor to provide the hospitality by which men earned status. Relations between men and women were defined in terms of mutual obligations and duties: husband and wife, brother and sister, mother and son-in-law.

The Kariba resettlement directly attacked these gender relationships. The Gwembe were transferred to a new settlement near an industrialized area. Initially, the houses were crude and crowded. Whereas previously women had depended upon kin for sanctuary from abusive husbands, the new conditions made this less a possibility; as a result, violence by husbands, themselves frustrated and angry over the move, increased greatly. Back in the village, popular opinion would help keep violence down, but in the more anonymous new setting this was not the case. While both men and women felt powerless in the new setting, ultimately it was women who lost whatever small power they once had. Since state officials assumed male ownership, men were allowed to demarcate their own lands by clearing them; a few women also made claims, but the majority were too confused or intimidated. Having had virtually no experience with industrial development and markets, women were unable to take advantage of what possibilities might have been available. Also, their perceptions of proper gender behavior restricted them. Clearing new fields, even those that would later belong to women, was always a man's job. In this new setting, where those who did the clearing received the land, men almost exclusively emerged as owners, so women had access to land only through their husbands. Although women may have worked less on the land in the first years, during which time they were almost completely disempowered, once lands were cleared women were expected to work them although they had lost all ownership rights. Other official actions, supposedly gender neutral, also favored men. Men were hired for road building and school construction, for example, while it was assumed that women were not employable.

Eritean Women in Canada

A different situation is evident in Atsuko Matsuoka and John Sorenson's (1999) study of Eritrean refugees in Canada. In the wake of one of the 20th century's longest wars, from 1961 to 1993, during which Ethiopia attempted to annex the former Italian colony of Eritrea, hundreds of thousands of refugees were forced to flee, mainly into neighboring Sudan and Somalia. Many were also scattered about the Middle East, Europe, and North America. By 1997, about 5,000 had settled in Canada, mainly in Toronto. Unlike the situation in the Kariba resettlement, where women's disempowerment partially derived from their lack of sophistication, the Eritrean women who made their way to Canada were mostly from the upper or middle-classes, were educated, and previously had jobs as professionals. Some refugees maintained links with the Eritrean People's Liberation Front (EPLF), which had emerged as the dominant political force when the country achieved independence. The EPLF came to power with a liberal agenda, including gender equality. Many of those who had settled overseas intended to return to Eritrea in the future, but in the wake of the war, the infrastructure lay in ruins and the country remained bogged down in the process of demilitarization and mired in acute shortages of food, water, housing, and employment.

During migration, almost all households, most of which had been made up of extended families, had been broken and scattered. Wives, husbands, children, and relatives had been separated for years. As a result, and because of the strangeness of the new environment, wives and husbands had to negotiate new relationships, far different from those in Eritrea. Formerly professional women often found it easier to get jobs than their husbands, who were left at home to take care of children and perform other "women's work" around the house. Even those men who found employment usually found themselves working at jobs of far lower status than those held in the home country. Unemployment and underemployment made it extremely hard to provide both for the household and for parents back in Eritrea. Thus, men found it difficult to perform culturally mandated obligations as husband, father, and son. For men, whose self-images were based on a patriarchal ideology, the radical change left them feeling devoid of status or power. In Eritrea, space was gendered; roughly, the domestic sphere belonged to women and the public sphere to men. To a great degree this was reversed in Canada. Even the former professional women had to reconceptualize their sense of appropriateness, as when they had to perform domestic chores pre-

viously done by servants. In Eritrea, raising children was highly differentiated along male/female lines, whereas the Canadian public school system
paid almost no attention to children's gender, forcing the refugees to either
impose rigid and unrealistic strictures on their children or relinquish them
to an alien value system. Many of the new generation of young men preferred to return to Eritrea in search of wives; Eritrean-Canadian women
were deemed too emancipated, too North American.

In the past, anthropologists have tended to view the household simplisti-
cally as a harmonious unit. Studies such as this require a new model of the
household as a place of contention and conflict among individuals with different objectives and values. At least in terms of gender relations, the household can be both conflictual and accommodative, as various individuals
constantly negotiate their roles.

Because of their temporary and uncertain status, refugees—whether in
camps or resettled in foreign countries—pose a special problem to anthropologists who have not traditionally dealt with transient or newly created
social structures. The great number of refugees today and, inevitably, in the
future, makes that challenge especially urgent.

PART III

Global/Local

Think globally, act locally.

Environmental slogan

The radical slogan of an earlier day, "Think globally, act locally," has been assimilated by transnational corporations with far greater success than in any radical strategy. The recognition of the local in marketing strategy, however, does not mean any serious recognition of the autonomy of the local. . . .

Arif Dirlik (1992: 34)

We are not a multinational, we are a multilocal.
    Coca Cola executive (Quoted in Wilson and Dissanayake 1992: 2)

Chapter 10

Globalization from the Ground Up

It should not again be necessary to emphasize that global process includes by definition and is even constituted by the articulation between local and global structures. The former is never a deduction from the latter.
Jonathan Friedman[1]

On average, food consumed in the United States has traveled 1,300 miles and changed hands a dozen times. This is not a peculiarly American phenomenon, but one that is increasingly global. As a result, production and distribution practices are invisible to the consumer, yet consumer culture holds a very strong power relation for quite distant people, shaping their lives in both obvious and subtle ways.

A study by Jane Collins (2000) reveals how European consumer preferences can impoverish even highly efficient small farmers and radically alter gender relations in Brazil. Grapes destined for Europe must be of consistently high quality. Because demand is year-round, northern countries depend on the Southern Hemisphere for winter production; the United States gets its grapes from Chile; Europe turns to South Africa and Brazil. In the São Francisco valley of Brazil, two-thirds of the crop is grown by eighteen large firms, while the remaining third is produced by about 300 farms of under six hectares. Because of close family management, these small farms produce significantly higher quality at considerably lower cost than the larger farms, yet they are constantly struggling to survive. While the labor-intensive production process favors the small farmer, the distribution system advantages the large-scale agribusiness. Grapes must be refrigerated in warehouses, trucks, and ships; lacking the bulk of the big firms, small farmers have access only if the "cold chain" is not already in use by the larger firms. Nor does the small farmer have direct access to foreign markets or to essential political and legal resources. Prices are set by two marketing boards, virtual cartels, that are more interested in profit and politics than the fate of the small farmer. In contrast to the presumption that capitalism leads to the rationalization of agriculture, here we see that real efficiency in production has become the victim of hugeness in distribution.

Another effect of São Francisco grape production has been to bring women into wage labor, completely transforming gender roles in a valley that had been devoted to cattle ranching until a dam was constructed only about two decades ago. Little mechanization can be applied to grapes, which require hand culling, trimming, harvesting, and packing, all with an eye toward maintaining quality for the European market. Women are preferred for these jobs for a number of reasons. By redefining once-skilled labor as unskilled—manual dexterity and small fingers are needed rather than skill—women have replaced men at much lower wages. Companies argue that women need "flexible schedules" because of their responsibilities at home, and thus labor laws requiring benefits can be circumvented. Unorganized and discriminated against by existing unions, women have little power of protest. Finally, women have been found to be less likely than men to openly protest the tight supervisory system that monitors every movement. What appears at first glance as a straightforward chain of trade turns out, on analysis, to involve a complex network of power relations.

FINDING THE GLOBAL IN THE LOCAL—AND VICE VERSA

There is nothing mere to the local.

Arjun Appadurai[2]

The more things come together, the more they remain apart.

Clifford Geertz[3]

Collins's study of Brazilian grape production is an example of *commodity chain analysis*, one method by which anthropologists trace the connections between the global and the local. A "commodity" is defined broadly as "any good that can be exchanged for other goods" (Stone, et al. 2000: 9). While ideologues of neoliberalism conceive of capitalism as a vast impersonal force, which when left to its own devices will be benign or beneficial, such studies present a less rosy picture, often revealing a subtle and invisibly distant exploitation. Such analysis can show how producers are affected by faraway consumer tastes and how even culture becomes commodified for international sale, as in the example of pseudo-Congolese music described in Chapter 3. One finding of such analysis is the falseness of the assumption by theorists of the modernization, dependency, and world systems schools that global flows emerge almost exclusively from an imperialist core to be imposed on a passive periphery. Both core and periphery are active participants. Commodities flowing in either direction may drastically change meaning as they move along a complex network of production, processing, advertising, distribution, and consumption. For the anthropological researcher, fieldwork may be just the beginning if the goal is a deep "system awareness" (Haugerud, et al., eds. 2000).

Those most directly affected by global processes—the small farmers, women workers, unions—may be aware of only a small part of the forces that are impacting their lives so drastically. There is nothing new about this. Eric Wolf (1982) provides numerous examples of how European expansion changed relatively bounded economic systems based on kinship into tributary and capitalist systems controlled from across oceans. Prior to the European encounter, the Mundurucú Indians of Brazil were a horticultural people whose system was tightly tied to patrilineal kinship. As European settlers moved into the area in the late 18th century, a series of changes was set in motion that transformed their way of life, as rubber tapping, rather than subsistence agriculture, became the primary occupation. Leadership shifted from native chief to white rubber trader. Entire villages dissolved as everyone moved to the rivers to be nearer the rubber trees. Probably few of the natives involved in these processes had any idea of the final destinations or uses of the rubber collected in buckets as sap.

This alienation of the worker from his product is basic to Marxist analysis, but there is also an alienation of the down-the-line distributor, such as the store owner who does the selling and the consumer who does the buying, in the sense that neither knows nor cares where the grapes or rubber came from. Under globalization, this process of distantiation of producer from consumer is not only increasing in terms of sheer distance and number of intermediaries, but also in terms of abstractness. It has been said that the logic underlying cargo cults in the Pacific was that islanders could not understand Western manufacturing and therefore assumed that manufactured goods were created by magic; in the First World, when plump, firm grapes magically appear in the produce section of a Copenhagen supermarket in mid-January, no one really thinks much about it. The villainous roles that not long ago were assigned by protesters to the United Fruit Company in Guatemala or International Telephone and Telegraph in Chile or Nestlé in

Africa seem anachronistic as transnationals (no longer mere *multi*nationals) become invisible through complexity, mobility, the multiplication of brand names, and sheer magnitude. Rather than targeting specific companies, protest is now directed toward the World Trade Organization or the International Monetary Fund, that is, at the level of the global system itself.

The global-local connection, which is at the heart of anthropological analysis, can be either blatant or subtle, obvious or hidden, complex or relatively direct. But it is never simple. The definition of "local" turns out to be as problematic as "global."

In Search of the Local

The great paradox of globalization is that it is creating a world that is more localized. This fractured unity is not new, but the very term *globalization* renders it a degree of analytical newness. Modernization theory postulated a Western-style industrialization—individualist, entrepreneurial, consumerist—as the inevitable end result for everyone who would participate. Dependency theory, while in many ways exactly the opposite of modernization theory, did not predict increased fragmentation; rather, the existing class system among nations and regions would be reinforced. World system theory envisioned only a very generalized division of labor between core, periphery, and semiperiphery. Articulation theory assumed diversity, but only to the extent that noncapitalist economic forms would continue to exist alongside capitalism. In the concept of globalization, however, we find a multitude of social, economic, political, and cultural localisms to be implicit: ethnicities, nationalisms, resistance movements, drug cartels, Web discussion groups, diaspora communities, transnational communities, NGOs, and interest groups. To the extent that localization is part of the definition of globalization, the separation of the two is artificial, though a heuristic necessity. While exclusive focus on macrostructures is inevitably distorting, the postmodern rejection of grand narratives of global structure leaves the local isolated and incomplete. The job of the anthropologist is to reveal the intersection and interaction of the macro and micro, of global and local (Cvetkovich and Kellner 1997: 2; Dirlik 1992: 23).

It should be obvious that traditional dictionary definitions of "local" are gone with the postmodern wind. My Microsoft Bookshelf dictionary defines "local" as, "Of, relating to, or characteristic of a particular place: a local custom; the local slang. b. Of or relating to a city, town, or district rather than a larger area: state and local government." No room here for Web discussion groups or Haitian transnationals in New York. According to Arjun Appadurai (1996: 178–199) *locality* is "primarily relational and contextual rather than scalar or spatial." For analytical purposes, the local is now something people carry with them; it has been deterritorialized. The local is thus more complex than previously conceived; it is not just a given of any situation, but must be produced. It must also be constantly reinforced, since its very malleability threatens it with dissolution. A particular locality is a *neighborhood*, a self-reproducing "life-world" of relatively stable associations and shared histories. Such a broad and fluid concept of locality allows for the spatially bounded communities of traditional ethnography, but also for transnational communities and for "virtual neighborhoods" based on fax machines, the Internet, and a commonality of films and television. Whereas in the past most localities were contained within nation-states, the forces of globalization have put the nation-state on the defensive, as it tries, futilely, to contain and control its localities.

For Ulf Hannerz (1996: 25–26), locality is an interpersonal connectedness made up of kinships, friendships, collegialities, ethnicities, and business relations. These comprise overlapping "habitats of meaning," based not on territoriality but on familiarity, that we carry with us from situation to situation. A tourist seeks the exotic in India but travels on tour busses with others like herself and stays in four-star hotels that replicate the American environment. For an Iowan, contacting a daughter in Germany via e-mail might become as routine as phoning her across town. Such habitats of shared meaning may be casual or emotionally intense. Business associates within a transnational corporation might have a long-term but entirely formal relationship, while a Tibetan may make his diaspora community the purpose and emotional center of his life. Despite, or perhaps because of, the challenge of creating and maintaining such localities in an increasingly deterritorialized world, the strength of identity politics and nationalist allegiances is increasing (Wilson and Dissanayake 1992: 5).

The Global-Local Nexus

It would be possible to suggest multiple localisms, in the same way that the contemporary analysts speak of multiple modernities. Certainly territorially bounded localities still exist, though they are getting rarer and more complex under the dual influences of travel and media, and they need to be distinguished from deterritorialized localities, which in turn can be subdivided into physical and virtual (localities defined by modern communication technology, such as Web chat groups). In the broadest terms, these multiple forms of locality might be classified according to their relationship to globalization, first, locality as a sight of resistance, and, second, locality as an articulation of the processes of globalization (Dirlik 1992: 22).[4] In the

first case, which might be called *reactive localization*, the ethnic group, union, nation, or diaspora community would be to a great extent a defensive
association against the universalistic tendencies of globalization. An ethnic
group, for example, deliberately fortifies boundaries and increases
in-group awareness in order to protect vital interests and salvage or reinforce a sense of identity in the face of assimilative threats. In the second
form, which might be termed *accommodative localization*, the local may be
seen as produced or shaped by neoliberal capitalism, as would be the case
with free trade zones in the Third World, *maquiladoras*, and transnational
corporate cultures.

A disclaimer that such classification is simplistic should be unnecessary;
taxonomies and especially dichotomies should automatically elicit a skeptical roll of the eyes. Obviously, reactiveness and accommodativeness are
matters of degree, and specific localities can be both reactive and accommodative at the same time. However, such distinctions do point up the need for
localities to adapt to global structures while at the same time seeking as
much wiggle room as possible. A great deal of anthropological data suggests that *unimpeded* neoliberal capitalism increases inequality, destroys indigenous cultures, promotes rampant consumerism, commodifies
everything, transfers wealth from the poor to the rich, eviscerates the environment, and disempowers the weak while further empowering the strong.
Unimpeded globalization does tend toward cultural homogenization of a
mostly, but not entirely, Western form, while at the same time it is as likely
"to polarize and exclude as it is to connect people and places" (Stone et al.
2000: 3). However, globalization is almost never unimpeded. Much of the
explosion of nationalism, ethnicity, nongovernmental associations, and
transnational communities can be understood as a defense against economic
and political marginality, cultural dissolution, and anomy. The situation is
roughly comparable to the period of industrial capitalism in the West after
1850, when child labor, low wages, miserable working conditions, and long
hours were opposed by the growth of unions, and tendencies toward central-
ization of power and wealth were countered by antimonopoly legislation.

Does the Local Determine the Global?

The claim that local and global are part of the same system should not be
construed as an assumption of equal power. To reinterpret Isaac Newton, every action has an opposite but not quite equal reaction. It may be true that both
must adapt to each other, but it is the local that does most of the adapting. Almost all national economies in the Third World and former Second World (the
old Soviet Bloc)—together comprising about 80% of the earth's popula-

tion—have been transformed within the last decades by neoliberal strictures mandated by various lending groups and by states giving foreign aid. The global system does its share of adjusting, say, to the economic crisis in Southeast Asia at the beginning of the 1990s and to continuing Mideast control of oil supplies, but it requires large-scale power to affect it significantly. None of this should suggest that globalization *determines* local behavior; quite the opposite. To the extent that local resistances are reactions to perceived threats, their particular manifestations are unpredictable from the higher level. While the local must respond to the global in some manner, the range of available responses is great—dissolution, cooptation, assimilation, armed resistance, unionization, ethnicization, the formation of political parties, regionalization. The global system is not threatened by resistances; this is a matter of magnitude, the elephant and the gnat syndrome. Since it is not threatened, the global can be quite accommodating. Ethnic wars and protest movements can be assimilated with barely a ripple in the system. Debt reschedulings, environmental protections, and changes in the IMF and WTO because of street protest actually prolong and strengthen the global system by protecting it from its own excesses (or as Marx would say, its internal contradictions). Such adaptive feedback relations are as much a part of the internal logic of global capitalism as technological change and the spread of consumerism.

The range of possible responses to globalization is influenced by numerous local factors: culture, colonial and postcolonial history, political leadership, class structure, preexisting organizations, gender differentials, accessible resources, available technology, and education levels, to name just a few. This makes top-down analysis usually futile. Not always. Ferguson's (1994) and Escobar's (1995: 113–153) studies of huge development projects in Lesotho and Colombia, described in Chapter 4, are quite revealing.[5] In most cases, however, a bottom-up analysis would be most amenable not only to anthropological fieldwork methodology but also to tracing linkages. The very specific cannot with any accuracy be predicted from the very general, especially when the number of active variables increases exponentially as one moves down the chain of cause and effect (Burawoy 2000a: 343). A postmodernist might claim that this justifies rejection of "totalizing" theories in favor of the concrete reality of the particular, but this fails to account for higher-level structures, without which the particular must remain arbitrary.

Deromanticizing the Local

If there is a tendency among those not on the neoliberal bandwagon to demonize the global, there is often an equal tendency to romanticize the local. The teleology of 1950s modernization theory assumed that all societies would be or should be brought up to the standards of the urban, industrialized civilization of capitalism, so the local was inevitably characterized in terms of rural stagnation, primitive technology, and simple social structures. Reactions to modernism, especially in the form of dependency theory, tended more toward the representation of the "traditional" in the abstract as a virgin local purity that was threatened by the destructive forces of modernity. The general bias in anthropology against hugeism—and globalization is about as huge as it gets—sets up a David-and-Goliath antagonism that is expressed, for example, in the poststructural insistence on the priority of local discourse over discourses of development.

A problem with this idealization of the local is that if all or nearly all localities have long been transformed by Western expansion, then the "traditional" of any locality is most likely an earlier stage of capitalism or, at the least, a stage of tributary relations with capitalism. Also, viewing the local as the primary site of opposition to globalization can lead one to overlook the internal divisions, oppression, violence, exploitation, environmental destruction, virulent racism, and gender inequities that may exist in a compressed state at the local level (Dirlik 1992: 23–38).

THE NATION-STATE: TRANSFORMATION OR DEMISE?

We need to think ourselves beyond the nation-state.

Arjun Appadurai[6]

[W]hen I use the notion "withering away of the nation," I do not assume that such a process would necessarily entail a withering away of the state as well.

Ulf Hannerz[7]

The search for the local might well start with a questioning of the nation-state, which is a conventional reference point for location and identity. One is Nigerian or Brazilian or Pakistani ("American" is a bit of a fluke, apparently less a matter of hemispheric megalomania—though that helps—than of the awkwardness of "United Statesian"). While regional and global organizations, such as the United Nations, NATO, ASEAN, NAFTA, the European Community, may have their own governing bodies and make overriding decisions, they are still made up of countries. National governments are still viewed as the main loci of power in relation to their citizens.

However, if theorists of globalization agree on very little else, there is a growing consensus that the nation-state is no longer the primary actor on the world stage. It is argued that the global order is less a structure of countries than of organizations that overlap national boundaries and override state sovereignty: transnational corporations, trade organizations, unofficial elite economic-political organizations such as the Trilateral Commission, financial institutions such as the World Bank and IMF, ecological movements, human rights organizations, HIV/AIDS associations, and developmental and antidevelopment pressure groups (Long 2000: 187). The only question is whether the state will disappear altogether or will be transformed into a subordinate organization mainly concerned with road construction and domestic policing. According to John Comaroff (1996: 172), globalization "threatens eventually to dissolve and decompose the nation-state." Appadurai (1996: 19) has "come to be convinced that the nation-state, as a complex modern political form, is on its last legs." Samuel Huntington (1996: 301–312) sees the U.S. nation-state as threatened under the dual onslaught of multiculturalism and moral decay. Within the field of transnationalist studies, "some observers have begun to speak of the demise of the nation-state's ability to form and discipline its subjects" (Glick Schiller, et al. 1995: 50). For Roger Rouse (1991), states are in the process of becoming deterritorialized.

While sympathetic to these views, I propose that the death of the nation-state may be highly exaggerated. The nation-state is indeed being transformed both from without and within, but this can be seen as an ongoing adaptation, a shifting of functions, rather than a fundamental alteration in the system of states. However, before making that argument, it is worthwhile glancing at some of the disappearing-state theorizers.

Arjun Appadurai (1996, 2000: 189) argues that "the nation-state relies for its legitimacy on the intensity of its meaningful presence in a continuous body of bounded territory" and that such boundaries are continually eroded by transnational communities and borderless media, such as movies, television, radio, and the Internet. After the Cold War, the world became unipolar in terms of economic integration, but also multicentric. Whereas previously states held a monopoly on internal financial decisions and relations with other states, these functions have been globalized. Modern nationalisms are not identified with the state; loyalties and identity have shifted to substate and international nationalisms and ethnicities. There are two fundamental dimensions of the decline of the nation-state. The first is ethical: States have become bloated, corrupt, violent, no longer willing or able to protect or support the minorities that are increasingly turning against them. The second dimension is the analytic: The state is besieged internally and from all sides by border wars, revolutions, inflation, the massive influx of immigrant populations, and serious flights of capital that threaten national sovereignty. Many states have become completely dependent on foreign labor, imported technical experts, and arms. In combination, such weakness adds up to a "terminal crisis" for the nation state (21).

Political scientist Samuel Huntington (1996) believes that the system of nation-states has already been replaced, at least ideologically and politically, by nine international "civilizations": Western, Latin American, African, Islamic, Sinic (Chinese), and the like. These follow patterns of culture, usually religion, and thus ignore national boundaries. Islamic civilization, for example, extends out of the Middle East north into Afghanistan, east to Indonesia, south deep into Africa. The unilateral modernizing influence of the West has seen its day; each civilization is turning inward upon itself and counterposing itself to the other civilizations. Future armed conflicts will be "fault-line" wars, fought where opposed civilizations rub up against each other. The United States is severely threatened from within by its acceptance of multiculturalism, which dilutes and destroys Western rationalism and democratic culture, the main sources of its strength. The signs of moral decay are expressed in burgeoning antisocial behavior, the demise of the family, declines in membership in voluntary associations, a weakening of the work ethic, and decreasing commitment to intellectual pursuits.

John Comaroff (1996) notes that nation-states are finding it increasingly difficult to meet the material demands of their citizens or to effect development policies that can feed, house, educate, and ensure their health. The global economy is undermining the nation-state in three ways: First, states have lost control of currency and trade, as both flow freely across borders; second, mobile markets and transnational corporations have dispersed production, so that companies are no longer firmly situated and can move about at will; third, a transnational division of labor has emerged, with workers, many of them illegal, traversing borders on a massive scale. "Taken together, these processes are leading to the erasure of anything that might be described as a national economy, if by that is meant a geopolitical bounded terrain within which production, exchange, and consumption sustain close connections with each other" (169).

Glick Schiller, Basch, and Blanc-Szanton (1995) note how recent an invention is the nation-state, and how fragile. The key idea underlying the nation-state is a myth, namely, that the state embraces a single people with a shared culture and that citizens are defined by their residence within a given territory and owe allegiance and undivided loyalty to a common government. If this was a myth in the past, when migrants were expected to assimilate, it is even more so today, when migrants tend to be transnational, maintaining their ethnicities through constant economic and social connections with a home country, never truly assimilating. What is emerging are deterritorialized nation-states without real borders, as has already occurred with Greece and Haiti.

Not Even Moribund

It is true that states have relinquished a good deal of economic control to transnational forces. This is especially so in regard to countries that in the past established strong import-substitution programs and nationalized industries (that is, virtually the entire Third World); the philosophy behind import substitution industrialization has been rendered irrelevant by global neoliberalism and IMF structural adjustment requirements. Even Southeast Asian countries, which developed strong economies very rapidly through state intervention and authoritarian governments, have given way to open markets and democratization. Few countries can go it alone in the global arena, with a result that most are either members of or seeking to be members of regional organizations; such membership requires even more concessions on the part of individual states. Increased localization, in the form of grassroots movements and heightened sociopolitical ethnicity, has weakened state control over the citizenry.

However, even while recognizing such reorienting of the state, arguments that the nation-state is "in demise" are not convincing. It is never quite clear what "demise" means, beyond a transfer of some functions or powers to local, regional, or global institutions and forces. What is to follow this demise is never clear (global government? anarchy? locally governed enclaves? multinational corporations? a deterritorialized citizenry?). In any case, such arguments reify and essentialize the nation-state, assuming that it is something it never was. While in most of the countries of Europe and in the United States, Canada, Australia, and Japan there really have been dominant, majority referent cultures, this has *never* been true in most Third World countries. If the nation-state nexus was a bit of a myth in the First World, it was little more than polite fiction elsewhere. Now that the USSR has collapsed, India may be the most multicultural country on earth, with fifteen major languages and 400 "scheduled tribes," yet as a state it is probably as strong today as it ever has been. The observation that many countries cannot feed or house their populations is quite true, but, then, they never could. In fact, a relatively small number of Third World countries, mainly in Southeast Asia, have made enormous strides in greatly raising the living standards of all sectors, and several countries of Latin America—Brazil and Mexico are the most obvious—have made significant advances toward industrialization.

There seems to be an illusion that Third World dictatorships were somehow "strong" and that the 1990s "decade of democratization" produced weakened states; this is simply not the case. The need for political killing, imprisonment, torture, and disappearance to maintain the state is a sign of extreme weakness in the sense that the available options for administrators—say, in how to spend funds or select among development alternatives—are far more limited than in more open societies. Few dictators hold any kind of absolute power; they must walk a narrow tightrope between a multitude of different interest groups: militaries divided between progressive and conservative factions, landed aristocracies, industrial elites, workers organizations, and external states.[8] The fact that such countries were able to keep their ethnicities in check through brute force is not a sign of strength (in retrospect, was the USSR *ever* internally strong?) so much as a blatant demonstration of lack of legitimacy. Countries like Indonesia, Zaire (now the Democratic Republic of the Congo), or Peru were never nation-states in the sense that they claimed some overriding loyalty from the majority of the population, so to argue now that their nation-stateness is in demise because of globalization is simply a non sequitur.

The argument makes more sense if the terms "nation" and "state" are separated. In the United States (but not most other First World countries), multiculturalism and transnationalism may indeed be diluting a sense of national culture, though, contra Huntington, this can be interpreted as more a matter of co-optation (rap and Latin music, Asian cuisine) than dilution. However, true nationalism has always been situational. On a day-to-day basis, people identify with their local communities or ethnic groups—probably always have, always will. Unifying nationalism comes to the fore mainly during wartime or what I call "negative rites of reinforcement," that is, patriotic rituals focused on tragedy, such as the assassination of President Kennedy, the Iran hostage crisis, the Challenger disaster, or the attacks on the World Trade Center. It should be noted also that unassimilated immigrants, such as the Cuban community in Miami or Kosovo refugees, often tend to be the most conservative and chauvinistic elements of the population, perhaps because they are more aware of the alternatives and have a clear external enemy. In Third World countries, voluntary migration may actually have the effect of strengthening the nation-state. Migration tends to funnel ethnic groups to diverse areas, and dispersed peoples are less likely to form nationalist or separatist aspirations than those that are all together in one place. Outmigration also serves to relieve internal pressure for jobs and other amenities while helping finance the state through remittances. Far from being weakened by outmigration, many impoverished states depend on it.

In abandoning parastatals and the strategy of import substitution, Third World countries lost an important source of financial control (as well as a primary source of graft). However, one of the main functions of the state within international capitalism has been the protection and encouragement of home-based companies. This function has not changed; in fact, the need for it is greater in a truly globalized economy. Sociologist Leslie Sklair (1995: 70–78) postulates a transnational capitalist class composed of corporate executives and their local affiliates, globalizing state bureaucrats, politicians and professionals, and consumerist elites (merchants, media). While the members of this class are transnational, they are firmly grounded in particular countries and would lose what power and influence they have if they were to abandon their national identifications. In this sense, many of the same global processes of self-interest that animate the local level also reinforce the state level. If there is a transnational grammar to the language of globalization, states still comprise the vocabulary, and there is little evidence this will change.

The number of sovereign states, far from diminishing, has quadrupled since the end of World War II, and territorial borders are more secure than in the past. Today, cross-border wars are almost nonexistent. The Gulf War, which was supported by perhaps the most global coalition ever contrived, announced loud and clear that established states of economic or strategic importance to the West are not to be attacked. Violent internal conflicts are legion, though in certain areas, such as Latin America, there are far fewer than fifteen years ago. Except for long-standing disputes, such as that between Peru and Ecuador, territorial borders are unchallenged from without, precisely because the global system is dedicated to protecting the state system.

The degrees and types of state intervention are indeed changing: Territorial boundaries do not function as containers of culture as well as they used to, new social movements are resisting or bypassing the state, and some state functions are being transferred to other organizations such as the World Bank and various NGOs, but this hardly suggests any pressing need to start writing the epitaph for the nation-state. In many ways, the state has been underresearched and undertheorized by anthropologists. The microeffects of state intervention, from passing laws to constructing roads to establishing immigration policies to running penal institutions to educating children, are so all-encompassing as to be taken for granted. The argument that global processes are leading to deterritorialized individuals and cultures does not go far enough; it is not only people and cultures that are being deterritorialized, so is the state. To be sure, the modern state continues to exist within well-defined map borders, but at the same time it extends in every direction through trade, regional organizations, military alliances, financial networks, and spying and covert meddling. The wave of the future is less likely to be a stateless globe than the globe that is already evident today,

a system made up of transnationalized states strongly anchored within protected physical territories.

Ethnicity and State Nationalism in Indonesia

One of the primary arguments for the decline or demise of the nation-state is that a multitude of ethnic groups challenges any national unity
that the state might claim. While ethnicity may overlap with nonstate aspirant "nations," it is a commonplace in anthropology that ethnicity and
state-nationalism are in opposition. Such a viewpoint might be expected
when fieldwork usually takes place within subordinated communities
where linkages with the state are confrontational. However, despite the anthropological stress on the disjunctive aspects of identity, ethnicity and
state-nationalism need by no means be mutually exclusive. C.W. Watson's
(1996) study of Indonesia reveals not only that the two identities may be
embodied in different, nonconflictive spheres of politics, economics, and
symbolism, but also that they may symbiotically reinforce each other.

Prior to the 1920s, Indonesian identity was largely encompassed in the
concept of *adat*, roughly "culture"—the distinctive language, behaviors, institutions, and ideologies associated with a particular region. One spoke of
adat Sunda, adat Minangkabau, or *adat Ambon.* The nationalist movement
against the Dutch colonizers, however, created a rough pan-Indonesian
identity that had never existed before, and this was elaborated by Indonesian politicians when colonialism came to an end. In the process of nation-building, local identities were subordinated. This process was made
possible by three common features that united all, or most, ethnic groups,
even those speaking different languages: first, the common experience of
Dutch occupation; second, the availability of Malay/Indonesian as a *lingua
franca* that facilitated communication between different groups; and third,
Islamic religion. The Indonesian language became the vehicle for the creation of new histories, which were spread by radio, national journals, television, telephones, and movies. These transformed local heroes in the
struggle against the Dutch into national heroes. A new vocabulary of egali-
tarianism—*saudara* or "sibling" and *bung* or "comrade brother"—became
common. A set of five principles of state was memorized by schoolchildren
and adults alike. The Indonesia-hosted Bandung Conference of 1955,
which codified the nonaligned movement of Asian and African nations, became a source of national pride.

Rather than breaking down ethnic differentiation, as modernization theorists were predicting, this growth of nationalism encouraged it. The nation-state was identified as a mosaic of valued traditional groups, so that

each region could see itself as contributing to a greater whole. Traditional dances and costumes were encouraged at national celebrations. Although there were periodic ethnic outbreaks, especially against the Javanese who were correctly perceived as a political and economic elite, by and large, ethnicity and state-nationalism belonged to different but overlapping spheres.

There existed, then, a dynamic tension in the relationship between the claims of nationalism and ethnicity. For the individual, the circumstances of the occasion very clearly dictated whether an ethnic or nationalist response was required. Nationalism was called upon in times of crisis and on special occasions and was only sporadically brought to the individual's consciousness—during times of war, national and international political conferences, championship sporting events, state holidays, and annual remembrance parades. Ethnicity, on the other hand, is constantly present, much closer to the bone, much quicker to realize itself in everyday domestic and professional contexts (Watson 1996: 110).

CONCLUSIONS

Although the local is at the center of the anthropology of globalization, the concept of the local requires rethinking to remove it from its associations with physical territory. In the studies of commodity chains or transnational communities, "local" becomes a term no more concrete than field or arena. It must be defined anew in each specific case. This redefinition becomes a problem of determining what relationships must be considered. Bereft of a neatly bounded local community that will embrace, all at once, kinship, friendship, sodalities, politics, and economics, only one or a few types of relationships must be chosen in order to circumscribe the ethnographic local, which may be spread widely. While globalization thus breaks down even ethnography's most fundamental sureties, it at the same time offers new freedoms to discover localities where we never looked for them before.

Chapter 11

Tribal Cultures: No Longer Victims

For all its conflicts and contradictions, global civil society is the realm most responsive to indigenous peoples.

Alison Brysk[1]

We want them to fight their own battles. What I consider a success is the Indians doing their own advocacy.

David Maybury-Lewis, founder of Cultural Survival[2]

Indigenous peoples throughout the world have for centuries been victim to outright genocide, decimation by European diseases, land theft, ecological destruction, forced removal, and a host of other depredations. Such abuses have been documented by anthropologists in books with titles like *Victims of Progress* (Bodley 1990) and *Victims of the Miracle* (Davis 1990). Oppression continues, of course, but in many cases it is no longer hidden or uncontested. This is especially true for some of the 200,000 Indians of the Amazon region of Brazil who, often with the help of anthropologists and transnational organizations, are learning new techniques of defending their cultures and homelands.

Until only a couple of decades ago, Brazilian Amazonian Indians were viewed by the government much as Indians in the first century of the United States, as barriers to progress to be removed by whatever means might be necessary, assuming that they were considered to exist at all. "Land without people for people without land" was the slogan for the Transamazon Highway, which was built in the 1970s in order to open the Amazon region to set-tlement. One hundred kilometers on either side of the road was declared state land for farming by the rural poor of the northeast. "Land without peo-ple" notwithstanding, this territory was already occupied by Indian horti-culturalists and rubber tappers. The expensive project merely succeeded in producing massive deforestation and erosion; thousands of Indians died of imported diseases and decimated ecosystems. Also during this time, Radam (Radar Amazonia) was established; remote sensing planes overflew the dense jungle in search of mineral resources. Mining increased greatly. Five hundred miners arrived in Yanomamo Indian territory, bringing with them deadly measles, tuberculosis, and venereal diseases; in one group, 50% of the population died.

In 1982, undiscouraged by previous disasters, Brazil commenced the ambitious Polonoroeste Project with a promised half billion dollars from the World Bank. This time, settlement along the new road was to be sup-ported by schools, shops, clinics, banks, sawmills, and factories. In 1985 alone, 200,000 settlers established farms in the region, displacing sev-enty-five Indian groups living in the area. The original plans, however, were not followed through; the road was built, but the supporting health services, markets, and schools never materialized. Within years, 80% of the settlers sold out their holdings to land speculators. By then, the formerly verdant rainforest was cleared and eroded to almost desert conditions, fit only for cattle.

It was within this unpromising context that the Kayapó of the upper Xingu River began to fight back. Traditionally the Kayapó relied on slash-and-burn agriculture, sometimes living in small villages, sometimes nomadic. As of the early 1990s, there remained 4,000 living in fourteen vil-lages. Though warriors in the past, the Kayapó had remained relatively qui-escent, as their territory, once the size of Austria, was gradually assimilated by the government, which recognized no indigenous legal claims to the land. By the 1960s, they had been "pacified" for a generation by the state In-dian agency and by missionaries, who together controlled their destiny. In 1980, gold was discovered in Kayapó territory, and miners poured in. Their fate seemed that of many other Indian groups in the same circumstances: political and economic marginalization in their own territory, prostitution, poverty, and decimation by disease.

With little to lose, in 1983, 200 Kayapó forcibly took over the gold mine, holding 3,000 miners captive and playing the publicity for all it was worth. Ultimately, the action helped force concessions from the government. By this time, the Kayapó had long experience with outsiders, not only mission-aries and government agents, but also with anthropologists, photographers, reporters, and cinematographers. These sympathetic intruders were instrumental in bringing an awareness of the political value of culture and identity. University of Chicago anthropologist Terence Turner taught them the use of video technology, helping them establish a video archive. Government officials knew that any negotiations would be videotaped, so that verbal promises could not be easily forgotten or rescinded. Kayapó cameramen stationed themselves prominently during confrontations with companies and with government agents to demonstrate that they were in charge of communications and to remind officials that the world would be watching. The Kayapó became increasingly sophisticated in the use of other modern technology, such as fax machines and e-mail. They recruited international allies to their cause, not only human rights and environmental organizations, but also the United Nations and the World Bank itself, from which they forced major concessions. By coordinating with other tribal peoples, they were able to create a united pan-tribal political force that amplified the protest of individual tribal groups.

All of this fit rather well with preexisting Kayapó philosophy. For them, moral force had always derived from representation; symbolic performances, oratory, and communal ceremonies had traditionally been a central part of their culture. Culture was affirmed and reality created through such collective expressions. As a result, television documentaries of their ritual and speeches were just a technological extension of previous practices.

It all came together at the Altimara Conference of Amazonian Indians. This large, highly publicized rally of Indians in traditional costume succeeded in halting a huge dam, financed by the World Bank, that would have flooded great areas of the Xingu River Valley. The event was attended by hundreds of reporters and official observers from around the world; Brazil itself was forced by the publicity to send its own high-level government officials. A documentary by Grenada TV, partially filmed at the Conference in close consultation with the Kayapó, quickly became a television and classroom standard (Beckham 1987). Altimara became a prototype for the political mobilization of "what could be described as a nascent global counter-civil society composed of non-governmental organizations, media, some politicians, some inter-governmental organizations, and last, but not least, anthropologists" (Turner 2001).

By the late 1990s, the Kayapó had their own reserve, were getting millions of dollars in profits from the mine on their territory, and were instrumental in forcing the World Bank to shut down funding of the Polonoroeste Project for several months while the project was reconsidered in the light of indigenous needs and demands. Such actions, along with pressures from numerous other groups, induced the World Bank to significantly change its policy on large-scale projects.[3] The formerly unknown Kayapó had firmly put themselves on the map as sophisticated activists and spokespersons for indigenous rights. Films about the Kayapó struggle, made by Americans and Europeans, are shown throughout the world. Videos they have made themselves are regularly presented at international film festivals.

TRIBAL SOCIETIES IN A GLOBAL WORLD

Demographic archeologists estimate that in neolithic times, before the rise of state societies, the world's population of 75 million was organized into a million and a half tribal nations, each politically autonomous, decentralized, economically self-sufficient (Bodley 1988: 1). The spread of states both decimated and incorporated the large majority of these societies, a process that was greatly amplified with the expansion of the conquering and colonizing West after the 15th century. Acknowledging that historical population estimates are highly and deservedly controversial, John Bodley (1990: 40) suggests a depopulation of almost 28 million in the Americas, Oceania, Australia, and the Congo (no figures are given for the rest of Africa). In the Western Hemisphere alone, declines ranged from 50% to 90% of regional populations due to disease, warfare, enslavement, social disruption, and ecological devastation. While the Center for World Historical Studies claims that presently existing "Fourth World" nations number 5,000 to 6,000, representing a third of mankind (CWIS 2001), the vast majority of these indigenous peoples are better described in terms of ethnicity than tribalism, having assimilated into dominant national cultures, often at the margins; most are peasants or are urbanized. Only about 200 million truly tribal peoples exist today, a tiny fraction of the world's 6 billion. These represent a wide range of levels of integration with the nation-state, from U.S. Indian reservations to isolated New Guinea villages. In many cases, such cultures continue to exist only because they have been pushed onto land that was not viewed as having any value by the dominant culture or because they were able to wrest some legal recognition for their territories. Typically, they will occupy only 10% to 30% of their original territories, assuming they have not been removed to less hospitable lands. They are often threatened with polluted or dammed-up water supplies, deforestation, erosion, mercury contamination from gold mining, oil spills, indiscriminant hunting by outsiders, disruptive tourism, and, above all, disease (Bodley 1988; Brysk 2000: 5–7).

The term "tribe" is contested, of course, as are most descriptive terms employed by anthropologists. Tribal, like indigenous or aboriginal, may have the unfortunate and unwarranted connotation of primitive, backward, stone age (Greaves 1996: 636). The term "tribe" has been employed in anthropology as a broad category in the classification of sociopolitical systems, standing between relatively definable bands and chiefdoms (the fourth category being state). Since numerous different structures fell within this class, definitions that attempted to cover all possibilities ranged from fuzzy to iffy, though many tribal groups did possess a core of common characteristics: They had unilineal kinship; subsistence was based on horticulture or pastoralism; they lacked a means of formal political succession; they were relatively egalitarian; and they were held together by pantribal sodalities, such as warrior societies, that crosscut kinship divisions (Lewellen 1992: 24–35). Today, many of these characteristics have disappeared. While tribes and ethnicities are both embedded in nation-states and are self-conscious of their uniqueness, the term "ethnicity" suggests a degree of integration not suggested by tribe. Ethnicities exist relative to a dominant culture and to other ethnicities. They may be transnational or at least spread throughout the country. The tribal group is more isolated from the larger society, on a reserve or reservation or within some such definite territory. Interactions with the larger society are usually less frequent.

While the tribal distinction is relatively clear in the case of the Kayapó, ethnicity overlaps with tribe in situations such as the North American reservation Navaho, who routinely move back and forth between native communities and the dominant Anglo culture. Alison Brysk (2000: 5) suggests the term "tribal village" to describe culturally defined communities based on a common location. Such communities are distinguished by face-to-face interactions, shared identity markers such as language, ritual, and costume, and a sense of common fate and intragroup accountability. Traditionally, kinship is the primary organizing mechanism, land is communally owned, and goods are exchanged through reciprocity rather than the market (though these economic forms often break down under the pressures of modernization). Taking the circumscribed village or community as the tribal unit avoids the problem of large groups, such as the African Yoruba, that may be dispersed through multiple subgroups and in which there is a wide range of individual assimilation into the dominant society.

TRIBAL MOBILIZATION

The problems faced by tribal peoples are very different from those of urban ethnicities, which is a primary reason for keeping the two separate. The governmental approach to tribes has largely been forced integration into the nation-state. The state, almost by definition, seeks control of both its lands and its people. Powerful commercial interests also want unimpeded access to resources. Often a landless peasantry, created by population growth and the commercialization of formerly subsistence lands, pressures the government to open "underused" tribal territories for settlement. Development of tribal lands, even if jobs and other benefits are promised, usually leads to displacement and environmental destruction. Tribal peoples almost invariably end up at the bottom of the social hierarchy, afforded only the lowest paying jobs, if employment is available at all. Democratization may exacerbate rather than solve such problems. In Amazonia, for example, 60% of the population is urban, living in such cities as Belém, Manaus, Santarém, and Porto Velho. Much of the rest of the population, though rural, is not native. As a result, the large majority of voters are nontribal and are most interested in employment, schools, roads, sanitation, electricity, and hospitals; they have little interest in Indian rights or environmentalism and, more likely than not, will vehemently oppose pro-Indian policies that restrict the opening of new lands to farming, ranching, mining, and lumbering (Lins Ribeiro and Little 1998: 184). Tribal populations are usually small and dispersed so they can seldom form effective voting blocs. Normal, state-sanctioned methods of political participation are blocked or so diluted that tribal peoples need to seek other means if they are to have any power at all.

The options for tribal political mobilization have been greatly increased by the recognition of indigenous rights by official global organizations and nongovernmental institutions. Although tribal peoples are not mentioned in the United Nations Universal Declaration of Human Rights, which focuses on individuals rather than groups, the UN continues to work on a Declaration on Indigenous Rights. A working draft, still in process, suggests that such rights should include freedom from genocide and dispossession, the right to maintain customs and culture, the right of self-governance, maintenance of traditional economic activities and land use, the protection of indigenous environments, and indigenous representation on governing bodies (Maybury-Lewis 1996: 640–641). Such formal rights are opposed by states that fear a relinquishment of control over their populations and territories.[4] However, the United Nations declaration of 1993 as the Year of Indigenous Peoples and 1995 to 2005 as the Decade of Indigenous Peoples has helped legitimize tribal resistance. In addition to the UN Working Group on Indigenous Populations, the Organization of American States has drafted a declaration on Indian issues, and both the World Bank and Inter-American Development Bank have established anthropological assessment divisions and guidelines for working with indigenous populations (Brysk 2000: 19).

A growing worldwide network of anthropologists has turned to advocacy to help indigenous peoples by providing funds, educating them in political matters and means of self-empowerment, intervening with governments, and lobbying official institutions. Systematic anthropological advocacy began at the 1971 Barbados Conference of anthropologists, who pledged to promote self-determination for tribal peoples and promised to involve themselves in politics to assist endangered cultures. This was reinforced by the establishment of a number of anthropological human rights organizations: Cultural Survival, based at Harvard; Survival International, which works out of London; the International Workshop for Indigenous Affairs in Copenhagen; and Germany's *Gesellschaft für Bedrohte Volker*. Indigenous peoples have formed their own local and regional organizations, such as COICA (*Coordinadora Indígena de la Cuenca Amazónica*), which represents Indians in nine Latin American countries. In addition, indigenous peoples often associate themselves with human rights organizations, such as Amnesty International, and with a host of feminist and environmental organizations.

Despite such resources, pressures on tribal peoples are intense, and success is by no means assured. A number of factors besides joining up with transnational advocacy organizations must come together for effective indigenous resistance and empowerment. Strong indigenous leaders must understand how the levers of power and influence work in their regions, their countries, and internationally. The media must be effectively employed to mobilize support among national voters and influential international leaders. Modern technology—especially the use of the Internet, e-mail, fax machines, and videos—can be used to solicit aid, inform distant groups, and coordinate efforts with others. Often favorable outcomes depend on judicial decisions; litigation is crucial to many efforts. All of this is costly, usually far more so than tribal groups can afford, which means that solicitation of funds, often internationally, is crucial.

MISKITO RESISTANCE IN NICARAGUA AND HONDURAS

The internationalization of tribal politics is seldom as manifest as among the Miskito Indians of Nicaragua. They have involved themselves with numerous international organizations, from the United Nations to the CIA to Cultural Survival, to establish and maintain their political rights.

The Atlantic Coast has been so isolated from the rest of the country that a large Creole population speaks English instead of Spanish. The Miskito themselves are more likely to be bilingual in their own language and English than Spanish, a reflection of British control until 1894 and U.S. influence since then. Moravian Protestantism, introduced in the 17th century, further distances the Miskito from the dominant Catholic mestizo culture of

Nicaragua. Throughout the long Somoza family dynasty, from 1937 to 1979, there was little attempt to integrate the Miskito, Sumu, and Rama Indians, who maintained a de facto autonomy, considering themselves part of the Anglo Zone of the Caribbean, rather than part of Hispanic Central America.

The Miskitos, a racial mixture of indigenous peoples and black runaway slaves, number about 150,000 in Nicaragua and 50,000 in Honduras. They have traditionally made their living by subsistence farming with some cash crops, hunting, fishing, and rubber tapping. More recently, they have worked as wage laborers for fruit and logging companies and have migrated, sending back remittances.

When the revolutionary Sandinistas came to power in 1979, the Miskito responded to the new government's goal of integrating the Atlantic coast into the broader state polity by forming MISURASATA, an organization that sought formal autonomy, including self-government. Though originally pro-revolution, the organization soon split three ways under three charismatic leaders, each supported by international allies. One faction, led by Hazel Law, sought accommodation with the Sandinistas, a goal that was supported by leftist internationalists, especially in Europe. With the outbreak of the U.S. proxy war against the Sandinistas, organized and funded by the CIA and originally led by former Somoza National Guardsmen who had escaped across the border into Honduras, Miskito leader Steadman Fagoth aligned his faction with the "Contras" against the Sandinistas. Brooklyn Rivera, who opposed both the Sandinistas and the participation in the war of former Somoza National Guard killers, took a much smaller group of Indians south into Costa Rica, where he ran low-level incursions across the border.

Miskitos in the Contra War

All factions in the war sought power and legitimacy through international alliances (Lewellen 1989). With the onset of the war between U.S.-backed Contras and the revolutionary state, Sandinista incursions into Miskito territory became increasingly aggressive, including the arrest of Indian leaders and the forced relocation of villages. In December 1983, as the war heated up, 3,000 Miskitos trekked north to Honduras. Ultimately, more than 40,000 became refugees outside of Nicaragua. KISAN, Brooklyn Rivera's group of intermittent fighters in Costa Rica, tried to distance itself from the blatantly CIA-run operations out of Honduras. With its more moderate approach, it sought and received international support from the Indian Law Resource Center, Cultural Survival, and the National Congress of

American Indians. Meanwhile MISURA, the 6,000 or so Honduran Miskito fighters, placed themselves under the direct control of the CIA.

The war, which was a full-scale test of President Reagan's doctrine of Low Intensity Conflict (LIC), avoided use of U.S. uniformed troops, although Honduras was virtually turned into a supply and training base for simultaneous support of efforts in El Salvador, Nicaragua, and Guatemala. LIC doctrine and practice included systematic destruction of the infrastructure, including CIA bombings and harbor minings, a massive national and international propaganda campaign, election fixing and other political manipulation, and massive economic destabilization. Despite the CIA funding, the Contras never in nine years of conflict fought a major battle, captured a town, or held any contested territory. They often had to be threatened with a cutoff of CIA aid before they would leave their Honduran camps, from which they ran death squad activities within Honduras. However, incursions into the rural areas of Nicaragua were sufficient to devastate the agricultural sector upon which the economy was largely dependent, as farmers were driven off their land and into fortified hilltop enclaves or city refugee camps. U.S. support was weakened by the Iran-Contra scandal, in which the Enterprise, a secret offshoot of the CIA, illegally sold missiles to Iran in order to continue financial support of the war when Congress had banned such aid.[5] Meanwhile, the Sandinistas were reappraising and moderating their approach to the Atlantic Coast indigenous population. Many Miskitos, increasingly convinced that victory was impossible, became disenchanted with their leadership.

Changing Strategies

In 1986, four years before the war officially came to an end with the electoral defeat of the Sandinistas, an agreement (opposed by the United States) for the autonomy of the Atlantic Coast was signed. This agreement was negotiated through the intervention of the president of Colombia and international nongovernmental organizations including Cultural Survival and the Unitarian Church. Representatives from Indian organizations in Ecuador, Peru, Colombia, Costa Rica, Canada, and the United States attended sessions during the negotiations. The Atlantic coast was divided into two autonomous, mostly ethnically distinct regions. Former President Jimmy Carter, acting as a freelance peacemaker, intervened to permit the Miskito organization YATAMA to participate in the 1990 elections in Nicaragua. In those elections, the Sandinistas were voted out, and the autonomous regions of the Atlantic Coast were represented by six out of sixty-four senators in the National Assembly. In 1991, with the help of the World Wildlife Fund and Cultural Survival, the east coast Indians formed Mikupia—"Miskito Heart"—to protect regional resources, and they negotiated the concession of the 3.2-million-acre Miskito Cays Protected Area.

With the help of international environmental organizations, Miskitos were able to block incursions by some foreign timber companies and to negotiate more amenable timber concessions with other companies. But it is a constant struggle to maintain control. They have gone to the Organization of American States to seek support in their conflicts with Korean and Spanish companies. Maintaining authority over their own "ethnodevelopment" is an ongoing and uphill battle. Meanwhile, increased political power has not been matched by social or economic betterment; unemployment is 70% in the Southern Autonomous Zone and 90% in the Northern zone, and life expectancy is even less than the fifty-six-year average for rural Nicaraguans as a whole.[6]

THE TRANSFORMATION OF COMMUNITY AND KINSHIP IN NEW GUINEA

Global incursions on tribal societies do not always result in a choice between cultural destruction or assimilation. If people are given the opportunity to adapt, an unpredictable synthesis of traditional and modern, of reciprocity and capitalism, may emerge. Even if the impact of capitalism is large and direct, it may be filtered through and transformed by preexisting social structures. This was the case among the isolated Faiwolmin people of the interior Fly River region of Papua New Guinea when a large multinational mining operation was established in the nearby mountains.

Until as late as the 1960s, the Faiwolmin were a remote backwater of Australian colonial rule. The people were mainly subsistence cultivators who organized around kinship and exchange. Because of the demands of taro cultivation on poor soil, cultivation tended to be highly mobile, and the population of the region was sparse. The organizing feature of exchange was kinship, with a classic pattern of reciprocity based on distance from the household: generalized reciprocity for the household core, balanced exchange at the tribal level, and negative reciprocity (based on bargaining) in the most distant areas of trade. Marriage was established, without ceremony, through the payment of brideprice.

Golgobip, the largest rural village in the area, was a two-day walk from the mine. When studied by Nicole Polier (2000), well after the completion of the Tabubil mine in 1988, Golgobip had established a curious blending of two socioeconomic structures. The mine employed 3,000 people at the peak of construction, but once in production relatively few workers were needed, since modern mining in frontier areas tends to be heavily capital-intensive, minimizing labor demands. Even though only a handful of Golgobip men actually worked the mine, social relations were more severely changed than through any other intervention, including by colonizing officials and a steady stream of Catholic and Protestant missionaries.

In Polier's analysis, the consequences of mine labor for social relations and exchange networks can be best understood in relation to four circuits. First was a circuit of commodity trade for the world market that resulted in the importation of extraction and transport machinery and the mine infrastructure. A second circuit was that of male-dominated labor power that was highly stratified along national, ethnic, racial, and regional lines, with the Faiwolmin at the bottom of a hierarchy that included North Americans and Australians at the top and Asians in middle positions. The third circuit was one of entrepreneurial activity, mainly by women, in the mine township; this included goods and services—imported foods and liquors, entertainment, banking, postal services, and travel. It was the fourth circuit that most directly affected the Faiwolmin by commodifying social relations and placing a money value on almost all exchanges.

Wage labor was inserted into a set of traditional values that were fundamentally communal and in many ways antithetical to capitalism, or at least to the individualist capitalism of the West. Since only a small group of men actually earned money in the mine while wives and families retained traditional households and kin networks, there was little pressure to radically change traditional values. The primary value was that of sharing and exchange. Although mine workers received extremely low pay, they were inundated with demands from unemployed relatives and friends to the extent that a common dream, seldom fulfilled, was to get a job much farther away from Golgobip where they could "live like a white man." This problem is extremely common whenever wage labor becomes available near a society that has previously remained largely outside the money economy. Traditionally, exchanges at all levels were treated not as objective and impersonal but as forming and maintaining social bonds. The solution for Golgobip mine workers was to squirrel away as much of the paltry wage as possible. Most deposited up to one-third in passbook savings accounts. Often these accounts were in informal credit associations of two or more workers, a strategy called "Sundaying" that provided smaller take-home pay but larger sums periodically, say for down-payment on a semipermanent corrugated-metal-roofed house (*haus kapa*), which could be used as a shop. The shop in turn could earn money for brideprice. In precolonial times, brideprice was paid in shell ropes, and these were still employed but only symbolically; now, brideprice had to be paid in money and purchased goods. The more that was given, the greater the prestige for both the husband and wife and their families.

The wage earner, who worked sixty-hour weeks, could hardly maintain a house and shop or carry on lengthy brideprice negotiations. Thus, a worker needed "managers." These were men who oversaw the assets and maintained the land. One worker had three managers in Golgobip: one handled brideprice savings and negotiations, one ran a small store from the worker's prefab house, and a third was established as "boss" over the gardens and maintained the worker's interest in social and cultural affairs in the village. There were six trade stores that sold processed foods and manufactured goods; while they provided a small income, their primary purpose was to "keep money out of circulation and in private control," that is, to hide money from friends and relatives. Even a *haus kapa* without shops required a full-time custodian who held the key, kept up repairs, and oversaw who would stay there. Thus the commodification of a small percentage of Golgobip's male labor had a ripple effect that ended up commodifying most other exchanges and monetizing the social and economic systems.

THE TRIBES THAT DID NOT DISAPPEAR

In the early 20th century, it was widely believed that "primitive" cultures would disappear. This belief stimulated a somewhat frantic descriptive anthropology, promoted by Franz Boas, dedicated to gathering as much information as possible on tribal cultures before they were erased from the face of the earth by the inexorable forces of modernization. This disappearing Indian theme, which has emerged in different versions around the world, formed the basis for various ideological trends in the United States as far back as the early 19th century; James Fenimore Cooper's *Last of the Mohicans*, published in 1826, and George Catlin's Indian paintings of the 1830s were representative of broad noble savage literary and artistic genres. However, at the beginning of the 21st century, tribal cultures, under whatever politically correct term is popular at the moment, are still with us and going strong. No longer primitive, many of these peoples are every bit as modern as the societies around them, but still have been able to maintain cultural, linguistic, and religious unity.

The processes of globalization both threaten tribal societies and provide the means of their survival. The spread of mining and lumbering into formerly tribal territory continues to physically menace once-isolated societies while cultures are enervated by the lure of cities, especially for young people, the necessity to seek employment outside the community, the influx of television and radio, and the ease of travel. However, as seen in the examples of the Kayapó and Miskito, it is more possible than ever to employ popular media and global institutions to stave off at least the more blatant threats, and the recognition of tribal rights as human rights has given these societies a moral and legal legitimization they never had before. More insidious forces are also at work to maintain tribal structures. While I have argued that the decline of the state is not a global process, the chaos in much of subsaharan Africa seems to be dissolving some always tenuously unified states back into their tribal components, though these are not the strong cultures of precolonial times but rather reconstituted warring factions. In any case, the global forces of localization are ensuring that the tribe will probably still be around at the turn of the next century.

Chapter 12

Peasants: Survivors in a Global World

The peasantry everywhere can be defined as a class of survivors. . . . The word survivor has two meanings. It denotes somebody who has survived an ordeal. And it also denotes a person who has continued to live when others disappeared or perished.

John Berger, *Pig Earth*[1]

The Lake Titicaca Basin is part of the *altiplano*, or high plain, that lies at an altitude of 12,500 feet between two high ranges in the central Andes and stretches from southern Peru deep into Bolivia. The area immediately around the 136-mile-long lake is one of the most densely populated peasant areas in Latin America, even though the climate and altitude only permit one harvest per year. The *altiplano* is mainly occupied by Aymara-speaking Indians; a much larger population of Quechua Indians starts at the north end of the lake and extends throughout Peru and into Ecuador. Historically, the Aymara were notoriously closed to outsiders. Because they had been able to maintain their household land rights when most of the rest of Peruvian Indians were enclosed within haciendas, they tended to be deeply suspicious of the dominant mestizos, who were perceived as an exploitative class. As a result, the Aymara were portrayed in travel literature and anthropological studies as dour and hostile. Through the 1950s, outsiders were not permitted to stay overnight in campesinos communities. As late as 1973, a cover article in *Science News* designated them—absurdly—the "meanest people in the world" (Trotter 1973: 76).[2]

It did not take long during my first trip to the region in 1976 to dispense with such stereotypes; the Aymara I met seemed to be just people, no better or worse than anybody else. However, the sense of an isolated peasantry mired in pre-Colombian tradition was pervasive. Another graduate student in anthropology at the University of Colorado, a Maryknoll missionary priest who was establishing an Aymara Institute in the village of Chucuito, had offered to finance my dissertation fieldwork there. A preliminary summer trip would permit me to observe the situation and get to know the missionaries who would be valuable contacts for entrance into the field. Traveling extensively throughout the region, I was able gain some feel for the area. Except for a scattering of corrugated tin roofs among the thatch, the image one received from driving the dirt roads and visiting homes was of a culture that had not changed much in hundreds of years. This impression was repeatedly confirmed by conversations with the missionaries, many of whom had lived in the *altiplano* for decades, and by the Aymara themselves, who portrayed their culture as conservative and traditional. I returned to Colorado to write up a research proposal that would employ systems theory to analyze why these people were so immune to the benefits of modernization.

On my return the following year, I had lived in the field with a peasant family for several months before I began to realize that something was drastically wrong with the scenario I had created for the Aymara based on previous anthropological studies, the anthropological theory of the day, and my own earlier visit. The conceptual vocabulary of peasant studies was composed of big and little traditions, folk-urban continuums, closed corporate communities, cargo systems, and images of limited good. I had deliberately set out to find a "traditional" community, since outside influences supposedly contaminated real culture. The community of Soqa should have been ideal; it was situated on an island in Lake Titicaca, connected to the shore by a 100–yard causeway that was under water most of the year. To get there from the nearest town and dirt road required an arduous fifteen-kilometer walk over a chain of rocky hills. Soqa was very seldom visited by mestizos and never by tourists or other gringos. There was no electricity or even a generator for a dozen miles in any direction. Given its isolation, "my" community should have been the very paragon of Aymara traditional culture.

Anomalies to this ideal image began to pop up rather quickly. For one thing, a defining trait of peasants was that they were supposed to transfer part of their surplus to the dominant culture, yet aside from the routine purchasing, fattening, and resale of cattle, no one seemed to be selling much of anything in markets; indeed, there did not seem to be any surplus. Nearly all the men and some of the women spoke Spanish, though most with a heavy

Aymara accent, and the two grade schools on the island, one public and one run by the Protestant Seventh Day Adventists, ensured that most of the next generation would be fluent in the second language. Two decades before, Soqa had restructured its political system away from the age-old Andean kin-and-religion-based *ayllu*; now it had a formal democratic government with a complex elected hierarchy of mayor, multiple sector leaders, education director, and liaisons with state functionaries. Although the large majority of people followed the ancient religion of *Pachamama* (Mother Earth), with an overlay of Catholicism, almost all major political positions were held by Adventists. Even those campesinos with little or no formal education were to some degree conversant about Peru and the larger world.

In order to understand the extent of nontraditional activities and the variation from area to area, I turned to the sociological technique of the questionnaire. Another anthropologist had made a formal survey in a nearby area fifteen years before, so for comparative purposes I incorporated his questions into my much longer questionnaire. After giving a preliminary version to a random sample of respondents to find out what questions were meeting resistance or were being misinterpreted, I hired and trained the leaders in three communities as interviewers; to motivate people to respond, the communities as a whole were paid on a per-respondent basis. It took more than six months to complete the sample of 353 households. I personally conducted selective follow-up interviews in the three communities to confirm the data and ask new questions.[3] Responses were transferred to code sheets, then analyzed using rudimentary statistics and a hand calculator. As the numbers began to take form, I was astonished at the degree to which my initial impressions were in error.[4]

The Aymara had undergone massive changes in just the previous twenty years. The major change was in money income. Two independent studies conducted in the area in the early 1960s found household income to be about US $37 per year. This did not mean, of course, that the people were "poor," only that subsistence agriculture was meeting their needs. A decade and a half later, the figure for Soqa, the most remote of the three communities I studied, was $633—fifteen times as much.[5] The causes of these changes were mainly population growth on a fixed agriculture base, already pushed to its limits, combined with the increasing division of land through inheritance and marriage. Subsistence agriculture, along with some fishing (the lake had been largely fished out to supply two German commercial processing factories), and raising chickens and guinea pigs could no longer sustain them. There were several options available for entering the money economy, such as increasing the number of cattle fattened on lake weed for resale and playing a brass instrument in fiesta dance bands. However, the only option that provided work for the large number of people being forced into the money economy was wage labor far away on the coast.

The idea of globalization was not even on the anthropological horizon at the time, but in retrospect, it is obvious that what was happening was that a formerly relatively closed system was opening to the world market, a market not only in labor and manufactured goods, but in ideas.

The increase in money came mostly from circular migration. The Peruvian government had hired Israeli advisors to help open the alluvial areas of the coastal desert to commercial farming, much of it in rice. While, in the past, very few campesinos traveled more than twenty miles from their communities in their entire lives, almost three-quarters of the men of Soqa now migrated twice every year to the coast, several hundred miles away, to work at planting and harvest in the rice fields of Camaná and Tambo; others were able to attain higher-pay construction jobs, requiring year-long contracts, in the larger cities. Although only about 60% of the money earned entered the community, the rest being spent at the place of work, there was an enormous increase in the number of manufactured household possessions such as tin roofs, metal beds, small kerosene stoves (previously cooking was done on dried cattle dung), treadle sewing machines, bicycles, and perhaps most important, battery radios. Bolivia had undergone a significant peasant revolution, and the rhetoric of political ideology sped across the lake on the air waves, along with regional and world news reports. Since the people had little concept of fiction, radio soap operas in Aymara were conceived as actually listening in on families with other ways of life. Because Peru had a strong import substitution program, and Peruvian-made goods were considered inferior, I was inundated with requests to bring back contraband Sony radios from my periodic trips to Bolivia.

The social and cultural effects on the home communities were sometimes conspicuous, sometimes subtle. The reason that the formerly ostracized and persecuted Adventists attained most elected positions in the new political hierarchy was that they had a two-generation head start on literacy and speaking fluency in Spanish; since the beginning of missionization in the early 20th century, converts were required to be able to read the Spanish Bible.[6] With the new openings toward the wider world, Protestants were well-positioned to lead the way as culture-brokers.

The three communities of my sample represented a wide range, from extremely conservative (a community that was still relatively self-sufficient) to progressive (Soqa). This was clearly reflected in responses to several attitudinal questions on the questionnaire. The Soqa sample was more "modern" in the sense that they felt greater control over their own fates, were more willing to expand women's roles, were less reliant on traditional ways of doing things, were less anxious about the world outside the *altiplano*, were more likely to borrow from the bank for investment, and tended to put a money value on time and labor not specifically devoted to household activities. Traditional associations had been severely weakened or had broken down altogether because so many men were away on the coast at crucial times; these included some semireligious fiesta dance groups and work groups for house building and community projects. However, new sodalities replaced them, such as school parent-teacher associations and soccer teams. In many ways, awareness of Peruvian soccer matches via conversations and the radio had more effect of giving the men a sense of belonging to the country of Peru than did politics or any recognition of a national culture.

Despite these changes, which even in the late 1970s had reached a level of stability in which every household had one foot in the countryside and another in the national economy, Aymara culture did not seem particularly threatened. Very few women worked outside their home communities; they maintained the land and households while the men were away and thus formed a base of stability. Kinship and *compadre* networks changed configuration, but were actually strengthened as they were extended to the coast and took on new functions as sources of information, protection, and jobs. While a considerable number of Indians, usually young men and some young women, migrated permanently to the cities of Ariquipa or Lima, their disappearance left the highland culture and society intact. The scarcity of land increased both its real and symbolic value, with the result that ties to land were maintained or amplified as a foundation of Aymara culture. There was no evidence that most Aymara were becoming, or had any desire to become, mestizos; in fact, there was a separate category for such people, *cholos*, who were virtually a separate class unto themselves. English terms like peasant, proletarianized peasant, semipeasant, and the like do not seem to really represent the simultaneous complexity of choices, networks, values, and cultural continuity that is compressed into the Spanish term *campesino*. The Aymara today live in multiple overlapping worlds—local, regional, national, global.

PEASANTS OR POST-PEASANTS?

The Titicaca Basin Aymara are somewhat atypical in their high-altitude adaptation, their remoteness, and their traditional hostility to outsiders, which protected them from the influences of modernity longer than peasants in most other areas. However, they do share with peasants throughout the world the increasingly diverse survival strategies that have led some scholars to question whether the term "peasant" is still meaningful.

A basic problem with the concept of peasant is that it never quite meant in reality what the dictionaries say it means, namely, someone who lives off the land by intensive agriculture (as opposed to horticulture) at a relatively low level of technological development (as opposed to modern farming). Although the term is comprehensive enough to include subsistence farmers, feudal serfs, sharecroppers, and agricultural laborers, it has been narrowed within anthropology to apply mainly to rural folk cultures that are separated by custom, history, and perhaps language from the dominant culture of the nation-state. Unlike tribal societies, which are relatively isolated and autonomous, peasants supposedly lived within a folk-urban continuum, transferring their surplus to the dominant class in exchange for whatever tidbits of modernity might be thrown their way (Redfield 1941; Greaves 1996: 915).

For Michael Kearney (1996: 5, 35), "the peasant is the most problematic social type within the social typology of anthropology." He argues that the anthropologized peasant was "invented" only after World War II with the emergence of the idea of development and within "the greater drama of containment of communism." Whereas the classic anthropological model set up a dualism of primitive versus civilized, the new bifurcation was between underdeveloped and developed, with primitive and peasant forming subcategories of underdeveloped (Figure 12.1). Thus, the peasant was defined in relation to development and situated within a whole set of dualisms, such as primitive/civilized, underdeveloped/developed, and traditional/modern. Within the social sciences, peasant theory was split between the "right wing romanticism" of peasants as fatalistic backward-looking victims of oppression and the "left wing romanticism" of dependency theory, which viewed peasants as a progressive and potentially revolutionary class.

It seems to me that this perspective simultaneously overcomplicates and oversimplifies peasants. Far from emerging after World War II, "peasant" is

Figure 12.1
Michael Kearney's Model of "Classical and Modern Anthropology"

Classical: PRIMITIVE .... CIVILIZED

Modern: TRADITIONAL
            UNDERDEVELOPED ....DEVELOPED

Primitive .... Peasant

Source: Kearney 1996: 36.

one of the oldest and most durable classifications in existence. Although field-workers compiled innumerable details about peasants, some of them unwisely generalized to the world peasant population, the anthropological view never really strayed far from the popular view: Peasants were traditional peoples who were rooted in the land. The concept of "primitive," a term now long out of fashion and justifiably so, is a much more complex category than peasant since it includes bands, tribes, and chiefdoms, hunter-gatherers, horticulturalists and pastoralists. While one must always admit to continuums, relatively speaking there is daylight between peasants and the tribal peoples discussed in the last chapter who are not involved in intensive agriculture and are more removed from direct structural integration into the nation-state. Historically, peasants have made up a fairly coherent category, relative to other anthropological classifications (race, tribe, nation, culture).

The Disappearing Peasant

This is less true today, however, when multiple and diverse strategies compete with agriculture. The continuum is not between peasant and primitive, but between peasant and modern. As the example of the Aymara shows, the contemporary peasant moves back and forth on a routine basis between a more or less traditional rurality and the modern world. To some extent, the peasant of the past was usually involved in self-sufficient subsistence agriculture, semifeudal hacienda-type labor, or sharecropping; these have disappeared in many places or are in the process of disappearing because of population increases that have overgrown subsistence resources, the growth of commercial agriculture, land reform, the increased need for money for the basics of survival, rising expectations, and pressures to grow for the market. The household itself may be quite fluid, with men and women, young and old moving in different directions at different times. It is now common to speak of landless peasants, worker-peasants, proletarian-peasants, or other hyphenated hybrids. In Mexico, many are involved in migration to the northern part of the country or across the border into California, while others have small businesses or work as taxi drivers or vendors in the urban informal economies.

So, should the category of peasant be abandoned altogether? The disappearance of the peasant was extensively debated in Mexico in the 1970s: the *proleterianistas* (or *descampesinistas*) held that the peasantry was inevitably being replaced, while the *campesinistas* argued the opposite. The belief in the disappearance of the peasant was closely related to Marx's evolutionary schema by which precapitalist modes of production must be subsumed by capitalism; the spread of capitalist agriculture would push peasants off their land, turning them into proletarians, or they would themselves become capitalists as they were forced to produce solely for the market. The argument on the other side was that peasants do not operate within the same rationalistic profitability system as capitalists, and thus they are not constrained by capitalist logic (Edelman 1999: 203).

Kearney argues that both are wrong; the "post-peasant" that has emerged does not fit either the peasant or proletarian category. He argues that we must first look at the "peasant essentialist" image that has been created and which is based on two criteria: first, that the peasant is defined in terms of subsistence rural production and an obsession with the land, and second, that he is subject to the dictates of a supraordinate state. It is clear that what we are calling peasants fit neither criterion. The post-peasant depends on numerous nonagricultural activities, which creates a multifaceted identity. There is little state control over these activities since some are transnational and others are in the informal economy, which is largely independent of state strictures. Such essentialisms emerge when complex people are forced into ambiguous categories (Kearney 1996: 59–69, 108–109).

The Surviving Peasant

And yet there is "an embarrassingly persistent failure of the peasantry to disappear" (Hewitt de Alcántara 1984: 185). For one thing, there is nothing new about the multiple survival strategies maintained by the contemporary peasant. As Peggy Barlett (1999: 1) observes: "Latin America's rural cultures have been formed in the crucible of past upheavals from forced labor, debt peonage, protracted civil war, and the ravages of disease. Is our sense of today's fluid lifeways built from an inattention to the fluidity of the past?" On the other hand, such fluidity, as measured by the amount of income from off-farm activities, can be exaggerated: In Africa, only 45% of income is generated away from home, in Asia 32%, and in Latin America 40% (FAO 2000). In other words, the land still provides most of the rural income. It seems to me that it is Kearney who is making the essentialist argument by so narrowly defining peasants that of course they do not exist.

But they do exist—at least in their own minds. In Latin America, the term *campesino* means more than just someone who works the land. It is true that it always implies having land or having a relation to land, and having some roots in a rural culture, but it by no means excludes the multiple activities that peasants normally require for survival. Among the Aymara, *campesino* is a term of self-identification that at once encompasses occupation, culture, ethnicity, and class (in more of a social than economic sense). In Peru, the term *Indio* is a derogatory ethnic slur; the Aymara would never apply it to themselves. They call themselves *campesinos*, which means that they see themselves as clearly set off from the other social groups or classes: *blancos* (supposedly more racially pure descendants of the European conquerors, but in truth a social category, not a race), mestizos, and *cholos*. The term *campesino*, then, designates a way of thinking, of differentiating oneself from other social categories, not just a relation to land or to the state. If a person becomes too modern or too assimilated into the dominant culture, if he changes his dress and speaks mainly Spanish, he becomes a *cholo*, and possibly his great-grandchildren will be mestizos. This is fairly universal in Latin America, whatever the terminology. In Costa Rica, as well as many other countries, rural organizations and resistance movements continue to include the word *Campesino* in their names (Edelman 1999: 190).

Kearney may be overgeneralizing from the Mexico situation, Mexico being one of a handful of NICs (Newly Industrializing Countries) in the Third World; it is modernizing much more rapidly and effectively than most. More traditional peasants are easily found in Ecuador, Bolivia, Guatemala, India, and many countries of Africa. In any case, as the Aymara data show, circular migration from a rural household is *not* a transitional form; it is an adaptive strategy that works over the long term. In countries where wage employment is seasonal, low paying, and uncertain, maintaining a base of land, no matter how small, provides a degree of economic, psychological, and cultural security not available by other means.

THE GLOBAL PEASANT

The role of peasants in the global economy is ambiguous and varies from region to region and country to country. On the producing end, most peasants are engaged to some extent in transnational agricultural markets, either as workers on large plantations or as small producers of export crops. On the receiving end, peasant production and employment are controlled by invisible market forces of supply and demand. The opening of markets to international trade may inundate a country with agricultural goods that undercut local producers; for example, under NAFTA, Mexico has become a prime target for the U.S. grain industry, which is capable of producing enormous surpluses at low cost. Associate producer contracts are common, having long replaced outright ownership of land by foreign companies; distant agroindustrial executives determine what is grown, where it is processed, and how it is transported, thus removing almost all aspects of control from the farmer.

Because a major stipulation of structural adjustments is that countries pay off their debts—that is, after all, the primary reason that the IMF lends money—governments are forced to encourage economic activities that will produce the most capital, which means, in the case of agriculture, policies stimulating the growth of large-scale, efficient farms devoted to export crops at the expense of subsistence farming or production of staples for local markets. No matter how desperate the need, in a supply-demand economy, poor people do not have sufficient money to create the demand that would override that of foreign purchasers. In El Salvador, for example, nearly all of the good land is devoted to products for export, mainly coffee but also sugarcane, oilseeds, cereals, vegetables, fruits, and beef. Despite the fertility of the land, much food must be imported at a cost that is prohibitive to the nearly half of the population that lives in poverty. An extensive and moderately successful land reform did not change this pattern; only 1% of the population still owns 40% of the arable land, and there are still 150,000 landless peasant families. The 25% of the rural poor who benefited from the land reform must grow for export in order to survive (Lewellen 1985a; López 1998).

Earlier predictions that peasants would form a labor force that could be transferred to industry for purposes of modernization, as was the case in many First World countries, turned out to be overly, if not blindly, optimistic. Industrial production has provided jobs for only a small fraction of the growing populations. To be sure, there has been a mass movement to cities, but this has not resulted in development, only in cities full of very poor people. In Latin America there are, for the first time in history, more impoverished people living in urban areas than in the countryside. However, because of population growth, in absolute numbers there are more rural poor than ever, and they tend to be the poorest of the poor (Loker 1999: 10). Peasants have been more marginalized by global processes than integrated into the global system, at least in the sense that if the majority of them simply disappeared off the face of the earth, the global system would be largely unaffected. The rural population is so much greater than what is needed for labor in an era of capital-intensive agriculture that the main effect of this reserve labor force is to keep agricultural wages at a bare subsistence or sub-subsistence level. Most jobs are seasonal, which is one reason why peasants put such a high value on having some land of their own, if only to grow subsistence crops to get them through to the next job.

Global trade has exacerbated a preexisting pattern of agricultural production that favors the large capital-intensive farm over the small-scale producer. It is true that certain labor-intensive crops, such as snow-peas or grapes, are actually more amenable to household production, but the larger producers still have either control of or more access to processing plants, transportation, loans, and markets. Efficiency in cropping is only one part of the whole process, and the small farmer is at a disadvantage in every other aspect. Government development programs usually privilege the urban sector, and what does filter out to the rural areas is largely, if not exclusively, concentrated in large-scale export farming. The dual impact of population growth and declining land for subsistence farming has forced many peasants to seek new lands through deforestation or to overintensify the use of fragile soils. Although "sustainability" has become the buzzword of agricultural development aid, in many ways the very structure of the global system is working against it.

Because most peasants labor in agriculture even when not working their own lands, they are at the mercy of global markets. In Guatemala, the Maya are involved in the market either through contract farming or field labor. In contract farming, small plots of land previously turned over to subsistence *milpa* production of corn, beans, and squash are used to produce broccoli or cauliflower for export. Whether working for oneself or for another, the process is risky. Crop failure due to weather can bring disaster, but so can exceptionally good weather, which can create a glut in the market and thus drop prices (Green 1998: 55). Export agriculture has always been subject to boom-and-bust cycles, but what might previously have been subject to supply and demand within a region or between two countries is now global in scale.

The global market and foreign agroindustrial control of commercial cropping has sped up two processes that have been going on for a long time: mechanization and rationalization. While some crops, such as coffee and cotton, remain labor-intensive, tractors, combines, and mechanical irrigation systems reduce the amount of labor required, so that it is impossible for agriculture to increase employment to the extent needed. In Latin America, the rationalization of agriculture, which involves the breaking of feudal bonds of mutual obligation between landowner and worker, has been going on since the collapse of the hacienda system, in some places starting early in the 19th century and in others, such as the Andean countries, as recently as a few decades ago. However, residual custom in many regions required some lingering reciprocal patron-client expectations, often formalized by vertical *compadrazgo* (fictive kin) relations between worker and landowner. Within such a local culture, the landowner might be expected to help out the worker or sharecropper with a loan, with legal help, or with days off for sickness in the family. Under fully capitalist agriculture, the only obligation of the land owner is to pay a wage and perhaps supply transportation (usually for a significant deduction from pay) to get to the fields. In most cases, shifting management, absentee ownership, primary obligations of the landowner to foreign agrobusiness, and migratory labor have broken down any lingering culture of reciprocity, leaving the peasant bereft of support outside his own family or community network.

In some cases, encouraged by governments, factories have come to the peasant. In Guatemala, numerous cement-block *maquilas*, mainly for apparel assembly, opened up along the Pan American Highway, in the heart of Maya country. In 1995, workers were hired for U.S. $4 a day, minus $.80 for transportation. Working conditions were harsh: poor ventilation, intense heat, routine verbal and physical harassment by supervisors, and rigid control of time. If the worker arrived late, half a days' pay was deducted; if one day was missed, two days' pay was deducted; and two missed days for any reason resulted in dismissal. Attempts to unionize were met with murder and disappearances. Although the construction of sweatshops within peasant regions permitted households to remain intact, the result was almost as disruptive as though the individual had migrated. Workers left at 4 A.M. to return at 9 P.M., with only Sundays off, leaving the individual with virtually no time to participate in household activities or community rituals. For most workers, a strategy emerged of taking six months off every year or two in order to recuperate and reconnect with family and community (Green 1998).

Globalization has increased possibilities for commercial cropping for some and entrepreneurial activities for others, but overall doors are closing faster than they are opening.

ADAPTATION, ORGANIZATION, RESISTANCE

Peasants are hardly passive victims of these processes; although often depicted as fatalistic and conservative, peasant survival has always depended on the ability to adapt and change when necessary. Resistance is never just reactive; the form that it takes will depend on numerous local, regional, state, and international variables, such as the legal ability to organize, the nature of political parties, local culture and leadership, and the political opportunities opened by changes in state policy. James Scott's *Weapons of the Weak* (1985) documents the myriad ways the peasants in Malaysia resisted the adverse effects of the Green Revolution through such tools as slander, arson, pilfering, petty sabotage, and foot-dragging. Outright peasant revolution (though often not peasant-led) is as common as always, although modern media and communications can sometimes stave off all-out war, as is the case with the Zapatistas in Mexico, who became masters at manipulating public opinion through press conferences, dramatic marches and rallies, and use of the Internet to propagate their views.

They were so successful, at least in public relations, that there emerged a craze for Zapatista dolls, pens, T-shirts, and other souvenirs. The signature Zapatista black mask, reminiscent of those worn by professional wrestlers, became a partly serious, partly comic symbol of protest throughout Mexico (Long 2000: 194).

In *Peasants Against Globalization*, Marc Edelman (1999) describes the multiple techniques employed by modern, highly sophisticated peasants when Costa Rica's "rush to free-market policies caused a crisis of legiti-macy for the state and left opponents of adjustments gasping for coherent political and economic alternatives" (91). Alliances between large and small producers emerged and disappeared, organizations with long acro-nyms were formed to confront particular situations and then dissolved, pressure groups were formed and political parties conscripted to the cause, riots and strikes were quickly and efficiently organized using computers and the media.

The complexity of the adjustments, adaptations, accommodations, and resistances that the peasant faces in the global arena is revealed in Michael Kearney's (1996: 174–185) study of the Mixtec of San Jerónimo, Mexico. He shows the process by which bounded communities become transna-tional, revealing the intricate interrelationship of labor, migration, identity, associations, and political strategy.

THE MIXTEC OF OAXACALIFORNIA

The community of San Jerónimo has, for centuries, been merely one among hundreds of similar traditional Mixtec towns and villages in the state of Oaxaca, Mexico. Each of these "closed corporate communities" (Wolf 1996) of mainly subsistence peasants was, to a great extent, a bounded so-cial universe in itself, with its own social structure and religious hierarchy. Increasingly, throughout the 20th century, peasants were forced by popula-tion growth, ecological deterioration, and the expansion of large-scale agri-culture to migrate for seasonal jobs to Northern Mexico and California. Mixtec identity became quite diverse, as many settled either permanently or temporarily in big-city shantytowns, took jobs in the informal economy as street vendors or part-time construction workers, became small-time mer-chants, entered the professions, or took jobs as civil servants.

Each of these transformations was accompanied by corresponding trans-formations in patterns of organization. Traditionally, political organizing was restricted largely to situational community petitions to government agencies, usually to settle disputes over land. Such restricted activity rein-forced the peasant identity, which, both internally and externally, was viewed as an asymmetrical power relationship based on peasantry as a class, the broad bottom of the pyramid perceived by Marxist anthropologists as peasant, proletariat, and bourgeoisie. Such identity, with all its implications of asymmetrical power, was accepted as normal by both peasants and nonpeasants. However, as Mixtec began to leave their homes in search of work, new associations became necessary. Women in cities formed street vendor associations for self-help, to prevent police intimidation, and to press for rights. Urban squatter associations established and organized shantytowns and pressed local governments for water, sewage, electricity, and roads.

Limited transnational Mixtec organizations emerged in the orchards and vegetable fields of California, where Mexican self-help associations already had a long history. These groups, which were quite parochial despite their cross-border credentials, were established by members of particular towns to raise money for community projects back home. In the 1970s, such associations became increasingly regional and political, embracing more than one ethnic group and pressing for land reform. One such group, the *Frente Oaxaqueña Binancional*, covered the entire state of Oaxaca and included not only Mixtec, but also Zapotec, Trique, Mixe, and Chinantec. While peasant identity—with its implications of bounded community and subsistence agriculture—had been under siege for some time, the panethnic, multijobbed identity implied by such organizations helped deal a final blow. The transnational space within which they moved became popularly known as *Oaxacalifornia*.

One major transformation was the shift from peasant self-identity to ethnic self-identity. This was inevitable given the increased internal differentiation and the more complex and fluid social organization brought about by the dissolution of bounded communities, by increasing transnationalization, and by greater and more direct subjection to global processes. Unlike the category of peasant, ethnicity is not defined by a particular form of production and thus is open to a wide variety of occupations, income levels, and interests. Ethnicity is also independent of space; it is tied to no particular community and can exist through a multitude of fields. No longer caught within the political classification of necessary subordination to the modern city and nation-state, the ethnic is freed to press for increasing regional autonomy and empowerment.

Two forces continue to push the Mixtec toward even more complex and encompassing organizations: first, common experiences in shantytowns and migrant agriculture that reach well beyond Oaxaca, and, second, the racism of mestizos, Anglos, and Chicanos on both sides of the border. One response is involvement in broad human rights and environmental movements, such as Amnesty International, Americas Watch, Greenpeace, and the Sierra Club. Unlike labor unions or peasant organizations, these truly global organizations bring together a wide variety of diverse people. They also bring a new perspective that universalizes local conditions. The murder, disappearance, torture, and intimidation of Mixtecs in Oaxaca, once viewed as individual crimes, are now seen as human rights issues, demanding world concern and world pressure on the government to do something. Pesticide pollution and deterioration of soil is no longer merely a family problem, but is a part of a much larger environmental picture. Such fusion between individual issues and global goals are made possible by the despatialization of organization, which is accomplished as electronic space takes over from local space, and the World Wide Web and e-mail make possible ongoing relationships and dialogues with people hundreds and thousands of miles away.

As we have seen in Chapter 5, from a theoretical point of view, the concept of ethnicity is highly problematic, since it cross-cuts widely different classes and occupations, indiscriminately drawing diverse agriculturalists, wage earners, and entrepreneurs into ostensibly unified groups. It is thus difficult to see that Kearney has accomplished much by reclassifying the Mixtec from peasant to ethnicity. Also, Kearney's generalization of this specifically Mexican research to suggest that peasants everywhere are disappearing as a useful type is not convincing. However, the processes revealed in this study of the Mixtec certainly suggest some widespread, if not universal, challenges and changes that peasants face in a globalized world.

Chapter 13

Afterthoughts, by Way of Conclusions

McWorld is the problem, not the solution.

Benjamin R. Barber[1]

Any conclusions to a book on globalization cannot help but convey an artificial sense of finality and closure. Thus, I hope the reader will settle not for any grand summation, but for a few personal impressions.

IS THERE A METANARRATIVE OF GLOBALIZATION?

After finishing the rough draft of this book, I reread an article from *Current Anthropology* titled "Ethnography and the Meta-Narratives of Modernity" by Harri Englund and James Leach (2000). A "metanarrative" is defined as "a set of organizing assumptions of which only some may be enunciated in a given anthropological narrative" (226). Because "the history of anthropology can be seen as a progression through a series of meta-narratives" (227), it would seem that the term, as employed in the article, is very close to some definitions of paradigm. In any case, the basic argument is that anthropological analyses employing the concept of modernity are replete with presuppositions that are never fully explored because they are never consciously articulated. Because modernization overlaps to a great degree with globalization, it was inevitable that I find some of these assumptions quite applicable to the present work. For instance, the idea that "modernity, full-fledged and recognizable, is everywhere" certainly has its correlative in globalization studies. The modernist assumptions that identities are fractured and decentered and that commodification erodes people's humanity would also be applicable to globalization research.

This led me to ask the question: Has a metanarrative of globalization emerged within anthropology that funnels research and analysis in particular directions? In other words, has anthropology already established the broad outlines of a model of globalization? The answer would clearly seem to be Yes! However, there is little about the model that is not contested.

The metanarrative of globalization would go something like this: *Globalization is impacting people everywhere by erasing local boundaries and transforming identities. Restrictive categories like tribal, peasant, community, local, and even culture are giving way to terms that emphasize blending, plasticity, and ongoing identity-construction: ethnic, hybrid, creole, national, and transnational. Fluidity and fragmentation rather than homogenization are the result of globalization, as people constantly move across former boundaries, erasing the distinctions between traditional and modern, urban and rural, developed and underdeveloped. Development itself is exposed as a hegemonic Western discourse that is on its way out. In this amorphous and deterritorialized world, people increasingly seek identities in the imagined communities of nationalism and ethnicity. Meanwhile the nation-state is weakening and possibly already moribund under the multiple external onslaughts of IMF-imposed structural adjustment policies, loss of control of the economy to transnational markets, subordination to global institutions such as the UN and WTO, and the loss of control of ideology to communications media that cross national borders at the speed of light. Internally, the nation-state is challenged by the rise of ethnicities, nationalisms, and multiple grassroots organizations that have taken over state functions. Emigration and immigration, often resulting in the formation of transnational diaspora communities, also erode state loyalties. Multiple modernities arise to challenge Western scientific and technologic modernity. The impact of global neoliberal capitalism is virtually always negative—as women are disempowered while being forced to add wage labor to household and subsistence work, communities are disrupted by circular or permanent migration, agriculture is concentrated in fewer and fewer large farms capable of efficiently exploiting available technology and distribution networks, and the displaced are funneled into sweatshops or the informal economy. However, capitalism does not impose itself in any pure way upon traditional or socialist economies, but is absorbed and transformed.*

How much of this is actually true? I have already criticized some of these assumptions as overstated or erroneous: Peasant and tribe remain useful categories, at least to the millions of people who describe themselves that way; the nation-state is not going to disappear in the foreseeable future; while valuable in focusing attention on local discourses, the polemical antidevelopment approach has not been particularly useful in its premise of a unitary development discourse that is about to disappear; transnationalism is an alternative to assimilation, but will not replace it. What about the rest of the model? The idea that seems to me to have the greatest impact is the emphasis on the *fluidity* of just about everything, from definitions to movements of people to identities. Looking back over these pages, I see that, unintentionally, *fluid* and its synonyms are probably the most used words in this book. If globalization is doing nothing else, it is dissolving boundaries. This, too, however, can be overdone: Some people—a lot of them actually—do stay home in relatively stable communities.

Most elements of the model will be true in some places, not true in others. For example, when IMF structural adjustments force a corrupt and inefficient government, that never did anything for its people anyway, to shape up a bit, the results can be more positive than negative. Many women have been empowered, not disempowered by globalization, as the availability of factory-labor jobs have provided options previously unavailable. It would be nice if word processors came equipped with a single key that spewed out the sentence, in italics: *"Some do; some don't!"* The fact is that the impact of globalization is highly variable, ranging from negligible to the extremely powerful, from negative to positive, from shallow to profound. Perhaps the greatest contribution of postmodernism lies in its admonition to be very careful about imposing generalizations on specific settings, at least before those settings are investigated in their own right. Which brings us to our next subject. . . .

BEWARE OF POSTMODERN ESSENTIALISMS

Way up there near the top of the list of characteristics that define postmodernism is an adamant opposition to "essentialism." This is "a belief in the real, true essence of things, the invariable and fixed properties which define the 'whatness' of a given entity" (Fuss 1989: xi–xii). The term is useful to feminists in the deconstruction of stereotyped concepts of women and womanhood. Postcolonial scholars have found it applicable to the often unconscious Western projections of commonality to invented groups such as Arab, African, and Indian. In anthropology, the charge of essentialism has been legitimately applied to tribe and peasant (categories that I have argued are still useful once we expose the underlying assumptions). Essentialism is a term that is sometimes thrown around with too much abandon, as an easy rebuke that requires no further explanation, but when employed judiciously, it can be of considerable value.

The problem is that postmodernism is replete with essentialisms. This derives partially, I think, from its freedom from making objective statements that are subject to empirical verification or that are constrained by hard data. In many postmodern writings, generalization follows upon generalization, sometimes with no referent to anything in the real world.[2] Standards and conventions tend to be those of English literary studies or culture studies, rather than those of the social sciences (which is only logical, since science, social or otherwise, may be rejected).

A sort of straw-man essentialism is evident in what postmodernists oppose—which is quite a bit. As I noted in Chapter 2, the routine dismissal of the anthropology of the past as imbued with Enlightenment values and as dominated by positivism reveals either (a) a misunderstanding of what these terms mean and the range of interpretations of their meanings or (b) an overly interpretive approach to the history of anthropological theory. Positivism, as the application of hard science methods and the search for scientific laws, exists in cultural anthropology but is the exception, not the rule. It is difficult to find much real positivism—unless that term is defined so broadly as to be virtually meaningless—in Boasian historical particularism, neoevolutionism, diffusionism, cultural and personality studies, structural-functionalism, the Manchester School, process theory, or symbolic anthropology. Marvin Harris's brand of cultural materialism *is* positivist (as he acknowledges), and some cultural ecology approaches might fit, but not much else. A basic assumption of the Enlightenment was social, moral, and scientific *progress*. There might have been a few anthropologists who briefly bought into that in the heyday of modernization theory in the 1960s, but they quickly outgrew it. By and large, anthropology has tended, if anything, to romanticize traditional cultures and defend them in their struggles *against* progress.

As discussed in Chapter 4, the assumption that development is or has been a unitary discourse is essentialism on a rather large scale. In many writings, modernization theory is essentialized as the easily refutable unilineal stage approach of W. W. Rostow; it was, and is, far more complex than that. Dependency "theory" is often rejected out of hand as an anachronism, with little regard for the fact that it was really a paradigm within which multiple and conflicting theories existed. The idea that the nation-state is on its last legs seems based on some essentialist notion of a rigid, intractable political structure that is incapable of adapting to the challenges of globalization.

It is not only rejected concepts that are essentialized. The term "hegemony" is tossed off with such casualness that one might think it needs no evidence or justification. American hegemony this, Western hegemony that. For Antonio Gramsci, hegemony was a fairly complex theory of the establishment of dominance by consent, but it is often employed to refer to military, cultural, financial, or ideological dominance, or simply an undefined and amorphous subjection. The term—an excellent one if its intricacies are recognized—should only be used if the writer is willing to define what aspect she is referring to, supply the evidence that such dominance exists, and specify how it is attained and maintained. Its casual use suggests that hegemony is simply a given, an attribute of the population under study, like the fact that they speak a certain language or have a predominance of type-A blood. The same might be said of Foucault's knowledge/power, an insightful concept that should never be used casually, without specification of how the nexus works in particular cases.

Among the valuable insights of postmodernism is the recognition of the way that apparently simple terms and ideas assume complex unconscious meanings that need to be consciously sorted out. Another is that generalizations must be treated with suspicion.

Doctor heal thyself.

ANTHROPOLOGY NEEDS TO GET ITS NERVE BACK

In their introduction to *African Political Systems* (1940), generally considered the foundation work in political anthropology, Meyer Fortes and E.E. Evans-Pritchard stated flatly, "We have not found that the theories of political philosophers have helped us to understand the societies we have studied and we consider them of little scientific value" (p. i). This sentiment might well have been the slogan of political anthropology in its developmental period. Until the mid-1960s, the theoretical framework of political anthropology, its methodology, its vocabulary, and its focus of interest owed little to political science, political sociology, or political psychology. . . . By and large . . . their point of view was resolutely anthropological.

Lewellen 1992: 3

This passage, from my *Political Anthropology: An Introduction*, by no means describes an ideal situation, but it does suggest a certain gutsiness. By deliberately cutting themselves off from outside political theories, these pioneers were forced to develop their theories inductively, from the ground up, as it were, based on their fieldwork. They did not really do that, of course, because they did not enter the field as theoretical vacuums but as professionals educated in the British Anthropology of the time, which was heavily influenced by Emil Durkheim by way of A. R. Radcliffe-Brown. Still, looking back to Boas, Mead, Kroeber, Malinowski, Gluckman, and Turner, one gets a sense of the priority of the concrete, the adventure of the real, the excitement of finding the meaningful in the day-to-day activities of people going about living their lives.

Critical anthropology wanted no part of such fieldwork romanticism. Fortes and Evans-Pritchard were revealed as lackeys of colonialism, and it turned out that Malinowski was writing literature, not social science. And, of course, the functionalisms of the time—structural and psychobiological—have not fared very well. But has contemporary anthropology really fared any better?

In many ways, anthropology's long period of critical self-appraisal has been more destructive than constructive. Fieldwork seems to have lost the authority it once had, and as a result, anthropologists have lost their theoretical nerve. In the past, theory was almost invariably closely tied to ethnography; today almost all of the basic ideas of postmodernism come originally from French philosophy. The present atmosphere is one of transnational and interdisciplinary borrowing. This is perhaps especially true in the anthropology of globalization, a subject area that overlaps with similar interests in political science, sociology, philosophy, and economics. Theoretical positions are staked out in highly abstract tomes, which are then applied downward to fieldwork, which assumes the job of fitting real people into the proper theoretical niches.

This is not always the case. Though quite rightly utilizing appropriate postmodern concepts, transnationalization studies and the reevaluation of peasantries derive their theoretical substance from the field. Such research and analyses demonstrate that anthropology really can establish its own viewpoint and become a leader, rather than a follower, in the study of globalization.

RECLAIMING ANTHROPOLOGY'S SOCIAL SCIENCE CREDENTIALS

The reevaluation of anthropology that has taken place over the last decades, and is perhaps best represented by the edited volume *Writing Culture: The Poetics and Politics of Ethnography* (Clifford and Marcus 1986), might have gone in any of several different directions. For example, the "crisis of representation" might have inspired that crucial question, *What are the criteria by which we can make judgments about the relative truth and falsity of anthropological claims?* This is a scientific question, a question of hard practicality, not a call to epistemological speculation or philosophical intuition. Anthropology would have been forced to confront the realism of its textbook methodologies and to develop methodologies that are practicable. If ethnographers are to continue to make cognitive claims about the way people think—a far more formidable goal than is often accounted—what methodologies would make such claims more plausible? A primary task would be to differentiate social science from the natural sciences. Against the cultural materialists, social science would have to abandon the search for laws, perhaps even abandon such prime metanarratives as the Marxist priority of infrastructure. It might have been recognized that there are simply too many variables in all human behavior to be reduced to universal laws. It might have been understood that a defining quality of the natural sciences is paradigm convergence, the agreement on the basics, within and among all disciplines, and that this will never be a part of social science. The questions of the situatedness and assumptions of the observer would have been of central importance, as would anthropological classification. Ideologies disattached from the collection and analysis of empirical data would have been looked at with skepticism. It might have been acknowledged that social science is fundamentally empirical and practical and that its facts and conclusions will always be more tentative than those of the natural sciences.

Such a direction would have made for a lively, factional, and often vehement dialogue, but it would have ended with anthropology more firmly anchored in the social sciences.

That was not the direction that was taken. For many reasons, not least that postmodernism was the dominant philosophy of the 1970s and a new generation brought up on Foucault and Baudrillard was entering graduate school, the anthropological crisis of identity took a different turn. The two sides were so far apart that there was often less dialogue than diatribe. Earlier, Clifford Geertz (1973) had rejected anthropology's social science pretensions, declaring it a branch of literary studies (which, if taken seriously, would have put anthropology at a severe disadvantage, since very few of us want to be judged on the quality of our writing styles). Basic to the postmodern argument was that either anthropology was not a science, social or otherwise, or all science was just another negotiated metanarrative, though an exceptionally powerful and hegemonic one. In any case, the argument about the nature of social science never really got joined.

If studies in the anthropology of globalization are exemplary of what is happening throughout the discipline, then the results of this clash of viewpoints is evolving in a direction unanticipated by either side, toward a sort of empirical postmodern social-science. Few of the writers in the field seem well-versed in, or even very interested in, the intricate complexities of postmodern philosophy, but many postmodern concepts have been adopted because they fit the more fluid (there's that word again) realities of globalization.

Abstract philosophy and epistemology seem merely effete and irrelevant in a Calcutta slum or among impoverished subsistence farmers in the Andes. Poverty and desperation are not amenable to vast epistemological generalizations or vague abstractions. Empiricism is the language of real people, and anthropology is—or should be—about real people.

THE FUTURE OF THE ANTHROPOLOGY OF GLOBALIZATION

The Skeptical Inquirer magazine regularly gathers the predictions of all the major U.S. media psychics to see how they fare over time. If we are to believe their predictions, in the 1990s: Singer Wynonna Judd quit country music to become a woman wrestler; the first successful human brain transplant was performed; marijuana replaced petroleum as the nation's chief source of energy; the Statue of Liberty lost both arms in a terrorist blast; and Soviet cosmonauts were shocked to discover an abandoned alien space station with the bodies of several extraterrestrials aboard (CSICOP 1999).

The moral in regard to predicting the future is: Don't!

I have no idea what the anthropology of globalization will look like in ten years. The subject is still in its youth, but, judging from the sheer number of articles and books already published, it is growing rapidly. However, it is not presently clear if there really is, or will be, an anthropology of globalization, in the sense of a subdiscipline to be taught as a college course, to have its own organization within the American Anthropological Association, and to have its own journals. The alternative is that globalization will be considered as context or as a theoretical perspective within existing subdisciplines such as peasant studies, economic anthropology, and political anthropology. This would be unfortunate. Globalization-as-context is useful and often necessary, but the multitude of studies discussed in these pages suggest the value of bringing globalization out of the chorus and onto center stage. While theoretical or paradigmatic unity may be neither possible nor desirable, there is already something of a unity of perspective, a positioning at that point of juncture between global and local. The anthropological niche is there; all we have to do is claim it.

Notes

CHAPTER 1. WHO IS ALMA?

1. Iglesias Prieto 1997: 99.

2. *Maquiladora*, or *maquila*, is from the Spanish word *maquilar*, which historically referred to the milling of wheat into flour. Today the term denotes a labor-intensive Mexican manufacturing plant operating under special customs laws that permit the duty-free import of machinery, equipment, parts, and components. The first *maquilas* were established in 1966 along the U.S. border. Since then they have spread throughout Mexico and much of Latin America.

3. I am aware that the term *Third World* is controversial. I devote an entire chapter in *Dependency and Development* (Lewellen 1995: Chapter 1) to justifying its use. It should be noted that the term *Second World*, which was supposed to have become anachronistic with the fall of the Soviet Union, is coming back into favor as it is realized that Russia and the countries of Eastern Europe, even sans communism, share characteristics that unite them while differentiating them from First or Third Worlds.

CHAPTER 2. SLOUCHING TOWARD GLOBALIZATION

1. Wilk 2000. This is a small sampling of made-up words satirizing the globalization fad. According to Wilk's introduction to this Web site: "In this globalized, global age, when everything has globated to the point where it is completely globulous, we obviously need some new vocabulary to describe the globish trends that are englobing us all."

2. A search of the Barnes and Noble on-line bookstore on June 1, 2001, brought up 776 titles listed under the keyword *globalization*. One hundred

twenty-four of them had been published within the first six months of 2001. The FirstSearch database WorldCat brought up 4,340 globalization sources, and the Google Internet search engine claimed 693,000 hits.

3. For example: "The expansion of the capitalist world market into areas previously closed to it . . . is accompanied by the decline of the nation-state and its power to regulate and control the flow of goods, people, information, and varied culture forms" (Cvetkovich and Kellner 1997: 3).

4. This division is based on Jameson 1998 and Held, et al. 1999: 10. Each has a good bibliography of the different positions.

5. See, for example, the special issue of *National Geographic* for August 1999. Global cultural homogenization is the theme of the entire issue.

6. A number of authors contributed to this section. In addition to those cited in the text, Beaud 1983, Stavrianos 1981, and Fieldhouse 1981 should be mentioned. A more extensive, continent-by-continent historical overview of the creation of the Third World can be found in Lewellen 1995, Chapter 2.

7. Because of this, and because of the sheer volume of globalization literature, I have made some attempt to focus on studies done after 1990, although many of the ethnographic examples of global processes come from the 1980s or earlier.

8. Loker 1999: 38.

9. My thanks to my economist colleague Jonathan Wight, who in several conversations has elaborated the often-forgotten moral dimension of Smith's theories. He has written a fascinating novel in which Smith, reincarnated in contemporary times, protests the distorted uses of his ideas (Wight 2002).

10. For example see Edelman 1999 and the numerous field studies in Loker, ed. 1999; Phillips, ed. 1998; and Haugerud et al., eds. 2000.

11. Giddens 1990: Chapter 1 and pages 149 to 150 also notes this tendency to confuse the condition itself with poststructuralist theory. Giddens rejects the idea of "post-modernity," preferring "radicalized-modernity." Table 2 on page 150 compares the two points of view.

12. A late version of this can be found in Francis Fukyama's (1989) celebration of the triumph of liberal democracy and world capitalism, appropriately and significantly titled "The End of History."

CHAPTER 3. THE ANTHROPOLOGY OF GLOBALIZATION

1. Stone et al. 2000.

2. Appadurai 1996: 27.

3. In Chapter 4, I will argue that the world system theory should be conceived as a subset of dependency theory.

4. Barrett 1999: 259.

5. See Shea 1998, Durham 1998, and Gibbs 1998.

6. The following material is based on multiple sources, including Graham, Doherty, and Malek 1992; Jameson 1988, 1990; Lemert 1997; Lennihan 1996; Lyotard 1984; Nugent 1996; Rorty 1994; Rosenau 1992; and Seidman 1994.

7. Respectively, Anthony Wallace and Eric Wolf, quoted by Cerroni-Long 1999: 9.

8. For those not up on the controversy, Alan Sokal (1996) wrote a nonsensical parody of postmodernism that was published, after peer review, as a serious article in the journal *Social Text*. He is also, with Jean Bricmont (1998), author of a book that parodies the postmodernist critique of science simply by citing long passages—some absolutely hilarious—by the postmodernists themselves.

9. Bourdieu is often claimed and cited by postmodernism, but he repudiates it, emphasizing the importance of scientific methodology.

10. This is similar to the criteria of frontier theoretical physics, where theories necessarily reach beyond what can be tested by means available today. It should be noted, however, that no theory in the natural sciences is accepted until it is empirically verified.

11. Laura Nader's preface and introduction to her edited volume *Naked Science: Anthropological Inquiry into Boundaries, Power, and Knowledge* (1996) provide a good overview of the postmodern approach. For the response from the scientific side, see Sokal and Bricmont 1998; Kuzner 1997; Gross and Levitt 1994; Gross, Levitt, and Lewis, eds. 1996; and Murphy and Margolis, eds. 1995.

12. Two of the most crucial differences are: (1) All physical sciences are ultimately based on a relatively small group of commonly accepted physical laws, which may change or be applicable at different scales (e.g., Newtonian vs. Einsteinian gravity), while no such laws exist in the social sciences. (2) Paradigm convergence—while each discipline such as chemistry or physics has its own set of paradigms, ultimately all physical sciences must agree with each other. There is no paradigm convergence among the social sciences; in fact, all radically disagree with each other.

13. This does not mean, as radical positivism would have it, that music, literature, art, philosophy, and religion do not have truths to express. The truths of a later Rembrandt self-portrait or Beethoven's Ninth Symphony are more subjectively powerful than anything science has to offer, but they are also incommensurable with anything science has to offer.

14. Examples include Basch, Schiller, and Szanton Blanc (1994) and Ferguson (1994). I also would include several of the ethnographic examples used throughout this book.

15. Thomas 1999: 263.

16. Barrett 1999: 267.

17. Friedman 1994: 74.

18. "Congo" is used here as a combinative term that the author of this study employs for two countries: the former Belgian Congo and the former French colony.

19. Song from ECD album *Big Youth*, lyrics by Egaitsu Hiroshi. Quoted in Condry 1999: 1.

20. Bhaskaran 1998: 106.

21. Barlett 1999: 8.

22. Hannerz 1998: 251.

23. This study is more fully described in Chapter 8.

24. In graduate school, I perused Boas's five-foot shelf of books on the Kwakiutl for a paper on the potlatch, but found the information so indiscriminate, untheorized, and random as to be only marginally useful.

25. Gupta and Ferguson's edited volume *Anthropological Locations* (1997) seems specifically devoted to deromanticizing and dethroning partici-pant-observation, although there are few concrete or elaborated suggestions for alternatives and almost no specific examples of other means of researching. Oddly, considering the date of publication and the interests of the editors, global-ization research is discussed only briefly and in passing in a couple of the essays.

CHAPTER 4. DEVELOPMENT, DEVOLUTION, AND DISCOURSE

1. Apter 1987: 7.

2. For example, Sachs 1992: 2; Esteva 1992: 6; Escobar 1995: 4. For the op-posed view, that development has had a much longer history, see Edelman 1999: 11 and Black 1999: 23.

3. Held, et al., 1999, Chapter 1.

4. For example, see Bodley, ed. 1988; Bodley 1990; Dentan, et al. 1997; Norberg-Hodge 1991.

5. Quoted in Dentan, et al. 1997: 103.

6. Some of the works on development to employ poststructuralist arguments, in various degrees, include Manzo 1991; Parajuli 1991; Escobar 1984–85, 1991, 1995, 1997; Hobart, ed. 1993; Ferguson 1994, 1997a; Gardner and Lewis 1996; Grillo and Stirrat, eds. 1997.

7. Ferguson's book has not gone without criticism. Objecting to the postulated dichotomy between developers and developed, Crewe and Harrison (1998: 176) argue that "the claim that development discourses and practices are entirely con-trolled by developers, predominantly from Europe and America, is becoming in-creasingly tenuous in the face of globalized information systems." Edelman (1999:8) objects to Ferguson's claim that the state and its dominant institutions are strengthened by the development process; the whole point of neoliberalism is to reduce the power of the state and the public sector.

8. Black 1999: 147.

9. Quoted in Unnithan and Srivastava 1997: 169.

CHAPTER 5. CONSTRUCTING IDENTITY

1. Fanton 1986: 109.

2. Quoted in Hale 1997: 571–572. The poster was on Hale's wall when Hale was writing his article.

3. Hall 1990: 309.

4. There are also a number of organizations that employ the more politically correct form: the Native American Rights Fund and the Native American Fine Arts Society, for example.

5. In this book, I employ both "Indian" and "Native American"—the latter when there might be a possibility that the reader would interpret the term *Indian* to refer to people from India.

6. Banks (1996: 186–187) provides a chart of a similar division in relationship to "ethnicity."

7. This is from a chart on a large map supplement in *National Geographic* (Swerdlow 1999). It is interesting to note that the long cover article that accompanies this map takes a strongly homogenizing view of "Global Culture," portraying indigenous cultures as threatened or "vanishing."

8. The term *premodern* is avoided, since it suggests modernity as an evolutionary end point, thus assuming that all must become modern in some globalized Western sense.

9. I include Xiaoping Li, although, as far as I know, her work has not been published. I have made extensive use of her insightful doctoral dissertation, "Transient Identities: Globalization and Contemporary Chinese Culture" (1996).

10. Information on the remarkable indigenous Nigerian video network comes from my colleague, Joe Obi, who spent a sabbatical studying this phenomenon.

11. Quoted in Rouse 1991: 8.

12. Friedman also includes *postmodernism* in his analytical framework. The argument is based on a Lévi-Straussian culture/nature dichotomy that I find rather confusing.

13. Tambiah 1996: 13.

14. In Lewellen (1995: 19), I make the argument that *Third World* is best defined as a relationship with the First World. This is somewhat incongruous (though not really contradictory), since the first chapter of the same book is devoted to defining the Third World as a demarcated group of nation-states.

15. Banks (1996: 182) observes that "whether ethnicity 'really' exists out there in the world or not, it has had a rather substantial and chimerical life within academic discourse in its own right." He suggests that the word is worth keeping as long as we recognize that it is a heuristic concept almost impossible to define.

16. Some might claim, however, that WASPs—white Anglo-Saxon Protestants—as well as "Anglos" and "Honkies" are indeed ethnic groups from the points of view of subordinated ethnicities.

17. See Wilmsen 1996: 2; Alonso 1994: 382–405; Appadurai 1996: 139–144; and Banks 1996: 11–48.

18. Pieterse (1996: 26–27) gives a somewhat different list of dynamics underlying ethnic politics today, putting more emphasis on the "retreat of the state" and
a general crisis of development.

19. This was something not sufficiently emphasized in Max Weber's classic
The Protestant Ethic and the Spirit of Capitalism (1993 [1905]). I tested the relationship between Protestantism, capitalism, and literacy among the Aymara Indians in the Peruvian altiplano, and my findings supported Benedict's
interpretation. A small minority of Protestants had emerged as a political elite in
many Aymara communities, which were mostly Catholic mixed with a
pre-Colombian religion. Only Protestants were required by their religion to be literate in Spanish; for Catholics, the priest is the mediator with God while for Protestants the Bible is the link. Although originally ostracized, as Aymara culture
increasingly opened to the wider mestizo world, Protestants—who could fluently
speak, read, and write Spanish—became the natural and obvious culture brokers
for bringing the Aymara into the modern world (Lewellen 1978, 1979).

20. Mountcastle 1997: 331.

CHAPTER 6. MIGRATION: PEOPLE ON THE MOVE

1. Mittelman 2000: 58.

2. Rouse 1991.

3. Altman (2001: 18) cites figures from *New Internationalist* (Sept. 1998:
16–17) of 100 million international migrants plus 20 million refugees in any
given year; among these, more than 35 million people work in foreign countries
and 10 million have been displaced by environmental degradation. These are
crude estimates, at best, as are all estimates of transnational migrations. Statistics
are unreliable even for First World countries (Castles 2000: 45).

4. Stone et al. (2000: 2) give 14% of the U.S. population as born abroad in
1900 and 8% today. Such percentages are based on census figures and therefore
do not include illegals. It has been estimated that there are as many as 5 million
undocumented immigrants and visa overstayers in the United States, a figure that
some consider exaggerated (Staring 2000: 205).

5. For example, Mangin 1970; Safa 1974; Du Toit and Safa 1975.

6. Camera and Kemper, eds. 1979; Cornelius 1978; Rosenthal-Urey 1982;
Mines and Massey 1985; Reichert 1981.

7. Bjerén 1997: 245.

8. Applied anthropology, as represented in the journal *Human Organization*,
has assimilated some of the postmodern vocabulary, but maintained a practical,
materialist, and developmental emphasis.

9. Specific pages from which this information is taken are Altman 2001: 11,
13–14, 101–102, 108–115.

CHAPTER 7. TRANSNATIONALISM: LIVING ACROSS BORDERS

1. Basch, Glick Schiller and Szanton Blanc 1994: 170.

2. Quoted in Richman 1992: 195; author's translation.

3. In the early 1970s, I worked as an advertising copywriter for elementary and high school textbooks for Holt, Rinehart, and Winston and American Book Companies. Immigrants were fashionable in social studies texts, with a strong emphasis on the idea that the United States was built on the assimilation of foreigners. At the same time, a budding multiculturalism was just becoming faddish, but only in the sense that ghetto subcultures were being recognized. An elementary school civics text targeted specifically at New York Black and Hispanic urban ghettos was so popular that I was given the assignment of advertising it for adoption in California schools. To my surprise, the campaign was successful. The acknowledgment of subcultures, but not of economic classes, was considered the cutting edge of liberal thinking in education at the time.

4. These researchers worked jointly and apparently equally on perhaps a score or more of articles, books, and edited volumes, which were authored under all possible sequences of their names: Basch, Glick Schiller and Szanton Blanc (1994); Glick Schiller, Basch, Blanc-Szanton (1992, 1995); Szanton Blanc, Basch, Glick Schiller (1995).

5. Quoted in Ong 1992: 136.

CHAPTER 8. DIASPORA: YEARNING FOR HOME

1. Gilroy 1994: 293.

2. Quoted in Fuglerud 1999: 68.

3. In lieu of common cultural identity, Van Hear (1998: 6) includes cultural, social, political, and/or economic exchange between spatially separated populations. Van Hear seems to conceive of transnationalism as an implicit aspect of diaspora. I question this. Many diasporas do not seem to be transnational; until recent openings to travel, Miami Cubans formed relatively enclosed enclaves, with virtually no possibility of contact with friends or relatives in Cuba and little need for contacts elsewhere. In the 1980s, Nicaraguan and Salvadoran exiles were seldom admitted legally to the United States, so they had to take advantage of a sort of "underground railroad" run mainly through churches and local human rights groups; thus they were dispersed as individuals, families, or small groups with little or no contact with each other and none with family and friends in the home country.

4. Several of the questions asked in this section are from Safran (1991: 95–96) and Shuval (2000: 43), although the development of these ideas does not follow theirs.

CHAPTER 9. REFUGEES: THE ANTHROPOLOGY OF FORCED MIGRATION

1. Malkki 1995: 503.
2. Sommers 1993: 16.
3. Harrell-Bond and Vourtira 1996: 1076–1077; Malkki 1995.
4. See chart Lewellen 1995: 186.
5. CORI has published, at this writing, seven collections of ethnographies on refugees and immigrants. Those consulted for this book are DeVoe, ed. 1992; Van Arsdale, ed. 1993; Mortland, ed. 1998; and Donnelly and Hopkins, eds. 1993.
6. These authors give two approaches, *maintenance* and *repair*, which roughly correspond to my *analytic* and *organizational*. The third approach seems different enough to me to deserve a separate classification.
7. In 1985, the United States was involved in wars in Afghanistan, Ethiopia, Angola, Nicaragua, Vietnam, Cambodia, El Salvador, Guatemala, Chad, Libya, and Zaire. At the same time, the Soviets were involved in Afghanistan, Ethiopia, Angola, and Nicaragua. Among the dictatorships that the United States supported during the Cold War (many of which it helped put into power) were Iran under the Shah, Guatemala, Haiti, Laos, Zaire, the Dominican Republic, Ecuador, Brazil, Indonesia, the Philippines, Uruguay, Argentina, and Chile. Among Third World dictatorships supported by the Soviets during the same period were Cuba, Albania, North Korea, Vietnam, Afghanistan, and Angola.

CHAPTER 10. GLOBALIZATION FROM THE GROUND UP

1. Friedman 1994: 232n.
2. Quoted in Kalb 2000: 12.
3. Clifford Geertz 1998, quoted in Kalb 2000: 12.
4. Dirlik, who elaborates these ideas in a slightly different manner, employs the phrases "critical localism" and "localism as ideological articulation of capitalism in its present phase."
5. It must be noted that neither study carries the analysis down to the local level; we never really see the effects of these behemoth aid projects on individuals or communities.
6. Appadurai 1996: 158.
7. Hannerz 1996: 81.
8. See the discussion of strong and weak states in Lewellen 1995: 125–153, especially the diagrams on page 136.

CHAPTER 11. TRIBAL CULTURES: NO LONGER VICTIMS

1. Brysk 2000: 245.
2. Quoted in Kolata 1987.

3. This section interweaves material from Turner 1995 and 2001; Brysk 2000: 218–220; and Kolata 1987.

4. For documents on this subject and the ongoing UN debate, go to the search page http://www.un.org/search/index.html and insert "indigenous rights."

5. I traveled and interviewed extensively throughout Nicaragua in 1980 and 1989 and viewed the physical destruction and social disruption wrought by both the revolution against Somoza and the Contra invasion. Sources on the Contra war abound. Sklair (1988) provides a detailed overview. The abridged edition of the U.S. Congressional Report on the Iran Contra Affair was published by the New York Times (1988). Sam Dillon's *Commandos* is a detailed study of the Contras, including their death squad activity in Honduras. My article "The Lie File" (Lewellen 1984) documents the U.S. propaganda campaign that was a crucial part of LIC doctrine toward Central America, and Lewellen 1989 analyzes U.S. manipulation of religion.

6. Sources for this section: Bourgois 1982; Hale 1992; Brysk 2000: 80–81, 112–116, 262–263.

CHAPTER 12. PEASANTS: SURVIVORS IN A GLOBAL WORLD

1. Berger 1992; quoted in Edelman 1999: 210.

2. The controversy over Aymara personality was fought out in the pages of *Current Anthropology*, with many experts joining in on both sides with extended comments. See Lewellen 1981, 1984, and Bolton 1984.

3. People were threatened by questions about how much money was earned outside the community, perhaps because of an egalitarian ethic and a fear that they might be taxed. Thus, the questionnaire merely asked where they worked and for how long. In the follow-up interview, conducted months later, people were not in the least bit hesitant in telling me what the wage rate was. By putting these two bits of information together, it was easy to determine how much money was earned.

4. Among the questions being researched was why a Protestant political elite had emerged not only in Soqa but throughout the region. Toward this goal, the questionnaire, along with many interviews, was designed to test a number of specific hypotheses based on what I believed to be true from book research. All of these hypotheses were refuted. This experience would become the basis for my later distrust of postmodernist and interpretive approaches that are not based on the systematic collection of information. Without the quantitative data, I would have interpreted quite differently, and quite erroneously.

5. Exchange rates against the dollar over time were taken into account.

6. Catholics need not be literate because the priest is the mediator between man and God; in Protestantism, the Bible is the only mediator. The Aymara data led me to rethink Max Weber's thesis of the relation between religion and European capitalism. Perhaps the key variable lay not in any "spirit of Protestantism" but in

the Protestant requirement for education. Benedict Anderson (1983) would seem to concur with his emphasis on the importance of "print capitalism."

CHAPTER 13. AFTERTHOUGHTS, BY WAY OF CONCLUSIONS

1. Barber 1995: 267.

2. The most extreme example of this that I have encountered is Roger Bartra's surrealistic *The Imaginary Networks of Political Power* (1992).

Bibliography

Alonso, Ana María. 1994. "The Politics of Space, Time, and Substance: State Formation, Nationalism, and Ethnicity." *Annual Review of Anthropology* 23: 397–405.

Altman, Dennis. 2001. *Global Sex.* Chicago: University of Chicago Press.

Alvares, Claude. 1996. "Science." *In* W. Sachs, ed., *The Development Dictionary: A Guide to Knowledge as Power.* London: Zed.

Anderson, Benedict. 1983. *Imagined Communities: Reflections on the Origin and Spread of Nationalism,* Revised Edition. London: Verso.

Appadurai, Arjun. 1991. "Global Ethnoscapes: Notes and Queries for a Transnational Anthropology." *In* R. Fox, ed., *Recapturing Anthropology.* Santa Fe, New Mexico: School of American Research.

———. 1996. *Modernity at Large: Cultural Dimensions of Globalization.* Minneapolis: University of Minnesota Press.

———. 2000. "Grassroots Globalization and the Research Imagination." *Public Culture* 12 (1): 12–19.

Apter, David E. 1987. *Rethinking Development: Modernization, Dependency, and Postmodern Politics.* Newberry Park, California: Sage.

Arce, Alberto, and Norman Long, eds. 2000. *Anthropology, Development, and Modernities: Exploring Discourses, Counter-Tendencies and Violence.* London: Routledge.

Banks, Marcus. 1996. *Ethnicity: Ethnological Constructions.* New York: Routledge.

Barber, Benjamin. 1995. *Jihad vs. McWorld: How Globalism and Tribalism Are Reshaping the World.* New York: Ballantine.

Barlett, Peggy F. 1999. "Introduction." *In* W.M. Loker, ed., *Globalization and the Rural Poor in Latin America.* Boulder, Colorado: Lynne Rienner.

Barrett, Stanley R. 1999. "Forecasting Theory: Problems and Exemplars in the Twenty-First Century." *In* E.L. Cerroni-Long, ed., *Anthropological Theory in North America*. Westport, Connecticut: Bergin and Garvey.

Bartra, Roger. 1992. *The Imaginary Networks of Political Power*. New Brunswick, New Jersey: Rutgers University Press.

Basch, Linda, Nina Glick Schiller, and Cristina Szanton Blanc. 1994. *Nations Unbound: Transnational Projects, Postcolonial Predicaments, and Deterritorialized Nation-States*. Langhorne, Pennsylvania: Gordon and Breach.

Beckham, Michael. 1987. *The Kayapó: Out of the Forest. Disappearing World Series* [videorecording]. Chicago: Films, Inc.

Benedict, Ruth. 1989 [1934]. *Patterns of Culture*. New York: Houghton-Mifflin.

Bennet, John W. 1990. "Anthropology and Development: The Ambiguous Engagement." *In* H.M. Mathur, ed., *The Human Dimension of Development: Perspectives from Anthropology*. New Delhi: Concept Publishing Company.

Berger, John. 1992 [1979]. *Pig Earth*. New York: Vintage.

Beaud, Michel. 1983. *History of Capitalism, 1500–1980*. Trans. T. Dickman and A. Lefebvre. New York: Monthly Review Press.

Bhagwati, Jagdish. 1966. *The Economics of Underdeveloped Countries*. New York: McGraw-Hill.

Bhaskaran, Dimple Suparna. 1998. *Made in India? Nationalized Genders and Colonized Sexualities*. PhD dissertation (Anthropology), University of Michigan.

Bjerén, Gunilla. 1997. "Gender and Reproduction." *In* T. Hammer, G. Brochmann, K. Tamas, and T. Faist, eds., *International Migration, Immobility and Development: Multidisciplinary Perspectives*. Oxford: Berg.

Black, Jan Knippers. 1999. *Development in Theory and Practice: Paradigms and Paradoxes*, Second Edition. Boulder, Colorado: Westview.

Blick, Jeffrey. 1988. "Genocidal Warfare in Tribal Societies as a Result of European-Induced Culture Conflict." *Man* 23 (Dec.): 654–670.

Bodley, John H. 1990. *Victims of Progress,* Second Edition. Mountain View, California: Mayfield.

Bodley, John H., ed. 1988. *Tribal Peoples and Development Issues: A Global Overview*. Mountain View, California: Mayfield.

Bohannan, Paul, Marie Womack, and Karen Saenz. 1999. "Paradigms Refound: The Structure of Anthropological Revolutions." *In* E.L. Cerroni-Long, ed., *Anthropological Theory in North America*. Westport, Connecticut: Bergin and Garvey.

Bolton, Ralph. 1984. "The Hypoglycemia-Aggression Hypothesis: Debate Versus Research." *Current Anthropology* 25 (1): 1–53.

Booth, David. 1993. "Development Research: From Impasse to a New Agenda." *In* F. Schuurman, ed., *Beyond the Impasse: New Directions in Development Theory*. London: Zed.

Bordewich, M. Fergus. 1996. *Killing the White Man's Indian: Reinventing Native Americans at the End of the Twentieth Century*. New York: Doubleday.

Bornschier, Volker, Christopher Chase-Dunn, and Richard Rubinson. 1978. "Cross-National Evidence on the Effects of Foreign Investment and Aid on Economic Growth and Inequality: A Survey of Findings and Analysis." *American Journal of Sociology* 84 (3): 694–699.

Bourdieu, Pierre. 1997. *Outline of a Theory of Practice*. Cambridge: Cambridge University Press.

———. 1980. *Distinctions: The Cultural Construction of Taste*. Cambridge, Massachusetts: Harvard University Press.

Bourdieu, Pierre, and Loïc J.D. Wacquant. 1992. *An Invitation to Reflexive Sociology*. Chicago: University of Chicago Press.

Bourgois, Philippe. 1982. "The Problematic of Nicaragua's Indigenous Minorities." *In* T.W. Walker, ed., *Nicaragua in Revolution*. New York: Praeger.

Boyer, Pascal. 1999. "Human Cognition and Cultural Evolution." *In* Henrietta L. Moore, ed., *Anthropological Theory Today*. Cambridge: Polity Press.

Breckon, Lydia. 1998. "To Rebuild Our Cambodia: An Examination of Khmer Americans' Sojourns in Cambodia." *In* C.A. Mortland, ed., *Diasporic Identity: Selected Papers on Refugees and Immigrants*, Vol. VI. Washington, D.C.: American Anthropological Association.

Breger, Rosemary, and Rosanna Hill. 1998. "Introducing Mixed Marriages." *In* R. Breger and R. Hill, eds., *Cross-Cultural Marriage: Identity and Choice*. Oxford: Berg.

Brettell, Caroline B. 2000. "Theorizing Migration in Anthropology: The Social Construction of Networks, Identities, Communities, and Globalscapes." *In* C.B. Brettell and J.F. Hollifield, eds., *Migration Theory: Talking Across Disciplines*. New York: Routledge.

Brohman, John. 1996. *Popular Development: Rethinking the Theory and Practice of Development*. Oxford: Blackwell.

Brumann, Cristoph. 1998. "The Anthropological Study of Globalization: Towards an Agenda for the Second Phase." *Anthropos* 93: 495–506.

Brysk, Alison. 2000. *From Tribal Village to Global Village: Indian Rights and International Relations in Latin America*. Stanford, California: Stanford University Press.

Buijs, Gina, ed. 1993. *Migrant Women: Crossing Boundaries and Changing Identities*. Oxford: Berg.

Burawoy, Michael. 2000a. "Grounding Globalization." *In* M. Burawoy, et al., *Global Ethnography: Forces, Connections, and Imaginations in a Postmodern World*. Berkeley: University of California Press.

———. 2000b. "Introduction." *In* M. Burawoy, et al., *Global Ethnography: Forces, Connections, and Imaginations in a Postmodern World.* Berkeley: University of California Press.

Burawoy, Michael, Joseph A. Blum, Sheba George, Zsuzsa Gille, Teresa Gowan, Lynne Haney, Maren Klawiter, Steven H. Lopez, Seán Ó Riain, and Millie Thayer. 2000. *Global Ethnography: Forces, Connections, and Imaginations in a Postmodern World.* Berkeley: University of California Press.

Calandra, Thom, and Phillip Matier. 1989. "A New Money Elite." *San Francisco Examiner,* Aug. 20: A1, A12–A14.

Camera, F., and Kemper, R.V., eds. 1979. *Migration Across Frontiers: Mexico and the United States.* Albany: SUNY Institute of Mesoamerican Studies.

Campbell, Patricia J., Debra Kreisberg-Voss, and Joy Sobrepeña. 1993. "The UNHCR and the International Refugee Protection System: Resources and Responses." *In* P. Van Arsdale, ed., *Refugee Empowerment and Organizational Change: A Systems Perspective.* Washington, D.C.: American Anthropological Association.

Carrier, James G., and Daniel Miller. 1999. "From Private Virtue to Public Vice." *In* H.L. Moore, ed., *Anthropological Theory Today.* Cambridge: Polity Press.

Castles, Stephen. 1998. "Globalization and Migration: Some Pressing Contradictions." *International Social Science Journal* 50 (2): 179–186.

———. 2000. "The Impacts of Emigration on Countries of Origin." *In* S. Yusuf, W. Wu, and S. Everett, eds., *Local Dynamics in an Era of Globalization.* Oxford: World Bank/Oxford University Press.

Cerroni-Long, E.L., 1999. "Anthropology at Century's End." *In* E.L. Cerroni-Long, ed., *Anthropological Theory in North America.* Westport, Connecticut: Bergin and Garvey.

Chaliand, Gérard, and Jean Pierre Rageau. 1995. *The Penguin Atlas of Diasporas.* New York: Penguin.

Clifford, James. 1994. "Diasporas." *Cultural Anthropology* 9 (3): 302–338.

Clifford, James, and George E. Marcus, eds. 1986. *Writing Culture: The Poetics and Politics of Ethnography.* Berkeley: University of California Press.

Cohen, Abner. 1969. *Custom and Politics in Urban Africa: A Study of Hausa Migrants in a Yoruba Town.* Berkeley: University of California Press.

Cohen, Robin. 1997. *Global Diasporas: An Introduction.* London: UCL Press.

Cohen, Ronald. 1970. "The Political System." *In* R. Naroll and R. Cohen, eds., *Handbook of Method in Cultural Anthropology.* Garden City, New York: Natural History Press.

———. 1978. "Ethnicity: Problem and Focus in Anthropology." *Annual Review of Anthropology,* Vol. 7.

Collins, Jane L. 2000. "Tracing Social Relations in Commodity Chains: The Case of Grapes in Brazil." *In* A. Haugerud, M.P. Stone, and P.D. Little, eds.,

Commodities and Globalization: Anthropological Perspectives. Oxford: Rowman & Littlefield.

Colson, Elizabeth. 1999. "Gendering Those Uprooted by 'Development.'" *In* D. Indra, ed., *Engendering Forced Migration.* New York: Berghahn.

Comaroff, John L. 1996. "Ethnicity, Nationalism, and the Politics of Difference in an Age of Revolution." *In* E.N. Wilmsen and P. McAllister, eds., *The Politics of Difference: Ethnic Premises in a World of Power.* Chicago: University of Chicago Press.

Condry, Ian. 1999. *Japanese Rap Music: An Ethnography of Globalization and Popular Culture.* Ph.D. dissertation (Anthropology), Yale University.

Cooper, Frederick, and Randall Packard. 1997. "Introduction." *In* F. Cooper and R. Packard, eds., *International Development and the Social Sciences.* Berkeley: University of California Press.

Cornelius, W. A. 1978. *Mexican Migration to the United States: Causes, Consequences and U.S. Response.* Boston: Center for International Studies, Massachusetts Institute of Technology.

Costa, Alberto C.G., Conrad P. Kottak, and Rosane M. Prado. 1997. "The Sociopolitical Context of Participatory Development in Northeastern Brazil." *Human Organization* 56 (2): 138–146.

Crewe, Emma, and Elizabeth Harrison. 1998. *Whose Development? An Ethnography of Aid.* London: Zed.

Crush, Jonathan, and David McDonald. 2000. "Transnationalism, African Immigration, and New Migrant Spaces in South Africa." *Canadian Journal of African Studies* 34 (1): 1–19.

CSICOP. 1999. "Skeptical Inquirer Magazine Releases: Failed Psychic Predictions 1999." Retrieved June 25, 2001, from the World Wide Web: http://www.csicop.org/articles/psychic-predictions/1999.html.

Cvetkovich, Ann, and Douglas Kellner. 1997. "Introduction: Thinking Global and Local." *In* A. Cvetkovich and D. Kellner, eds., *Articulating the Global and the Local: Globalization and Cultural Studies.* Boulder, Colorado: Westview.

CWIS. 2001. "Background on the Term 'Fourth World'." Retrieved May 10, 2001, from the World Wide Web: http://www.cwis.org/fourthw.html.

D'Andrade, Roy. 1999. "Culture Is Not Everything." *In* E.L. Cerroni-Long, ed., *Anthropological Theory in North America.* Westport, Connecticut: Bergin and Garvey.

Daramola, Olusegun A., and Timothy U. Mozia. 1993. "Toward Understanding the Refugee Dilemma: Migration Theory and the Principles of Empowerment." *In* P. Van Arsdale, ed., *Refugee Empowerment and Organizational Change: A Systems Perspective.* Washington, D.C.: American Anthropological Association.

Davis, Shelton H. 1990. *Victims of the Miracle.* Cambridge, England: Cambridge University Press.

Dentan, Robert Knox, Kirk Endicott, Alberto Gomes, and M. B. Hooker. 1997. *Malaysia and the "Original People": A Case Study of the Impact of Development on Indigenous Peoples*. Boston: Allyn and Bacon.

DeVoe, Pamela A., ed. 1992. *Selected Papers on Refugee Issues*. Washington, D.C.: American Anthropological Association.

Dillon, Sam. 1991. *Commandos: The CIA and Nicaragua's Contra Rebels*. New York: Henry Holt.

Dirlik, Arif. 1992. "The Global in the Local." *In* R. Wilson and W. Dissanayake, eds., *Global/Local: Cultural Production and the Transnational Imaginary*. Durham, North Carolina: Duke University Press.

Doherty, Joe, Elspeth Graham, and Mo Malek, eds. 1992. *Postmodernism and the Social Sciences*. New York: St. Martin's Press.

Donnelly, Nancy D., and Mary Carol Hopkins. 1993. "Introduction." *In* M.C. Hopkins and N.D. Donnelly, eds., *Selected Papers on Refugee Issues II*. Washington, D.C.: American Anthropological Association.

Durham, William H. 1998. "Department of Anthropological Sciences–Vision Statement." *Anthropology Newsletter*, October: 21–22.

Du Toit, Brian, and Helen I. Safa. 1975. *Migration and Urbanization: Models and Adaptive Strategies*. The Hague: Mouton.

Edelman, Marc. 1999. *Peasants Against Globalization: Rural Social Movements in Costa Rica*. Stanford, California: Stanford University Press.

Edgerton, Robert B. 1999. "Maladaptation: A Challenge to Relativism." *In* E.L. Cerroni-Long, ed., *Anthropological Theory in North America*. Westport, Connecticut: Bergin and Garvey.

Edwards, Michael. 1989. "The Irrelevance of Development Studies." *Third World Quarterly* 11 (1): 116–136.

———. 1993. "How Relevant Is Development Studies?" *In* F. Schuurman, ed., *Beyond the Impasse: New Directions in Development Theory*. London: Zed.

Englund, Harri, and James Leach. 2000. "Ethnography and the Meta-Narratives of Modernity." *Current Anthropology* 41:225–248.

Epstein, Thomas Hylland. 1978. *Ethnos and Identity: Three Studies in Ethnicity*. London: Tavistock.

Erikson, Thomas Hyland. 1993. *Ethnicity and Nationalism: Anthropological Perspectives*. London: Pluto Press.

Escobar, Arturo. 1984–1985. "Discourse and Power in Development: Michel Foucault and the Relevance of His Work to the Third World." *Alternatives* 10: 377–400.

———. 1991. "Anthropology and the Development Encounter: The Making and Marketing of Development Anthropology." *American Ethnologist* 18 (4): 658–682.

———. 1995. *Encountering Development: The Making and Unmaking of the Third World*. Princeton, New Jersey: Princeton University Press.

————. 1997. "Anthropology and Development." *International Social Science Journal* 49 (4): 497–515.

————. 1998. Personal Correspondence, October14, 1998.

Esteva, Gustavo. 1992. "Development." *In* W. Sachs, ed., *The Development Dictionary: A Guide to Knowledge as Power.* London: Zed.

Fanton, Frantz. 1986. *Black Skin, White Masks.* London: Pluto Press.

FAO (Food and Agriculture Organization of the United Nations). 2000. "Contemporary Thinking on Land Reform." Retrieved May 26, 2001, from the World Wide Web: http://www.fao.org/WAICENT/FAOINFO/SUSTDEV/LTdirect/LTan0037.htm.

Featherstone, Mike. 1992. "Localism, Globalism, and Cultural Identity." *In* R. Wilson and W. Dissanayake, eds., *Global/Local: Cultural Production and the Transnational Imaginary.* Durham, North Carolina: Duke University Press.

Ferguson, James. 1994. *The Anti-Politics Machine: "Development," Depoliticization and Bureaucratic Power in Lesotho.* Cambridge: Cambridge University Press.

————. 1997a. "Anthropology and Its Evil Twin: 'Development' in the Constitution of a Discipline." *In* F. Cooper and R. Packard, eds., *International Development and the Social Sciences.* Berkeley: University of California Press.

————. 1997b. "Development and Bureaucratic Power in Lesotho." *In* M. Rahnema, ed., *The Post-Development Reader.* London: Zed.

Fieldhouse, David K. 1981. *Colonialism, 1870–1945: An Introduction.* New York: St. Martin's Press.

Fortes, Meyer, and E. E. Evans-Pritchard, eds. 1940. *African Political Systems.* Oxford: Oxford University Press.

Foucault, Michel. 1972 [Orig. 1969]. *The Archeology of Knowledge and the Discourse on Language.* Translated by A.M. Sheridan Smith. New York: Pantheon.

————. 1973 [1963]. *The Birth of the Clinic: An Archeology of Medical Perception.* Translated by A.M. Sheridan Smith. New York: Pantheon.

————. 1988 [1961]. *Madness and Civilization.* Translated by Richard Howard. New York: Vintage.

————. 1995 [1975]. *Discipline and Punish: The Birth of the Prison.* Translated by A. M. Sheridan Smith. New York: Pantheon.

Frank, Andre Gunder. 1967. *Capitalism and Underdevelopment in Latin America.* New York: Monthly Review Press.

————. 1969. *Latin America: Underdevelopment or Revolution.* New York: Monthly Review Press.

Fried, Morton. 1967. *The Evolution of Political Society.* New York: Random House.

Friedman, Jonathan. 1994. *Cultural Identity and Global Processes.* London: Sage.

Fuglerud, Øivind. 1999. *Life on the Outside: The Tamil Diaspora and Long Distance Nationalism*. London: Pluto Press.

Fukuyama, Francis. 1989. "The End of History." *The National Interest* 16 (Summer): 3–18.

Fuller, Buckminster. 1969. *Operating Manual for Spaceship Earth*. Carbondale: Southern Illinois University Press.

Fuss, Diana. 1989. *Essentially Speaking: Feminism, Nature and Difference*. London: Routledge.

Galtung, Johan. 1971. "A Structural Theory of Imperialism." *Journal of Peace Research* 2: 81–116.

García Canclini, Néstor. 1995. *Cultural Hybridity: Strategies for Entering and Leaving Modernity*. Minneapolis: University of Minnesota Press.

Gardner, Katy, and David Lewis. 1996. *Anthropology, Development and the Post-Modern Challenge*. London: Pluto Press.

Gates, Marilyn. 1966. "Anthropology and the Development Encounter." *Current Anthropology* 37 (3): 575–577.

Geertz, Clifford. 1973. *The Interpretation of Cultures*. New York: Basic Books.

Gellner, Ernest. 1983. *Nations and Nationalism*. Oxford: Basil Blackwell.

George, Sheba. 2000. "'Dirty Nurses' and 'Men Who Play': Gender and Class in Transnational Migration." *In* M. Burawoy, et al., *Global Ethnography: Forces, Connections, and Imaginations in a Postmodern World*. Berkeley: University of California Press.

Georges, Eugenia. 1990. *The Making of a Transnational Community: Migration, Development, and Cultural Change in the Dominican Republic*. New York: Columbia University Press.

Gibbs, James Lowell. 1998. "Stanford Anthropology Department Splits." *Anthropology Newsletter*, October: 21–22.

Giddens, Anthony. 1990. *The Consequences of Modernity*. Stanford, California: Stanford University Press.

———. 1999. *Runaway World*. London: Routledge.

Gilroy, Paul. 1991. "It Ain't Where You're From, It's Where You're At . . . : The Dialectics of Diasporic Identification." *Third Text* 13: 3–16.

———. 1994. "Diaspora." *Paragraph* 17 (1): 207–212.

Glick Schiller, Nina, Linda Basch, and Cristina Blanc-Szanton. 1992. "Transnationalism: A New Analytic Framework for Understanding Migration." *In* N. Glick Schiller, L. Basch, and C. Blanc-Szanton, eds., *Towards a Transnational Perspective on Migration: Race, Class, Ethnicity, and Nationalism Reconsidered*. New York: Annals of the New York Academy of Sciences, Vol. 645.

———. 1995. "From Immigrant to Transmigrant: Theorizing Transnational Migration." *Anthropological Quarterly* 68 (1): 48–63.

Glick Schiller, Nina, Linda Basch, and Cristina Blanc-Szanton, eds. 1992. *Towards a Transnational Perspective on Migration: Race, Class, Ethnic-*

ity, and Nationalism Reconsidered. New York: Annals of the New York Academy of Sciences, Vol. 645.

Gmelch, George, and Sharon Bohn Gmelch. 1995. "Gender and Migration: The Readjustment of Women Migrants in Barbados, Ireland, and Newfoundland." *Human Organization* 54 (4): 470–474.

Gow, David D. 1990. "Development Anthropology: Quest of a Practical Vision." *In* H. M. Mathur, ed., *The Human Dimension of Development: Perspectives From Anthropology.* New Delhi: Concept Publishing Company.

———. 1996. "The Anthropology of Development: Discourse, Agency, and Culture." *Anthropological Quarterly* 69 (3): 165–172.

Graham, Elspeth, Joe Doherty, and Mo Malek. 1992. "Introduction: The Context and Language of Postmodernism." *In* J. Doherty, E. Graham, and M. Malek, eds., *Postmodernism and the Social Sciences.* New York: St. Martin's Press.

Greaves, Thomas C. 1996. "Indigenous Peoples." *In* D. Levinson and M. Ember, eds., *The Encyclopedia of Cultural Anthropology.* New York: Henry Holt.

Green, Linda. 1998. "The Localization of the Global: Contemporary Production Practices in a Mayan Community in Guatemala." *In* L. Phillips, ed., *The Third Wave of Modernization in Latin America: Cultural Perspectives on Neoliberalism.* Wilmington, Delaware: Scholarly Resources.

Griffith, David. 1998. "Experiencing Refugees: A Review Essay." *Reviews in Anthropology* 27: 407–424.

Grillo, R.D. 1997. "Discourses of Development: The View From Anthropology." *In* R.D. Grillo and R.L. Stirrat, eds., *Discourses of Development.* New York: Oxford.

Grillo, R. D., and R. L. Stirrat, Eds. 1997. *Discourses of Development.* New York: Oxford.

Griswold, Daniel. 2000. "The Blessings and Challenges of Globalization." *World and I* 15 (9). Retrieved Jan. 26, 2001, from the InfoTrac on-line database on the World Wide Web: http://web3.infotrac.galegroup.com/itw/infomark.

Gross, Paul R., and Norman Levitt. 1994. *Higher Superstition: The Academic Left and Its Quarrel with Science.* Baltimore, Maryland: Johns Hopkins University Press.

Gross, Paul R., Norman Levitt, and Martin W. Lewis, eds. 1996. *The Flight from Science and Reason.* New York: New York Academy of Sciences.

Gupta, Akhil, and James Ferguson. 1997. "Discipline and Practice: 'The Field' as Site, Method, and Location in Anthropology." *In* A. Gupta and J. Ferguson, eds., *Anthropological Locations: Boundaries and Grounds of a Field Science.* Berkeley: University of California Press.

Gupta, Akhil, and James Ferguson, eds. 1997. *Anthropological Locations: Boundaries and Grounds of a Field Science.* Berkeley: University of California Press.

————. 1997a. *Culture, Power, Place: Explorations in Critical Anthropology.* Durham, N.C.: Duke University Press.

Hale, Charles R. 1992. *Resistance and Contradiction: Miskitu Indians and the Nicaraguan State.* Stanford, California: Stanford University Press.

————. 1997. "Cultural Politics of Identity in Latin America." *Annual Review of Anthropology* 26: 567–590.

Hall, Stuart. 1990. "Cultural Identity and Diaspora." *In* J. Rutherford, ed., *Identity, Community, Culture, Difference.* London: Lawrence and Wishart.

Hammar, Tomas, Grete Brochmann, Kristof Tamas, and Thomas Faist, eds. 1997. *International Migration, Immobility and Development: Multidisciplinary Perspectives.* Oxford: Berg.

Hammar, Tomas, and Kristof Tamas. 1997. "Why Do People Go or Stay?" *In* T. Hammar, G. Brochmann, K. Tamas, and T. Faist, eds., *International Migration, Immobility and Development: Multidisciplinary Perspectives.* Oxford: Berg.

Handleman, Don. 1977. "The Organization of Ethnicity." *Ethnic Groups* 1: 187–200.

Hannerz, Ulf. 1996. *Transnational Connections: Culture, People, Places.* London: Routledge.

————. 1998. "Transnational Research." *In* R. Bernard, ed., *Handbook of Methods in Cultural Anthropology.* Walnut Creek, California: Altamira Press.

Harrell-Bond, Barbara, and Efithia Vourtira. 1996. "Refugees." *In* D. Levinson and M. Ember, eds., *The Encyclopedia of Cultural Anthropology.* New York: Henry Holt.

Harris, Marvin. 1999a. *Theories of Culture in Postmodern Times.* Walnut Creek, California: Altimara.

————. 1999b. "Science, Objectivity, Morality." *In* E.L. Cerroni-Long, ed., *Anthropological Theory in North America.* Westport, Connecticut: Bergin and Garvey.

Harris, Olivia. 1996. "The Temporalities of Tradition: Reflections on a Changing Anthropology." *In* Václav Hubinger, ed., *Grasping the Changing World: Anthropological Concepts in the Postmodern Era.* London: Routledge.

Harvey, David. 1990. *The Condition of Postmodernity.* Cambridge, Massachusetts: Blackwell.

Haugerud, Angelique, M. Priscilla Stone, and Peter D. Little, eds. 2000. *Commodities and Globalization: Anthropological Perspectives.* Oxford: Rowman & Littlefield.

Heisler, B. Schmitter. 1992. "The Future of Immigrant Incorporation: Which Models? Which Concepts?" *International Migration Review* 26: 623–645.

Heisler, Barbara Schmitter. 2000. "The Sociology of Immigration: From Assimilation to Segmented Integration, from the American Experience to the

Global Arena." *In* C.B. Brettell and J.F. Hollifield, eds., *Migration Theory: Talking Across Disciplines*. New York: Routledge.

Held, David, Anthony G. McGrew, David Goldblatt, and Jonathan Perraton. 1999. *Global Transformations: Politics, Economics and Culture*. Stanford, California: Stanford University Press.

Hewitt de Alcántara, Cynthia. 1984. *Anthropological Perspectives on Rural Mexico*. London: Routledge and Kegan Paul.

Hobart, Mark. 1993. "Introduction: The Growth of Ignorance." *In* M. Hobart, ed., *An Anthropological Critique of Development: The Growth of Ignorance*. London: Routledge.

Hopkins, Mary Campbell, and Nancy D. Donnelly, eds. 1993. *Selected Papers on Refugee Issues II*. Washington, D.C.: American Anthropological Association.

Horowitz, Michael M. 1996. "Development Anthropology." *In* D. Levinson and M. Ember, eds., *The Encyclopedia of Cultural Anthropology*, Vol. 1. New York: Holt

Hsu, Francis L. K. 1972. "American Core Value and National Character." *In* F. Hsu, ed., *Psychological Anthropology*. Morristown, New Jersey: Shenkman Books.

Huntington, Samuel. 1996. *The Clash of Civilizations: Remaking of the World Order*. New York: Simon and Schuster.

Iglesias Prieto, Norma. 1997. *Beautiful Flowers of the Maquiladora*. Translated by Michael Stone. Austin: University of Texas Press.

Indra, Doreen. 1999. "Not a 'Room of One's Own': Engendering Forced Migration Knowledge and Practice." *In* D. Indra, ed., *Engendering Forced Migration*. New York: Berghahn.

Indra, Doreen, ed. 1999. *Engendering Forced Migration*. New York: Berghahn.

Jameson, Frederic. 1988. "Cognitive Mapping." *In* C. Nelson and L. Grossberg, eds., *Marxism and Interpretation of Culture*. Urbana: University of Illinois Press.

———. 1990. *Postmodernism, or, the Cultural Logic of Late Capitalism*. Durham, North Carolina: Duke University Press.

———. 1998. "Notes on Globalization as a Philosophical Issue." *In* Frederic Jameson and Miyoshi Masao, eds., *The Cultures of Globalization*. Durham, North Carolina: Duke.

Joshi, Mary Sissons, and Meena Krishna. 1998. "English and North American Daughters-in-Law in the Hindu Joint Family." *In* R. Breger and R. Hill, eds., *Cross-Culttural Marriage: Identity and Choice*. Oxford: Berg.

Kalb, Don. 2000. "Localizing Flows: Power, Paths, Institutions, and Networks." *In* D. Kalb, M. van der Land, R. Staring, B. van Steenbergen, and N. Wilterdink, eds., *The Ends of Globalization: Bringing Society Back In*. Lanham, Maryland: Rowman and Littlefield.

Kearney, Michael. 1986. "From the Invisible Hand to Visible Feet: Anthropological Studies of Migration and Development." *Annual Review of Anthropology* 15: 331–361.

———. 1995. "The Local and the Global: The Anthropology of Globalization and Transnationalism." *Annual Review of Anthropology* 24: 547–565.

———. 1996. *Reconceptualizing the Peasantry: Anthropology in a Global Perspective*. Boulder, Colorado: Westview.

Keller, Stephen L. 1975. *Uprooting and Social Change: The Case for a Development Oriented Strategy*. Delhi: Manohar.

Kepel, Gilles. 1997. *Allah in the West: Islamic Movements in America and Europe*. Stanford, California: Stanford University Press.

Khatib-Chahidi, Jane, Rosanna Hill, and Renée Paton. 1998. "Chance, Choice and Circumstance: A Study of Women in Cross-Cultural Marriages." *In* R. Breger and R. Hill, eds., *Cross-Cultural Marriage: Identity and Choice*. Oxford: Berg.

Kiely, Ray. 1995. *Sociology and Development: The Impasse and Beyond*. London: UCL Press.

———. 1998. *Industrialization and Development: A Comparative Analysis*. London: UCL Press.

Kolata, Gina. 1987. "Anthropologists Turn Advocates for the Brazilian Indians." *Science* 236: 1183–1188. Retrieved May 28, 2001, from the InfoTrac database on the World Wide Web: http://web4.infotrac.galegroup.com/.

Krulfeld, Ruth M. 1992. "Cognitive Mapping and Ethnic Identity: The Changing Concepts of Community in the Laotian Diaspora." *In* P.A. DeVoe, ed., *Selected Papers on Refugee Issues*. Washington, D.C.: American Anthropological Association.

———. 1993. "Bridling Leviathan: New Paradigms of Method and Theory in Culture Change from Refugee Studies and Related Issues of Power and Empowerment." *In* M.C. Hopkins and N.D. Donnelly, eds., *Selected Papers on Refugee Issues II*. Washington, D.C.: American Anthropological Association.

Kuhn, T.S. 1970. *The Structure of Scientific Revolutions,* Second Edition. Chicago: University of Chicago Press.

Kuzner, Lawrence. 1997. *Reclaiming a Scientific Anthropology*. Walnut Creek, California: Altimira.

Lavenda, Robert H., and Emily A. Schultz. 1999. *Core Concepts in Cultural Anthropology*. Mountain View, California: Mayfield.

Lavie, Smadar, and Ted Swedenburg. 1996. "Introduction: Displacement, Diaspora, and Geographies of Identity." *In* S. Lavie and T. Swedenburg, eds., *Displacement, Diaspora, and Geographies of Identity*. Durham, North Carolina: Duke University Press.

Lavie, Smadar, and Ted Swedenburg, eds. 1996. *Displacement, Diaspora, and Geographies of Identity*. Durham, North Carolina: Duke University Press.

Lawrence, Christopher. 2000. "The World Bank, Transnational Migration, and the Development of Inequality." Paper presented at the Annual Meeting of the American Anthropological Association, San Francisco, November 2000.

Leach, Edmund. 1954. *Political Systems of Highland Burma*. Boston: Beacon Press.

Lemert, Charles C. 1997. *Postmodernism Is Not What You Think*. London: Blackwell.

Lennihan, Louise D. 1996. "The Anthropology of Modernity and the Postmodernist Anthropology of 'Development' Discourse." *Reviews in Anthropology* 25: 125–135.

Lewellen, Ted C. 1978. *Peasants in Transition: The Changing Economy of the Peruvian Aymara*. Boulder, Colorado: Westview Press.

———. 1979. "Deviant Religions and Cultural Evolution: The Aymara Case." *Journal for the Scientific Study of Religion* 18: 243–251.

———. 1981. "Aggression and Hypoglycemia in the Andes: Another Look at the Evidence." *Current Anthropology* 22 (4): 347–361.

———. 1984. "'Comment' on 'The Hypoglycemia-Aggression Hypothesis: Debate versus Research'" by Ralph Bolton. *Current Anthropology* 25 (1): 35–40.

———. 1985a. "Structures of Terror: A Systems Analysis of Repression in El Salvador." *In* G.W. Shepherd and V.P. Nanda, eds., *Human Rights and Third World Development*. Boulder, Colorado: Westview.

———. 1985b. *The Missing Statistic: Income, Development and Basic Needs In the Third World*. Project 40 Monographs: Global Development. World Academy of Development and Cooperation.

———. 1986. "The Lie File: The Political Manipulation of Central American Data, 1981–1984." *Scandinavian Journal of Development Alternatives* 5 (1): 29–49.

———. 1989. "Holy and Unholy Alliances: The Politics of Catholicism in Revolutionary Nicaragua." *Journal of Church and State* 31 (1): 15–34.

———. 1992. *Political Anthropology: An Introduction*, Second Edition. Westport, Connecticut: Bergin and Garvey.

———. 1995. *Dependency and Development: Introduction to the Third World*. Westport, Connecticut: Bergin and Garvey.

———. 2000. "What's Hot? What's Not? in Anthropology." *Anthropology News*, March, p. 80.

Lewis, Herbert S. 1999. "The Misrepresentation of Anthropology and Its Consequences." *American Anthropologist* 100 (3): 716–731.

Li, Xiaoping. 1996. *Transient Identities: Globalization and Contemporary Chinese Cultures*. PhD dissertation (Anthropology), York University, New York/Ontario.

Life. 1994. "Eyewitness to Rwanda." September: 74–80.

Lins Ribeiro, Gustavo. 1988. "Developing the Moonland: The Yacreta Hydroelectric High Dam and Economic Expansion in Argentina." PhD dissertation (Anthropology), City University of New York.

———. 1995. "Ethnic Segmentation of the Labor Market and the 'Work Site Animal': Fragmentation and Reconstruction of Identities with the World
System." *In* J. Schneider and R. Rapp, eds., *Articulating Hidden Histories: Exploring the Influence of Eric R. Wolf.* Berkeley: University of
California Press.

Lins Ribeiro, Gustavo, and Paul E. Little. 1998. "Neoliberal Recipes, Environmental Cooks: The Transformation of Amazonian Agency." *In* L. Phillips, ed., *The Third Wave of Modernization in Latin America: Cultural
Perspectives on Neoliberalism.* Wilmington, Delaware: Scholarly Resources.

Loker, William M. 1999. "Grit in the Prosperity Machine: Globalization and the
Rural Poor in Latin America." *In* W.M. Loker, ed., *Globalization and
the Rural Poor in Latin America.* Boulder, Colorado: Lynne Rienner.

Loker, William M., ed. 1999. *Globalization and the Rural Poor in Latin America.*
Boulder, Colorado: Lynne Rienner.

Lombardi, Gerald S. 1999. *Computer Networks, Social Networks, and the Future
of Brazil.* PhD dissertation (Anthropology), New York University.

Long, Norman. 2000. "Exploring Local/Global Transformations: A View from
Anthropology." *In* A. Arce and N. Long, eds., *Anthropology, Develop-
ment, and Modernities: Exploring Discourses, Counter-Tendencies and
Violence.* London: Routledge.

López, Ramón. 1998. "Rural Poverty: A Quantitative Analysis." Annex 3 to *El Salvador: Rural Development Study,* The World Bank. Retrieved May 26,
2001, from the World Wide Web: http://wbln0018.worldbank.org/Net-
works/ESSD/icdb.nsf/.

Lugo, Alejandro. 1997. "Reflections on Border Theory, Culture, and the Nation."
In S. Michaelsen and D.E. Johnson, eds., *Border Theory: The Limits of
Cultural Politics.* Minneapolis: University of Minnesota Press.

Lutz, Catherine, and Donald Nonini. 1999. "The Economies of Violence and the
Violence of Economies." *In* H.L. Moore, ed., *Anthropological Theory
Today.* Cambridge: Polity Press.

Lyotard, Jean-François. 1984. *The Postmodern Condition.* Minneapolis: University of Minnesota Press.

Magnarella, Paul J. 1999. "Human Materialism: A Paradigm for Analyzing
Sociocultural Systems and Understanding Human Behavior." *In* E.L.
Cerroni-Long, ed., *Anthropological Theory in North America.* Westport,
Connecticut: Bergin and Garvey.

Malinowski, Bronislaw. 1961 [1922]. *Argonauts of the Western Pacific.* New
York: E.P. Dutton.

Malkki, Liisa H. 1995. "Refugees and Exile: From 'Refugee Studies' to the National Order of Things." *Annual Review of Anthropology* 24: 495–523.

————. 1996. "Speechless Emissaries: Refugees, Humanitarianism, and Dehistoricization." *Cultural Anthropology* 11 (3): 377–404.

————. 1997. "News and Culture: Transitory Phenomena and the Fieldwork Tradition." *In* A. Gupta and J. Ferguson, eds., *Anthropological Locations: Boundaries and Grounds of a Field Science*. Berkeley: University of California Press.

Malley, Robert. 1999. "The Third Worldist Moment." *Current History* 98: 359–369.

Malmberg, Gunnar. 1997. "Time and Space in International Migration." *In* T. Hammar, G. Brochmann, K. Tamas, and T. Faist, eds., *International Migration, Immobility and Development: Multidisciplinary Perspectives*. Oxford: Berg.

Mangin, W., ed. 1970. *Peasants in Cities: Readings in the Anthropology of Urbanization*. Boston: Houghton-Mifflin.

Manzo, Kate. 1991. "Modernist Discourse and the Crisis of Development Theory." *Studies in Comparative Development* 26 (2): 3–36.

Marcus, George E. 1995. "Ethnography in/of the World System: The Emergence of Multi-Sited Ethnography." *Annual Review of Anthropology* 24: 95–117.

Mariátegui, José Carlos. 1971 [1928]. *Seven Interpretive Essays on Peruvian Reality*. Austin: University of Texas Press.

Matsuoka, Atsuko, and John Sorenson. 1999. "Eritrean Canadian Refugee Households as Sites of Gender Renegotiation." *In* D. Indra, ed., *Engendering Forced Migration*. New York: Berghahn.

Maxwell, Joseph A. 1999. "A Realist/Postmodern Concept of Culture." *In* E.L. Cerroni-Long, ed., *Anthropological Theory in North America*. Westport, Connecticut: Bergin and Garvey.

Maybury-Lewis, David. 1996. "Indigenous Rights." *In* D. Levinson and M. Ember, eds., *The Encyclopedia of Cultural Anthropology*. New York: Henry Holt.

McCall, Grant. 1994. "Anthropology and Global Change." *Current Anthropology* 35 (2): 190–191.

McLuhan, Marshall, and Bruce R. Powers. 1992. *The Global Village: Transformations in World Life and Media in the Twenty-First Century*. Oxford: Oxford University Press.

Meillassoux, Claude. 1981. *Maidens, Meals and Money*. Cambridge: Cambridge University Press.

Merchand, Marianne H., Morten Bøås, and Timothy Shaw. 1999. "The Political Economy of New Regionalisms." *Third World Quarterly* 20 (5): 897–910.

Miller, Daniel. 1997. *Capitalism: An Ethnographic Approach*. Oxford: Berg.

Mines, R., and Massey, D. 1985. "Patterns of Migration to the United States from Two Mexican Communities." *Latin American Research Review* 20 (2): 104–123.

Mittelman, James. 2000. *The Globalization Syndrome: Transformation and Resistance*. Princeton, New Jersey: Princeton University Press.

Moore, Henrietta L. 1999. "Anthropological Theory at the Turn of the Century." *In* H.L. Moore, ed., *Anthropological Theory Today*. Cambridge: Polity Press.

———. 1999. "Whatever Happened to Women and Men? Gender and Other Crises in Anthropology." *In* H.L. Moore, ed., *Anthropological Theory Today*. Cambridge: Polity Press.

Mortland, Carol A. 1998. "Introduction." *In* C.A. Mortland, ed., *Diasporic Identity: Selected Papers on Refugees and Immigrants*, Vol. VI. Washington, D.C.: American Anthropological Association.

Mortland, Carol A., ed. 1998. *Diasporic Identity: Selected Papers on Refugees and Immigrants,* Vol. VI. Washington, D.C.: American Anthropological Association.

Mountcastle, Amy. 1997. *Tibetans in Exile: The Construction of Global Identities*. PhD dissertation (Anthropology), State University of New Jersey, New Brunswick.

Murphy, Martin F., and Maxine L. Margolis, eds. 1995. *Science, Materialism, and the Study of Culture*. Gainesville: University of Florida Press.

Nader, Laura. 1996. *Naked Science: Anthropological Inquiry into Boundaries, Power, and Knowledge*. London: Routledge.

Nash, June. 1994. "Global Integration and Subsistence Insecurity." *American Anthropologist* 96 (1): 7–30.

Norberg-Hodge, Helena. 1991. *Ancient Futures: Learning from Ladakh*. San Francisco: Sierra Club Books.

Nugent, Stephen. 1996. "Postmodernism." *In* A. Barnard and J. Spencer, eds., *Encyclopedia of Social and Cultural Anthropology*. London: Routledge.

Ong, Aihwa. 1992. "Limits to Cultural Accumulation: Chinese Capitalists on the American Pacific Rim." *In* N. Glick Schiller, L. Basch, and C. Blanc-Szanton, eds., *Towards a Transnational Perspective on Migration: Race, Class, Ethnicity, and Nationalism Reconsidered*. New York: Annals of the New York Academy of Sciences, Vol. 645.

———. 1993. "On the Edge of Empires: Flexible Citizenship among Chinese in Diaspora." *Positions* 1 (3): 745–778.

———. 1999. *Flexible Citizenship: The Cultural Logics of Transnationality*. Durham, North Carolina: Duke University Press.

Parajuli, Pramod. 1991. "Power and Knowledge." *International Social Science Journal* 43 (1): 173–190.

Patterson, Thomas. 1999. Change and Development in the Twentieth Century. Oxford: Berg.

Petkofsky, Andrew. 1995. "Indian Poster Benefits Fund—Chiefs of 8 Tribes Pictured." *Richmond Times Dispatch* July 3: B-1.

Petras, James. 1999. "Globalization: A Critical Analysis." *Journal of Contemporary Asia* 29 (1):3 ff. Retrieved January 12, 2001, from the InfoTrac

on-line database on the World Wide Web: http://web3.infotrac.
galegroup.com/itw/infomark/.

Phillips, Lynne. 1998. "Conclusion: Anthropology in the Age of Neoliberalism." *In* L. Phillips, ed., *The Third Wave of Modernization in Latin America: Cultural Perspectives on Neoliberalism.* Wilmington, Delaware: Scholarly Resources.

Pieterse, Jan Nederveen. 1996. "Varieties of Ethnic Politics and Ethnicity Discourse." *In* E.N. Wilmsen and P. McAllister, eds., *The Politics of Difference: Ethnic Premises in a World of Power.* Chicago: University of Chicago Press.

Piot, Charles. 1999. *Remotely Global: Village Modernity in West Africa.* Chicago: University of Chicago Press.

Polier, Nicole. 2000. "Commoditization, Cash, and Kinship in Postcolonial Papua, New Guinea." *In* A. Haugerud, M.P. Stone, and P.D. Little, eds., *Commodities and Globalization: Anthropological Perspectives.* Oxford: Rowman & Littlefield.

Portes, Alejandro. 2000. "Globalization from Below: The Rise of Transnational Communities." *In* D. Kalb, M. van der Land, R. Staring, B. van Steenbergen, and N. Wilterdink, eds., *The Ends of Globalization: Bringing Society Back In.* Lanham, Maryland: Rowman and Littlefield.

Rabinow, Paul. 1996. *Essays on the Anthropology of Reason.* Princeton: Princeton University Press.

Rahnema, Majid, Ed. 1997. *The Post-Development Reader.* London: Zed.

Redfield, Robert. 1941. *The Folk Culture of the Yucatan.* Chicago: University of Chicago Press.

Reichert, J. S. 1981. "The Migrant Syndrome: Seasonal U.S. Wage Labor and Rural Development in Central Mexico." *Human Organization* 40 (1): 56–66.

Richman, Karen. 1992. "'A Lavalas at Home/A Lavalas for Home'. Inflections of Transnationalism in the Discourse of Haitian President Aristide." *In* N. Glick Schiller, L. Basch, and C. Blanc-Szanton, eds., *Towards a Transnational Perspective on Migration: Race, Class, Ethnicity, and Nationalism Reconsidered.* New York: Annals of the New York Academy of Sciences, Vol. 645.

Rorty, Richard. 1994. "Method, Social Science, and Social Hope." *In* S. Seidman, ed., *The Postmodern Turn.* Cambridge: Cambridge University Press.

Rosaldo, Renato. 1995. "Forward." *In* N. García Canclini, *Cultural Hybridity: Strategies for Entering and Leaving Modernity.* Minneapolis: University of Minnesota Press.

Rosenau, Pauline Marie. 1992. *Post-Modernism and the Social Sciences: Insights, Inroads, and Intrusions.* Princeton: Princeton University Press.

Rosenthal-Urey, Ina. 1982. *Migrants and Stay-At-Homes: A Comparative Study of Rural Migration from Michoacan, Mexico.* La Jolla, California: Center for U.S.-Mexican Studies, University of California, San Diego.

Rostow, W.W. 1960. *The Stages of Economic Growth*. London: Cambridge University Press.

Rouse, Roger. 1991. "Mexican Migration and the Social Space of Postmodernism." *Diaspora* 1 (1): 8–23.

Sachs, Wolfgang. 1992. "Introduction." *In* W. Sachs, ed., *The Development Dictionary: A Guide to Knowledge as Power*. London: Zed.

Sachs, Wolfgang, ed. 1992. *The Development Dictionary: A Guide to Knowledge as Power*. London: Zed.

Sadowski, Yahya. 1998. "Ethnic Conflict." *Foreign Policy* 111: 12–23.

Safa, Helen Icken. 1974. *The Urban Poor of Puerto Rico: A Study in Development and Inequality*. New York: Holt, Rinehart and Winston.

Safran, William. 1991. "Diasporas in Modern Societies: Myths of Homeland and Return." *Diaspora* 1 (1): 83–99.

Said, Edward W. 1979. *Orientalism*. New York: Vintage.

Schuurman, Frans. 1993. "Introduction: Development Theory in the 1990s." *In* F. Schuurman, ed., *Beyond the Impasse: New Directions in Development Theory*. London: Zed.

Scott, James. 1985. *Weapons of the Weak: Everyday Forms of Peasant Resistance*. New Haven, Connecticut: Yale University Press.

Seidman, Steven. 1994. "Introduction." *In* S. Seidman, ed., *The Postmodern Turn*. Cambridge: Cambridge University Press.

Seton, Kathy. 1999. "Fourth World Nations in the Era of Globalization: An Introduction to Contemporary Theorizing Posed by Indigenous Nations." *Fourth World Journal*, 4 (1). Retrieved May 19, 2001, from the World Wide Web: http://www.cwis.org/fwj/.

Sharp, Lauriston. 1952. "Steel Axes for Stone-Age Australians." *Human Organization* 11(2): 17–22.

Shea, Christopher. 1998. "Tribal Skirmishes in Anthropology." *Chronicle of Higher Education*, Sept. 11, 1998, pp. A17, A20.

Sheffer, Gabriel. 1995. "The Emergence of New Ethno-National Diasporas." *Migration* 28: 5–28.

Sheffer, Gabriel, ed. 1986. *Modern Diasporas in International Politics*. New York: St. Martin's Press.

Sheridan, Alan. 1980. *Michel Foucault: The Will to Truth*. New York: Tavistock.

Shumway, David R. 1989. *Michel Foucault*. Charlottesville: University Press of Virginia.

Shuval, Judith. 2000. "Diaspora Migration: Definitional Ambiguities and a Theoretical Paradigm." *International Migration* 38 (5): 41–55.

Sissons Joshi, Mary, and Meena Krishna. 1998. "English and North American Daughters-in-Law in the Hindu Joint Family." *In* R. Breger and R. Hill, eds., *Cross-Cultural Marriage: Identity and Choice*. Oxford: Berg.

Skinner, Elliott P. 1993. "The Dialectic between Diasporas and Homelands." *In* J.E. Harris, ed., *Global Dimensions of the African Diaspora*. Washington, DC: Howard University Press.

Sklair, Holly. 1988. *Washington's War on Nicaragua*. Boston: South End Press.

Sklair, Leslie. 1991. *Sociology of the Global System*. Baltimore, Maryland: Johns Hopkins University Press.

———. 1995. *Sociology of the Global System*, Second Edition. Baltimore, Maryland: Johns Hopkins University Press.

Smith, Adam. 1976 [1776]. *An Inquiry into the Nature and Causes of the Wealth of Nations*. Oxford: Oxford University Press.

Smith, Anthony. 1986. *The Ethnic Origins of Nations*. Oxford: Basil Blackwell.

Sokal, Alan. 1996. "Transgressing the Boundaries: Toward a Transformative Hermeneutics of Quantum Gravity." *Social Text* 46 (47): 217–252.

Sokal, Alan, and Jean Bricmont. 1998. *Fashionable Nonsense: Postmodern Intellectuals' Abuse of Science*. New York: Picador USA.

Sommers, Marc. 1993. "Coping with Fear: Burundi Refugees and the Urban Experience in Dar Es Salaam, Tanzania." *In* M.C. Hopkins and N.D. Donnelly, eds., *Selected Papers on Refugee Issues II*. Washington, D.C.: American Anthropological Association.

Spindler, George and Louise. 1990. *The American Cultural Dialogue and Its Transmission*. Bristal, Pennsylvania: Falmer Press.

Stahl, Charles W., and Fred Arnold. 1986. "Overseas Workers' Remittances in Asian Development." *International Migration Review* XX (4): 899–925.

Staring, Richard. 2000. "Flows of People: Globalization, Migration, and Transnational Communities." *In* D. Kalb, M. van der Land, R. Staring, B. van Steenbergen, and N. Wilterdink, eds., *The Ends of Globalization: Bringing Society Back In*. Lanham, Maryland: Rowman and Littlefield.

Stavrianos, L.S. 1981. *Global Rift: The Third World Comes of Age*. New York: William Morrow.

Stone, Priscilla, Angelique Haugerud, and Peter Little. 2000. "Commodities and Globalization: Anthropological Perspectives." *In* A. Haugerud, M.P. Stone, and P.D. Little, eds., *Commodities and Globalization: Anthropological Perspectives*. Oxford: Rowman & Littlefield.

Swerdlow, Joel L., et al. 1999. "Global Culture." *National Geographic* 196 (2): 2–89.

Szanton Blanc, Cristina, Linda Basch, and Nina Glick Schiller. 1995. "Transnationalism, Nation-States, and Culture." *Current Anthropology* 36 (4): 683–686.

Tambiah, Stanley J. 1996. "The Nation-State in Crisis and the Rise of Ethnonationalism." *In* E.N. Wilmsen and P. McAllister, eds., *The Politics of Difference: Ethnic Premises in a World of Power*. Chicago: University of Chicago Press.

Tedlock, Barbara. 1996. "Diasporas." *In* D. Levinson and M. Ember, eds., *The Encyclopedia of Cultural Anthropology*, Vol. 1. New York: Henry Holt.

Thomas, Nicholas. 1999. "Becoming Undisciplined: Anthropology and Cultural Studies." *In* H.L. Moore, ed., *Anthropological Theory Today*. Cambridge: Polity Press.

Trotter, Robert J. 1973. "Aggression: A Way of Life for the Qolla." *Science News* 103: 76–77.

Trouillot, Michel-Rolph. 2001. "The Anthropology of the State in the Age of Globalization: Close Encounters of the Deceptive Kind." *Current Anthropology* 42 (1): 125–138.

Turner, Terence. 1995. "An Indigenous People's Struggle for Socially Equitable and Ecologically Sustainable Production: The Kayapó Revolt Against Extractivism." *Journal of Latin American Anthropology* 1 (1): 98–121.

———. 2001. "Self-representation, Media and the Construction of a Local-Global Continuum by the Kayapó of Brazil." Retrieved May 18, 2001, from the World Wide Web: http://lime.weeg.uiowa.edu/~anthro/fulbright/abstracts/turner.html.

Turner, Victor. 1974. *Dramas, Fields, and Metaphors*. Ithaca, New York: Cornell University Press.

U.S. Congress. 1988. *Report of the Congressional Committees Investigating the Iran-Contra Affair with the Minority View*. New York: Times Books.

U.S. Department of State. 2000. "Background Notes: El Salvador." Retrieved May 27, 2002, from the World Wide Web: http://www.state.gov/www/background_notes/elsal_0008_bgn.html.

UNDESIPA (United Nations Department for Economic and Social Information and Policy Analysis, Population Division). 2001. "Countries with the Highest Percentage of International Migrants in Total Population, 1990." Retrieved March 26, 2001, from the World Wide Web: http://www.undp.org/popin/wdtrends/migpol95/impcht2.htm.

UNDP (United Nations Development Programme). 1993. *Human Development Report 1993*. New York: United Nations.

UNHCR (United Nations High Commissioner for Refugees). 1988. *Collection of International Instruments Concerning Refugees*. Geneva: UNHCR.

Unnithan, Maya, and Kavita Srivastava. 1997. "Gender Politics, Development and Women's Agency in Rajasthan." *In* R.D. Grillo and R.L. Stirrat, eds., *Discourses of Development: Anthropological Perspectives*. Oxford: Berg.

Uribe, Consuelo. 1986. "Limitations and Constraints of Colombia's National Food and Nutrition Plan (PAN)." *Food Policy* 11 (1): 47–70.

Van Arsdale, Peter W. 1993. "Empowerment: A Systems Perspective." *In* P. Van Arsdale, ed., *Refugee Empowerment and Organizational Change: A Systems Perspective*. Washington, D.C.: American Anthropological Association.

Van Arsdale, Peter, ed. 1993. *Refugee Empowerment and Organizational Change: A Systems Perspective*. Washington, D.C.: American Anthropological Association.

Van Hear, Nicholas. 1998. *New Diasporas: The Mass Exodus, Dispersal, and Regrouping of Migrant Communities*. London: UCL Press.

Vertovec, Steven, and Robin Cohen. 1999. "Introduction." *In* S. Vertovec and R. Cohen, eds., *Migration, Diasporas and Transnationalism*. Cheltenham, UK: Edward Elgar.

Vertovec, S., and R. Cohen, eds. 1999. *Migration, Diasporas and Transnationalism*. Cheltenham, UK: Edward Elgar.

Wallerstein, Immanuel. 1974. *The Modern World System: Capitalist Agriculture and the Origins of the European World Economy in the Sixteenth Century*. New York: Academic Press.

Warren, Kay B., and Susan C. Bourque. 1991. "Women, Technology, and International Development Ideologies: Analyzing Feminist Voices." *In* M. di Leonardo, ed., *Gender at the Crossroads of Knowledge: Feminist Anthropology in the Postmodern Era*. Berkeley: University of California Press.

Watson, C.W. 1996. "Anthropology and the Contemporary Construction of Ethnicity in Indonesia and Britain." *In* V. Huhinger, ed., *Grasping the Changing World: Anthropological Concepts in the Postmodern Era*. London: Routledge.

Weber, Max. 1993 [1905]. *The Protestant Ethic and the Spirit of Capitalism*. London: Routledge.

White, Bob. 2000. "*Soukouss* or Sell-Out? Congolese Popular Dance Music as Cultural Commodity." *In* A. Haugerud, M.P. Stone, and P.D. Little, eds., *Commodities and Globalization: Anthropological Perspectives*. Oxford: Rowman & Littlefield.

Wight, Jonathan. 2002. *Saving Adam Smith: A Tale of Wealth, Virtue, and Transformation*. New York: Prentice-Hall.

Wilk, Richard. 2000. "Globobabble." Retrieved August 10, 2000, from the World Wide Web: http://www.indiana.edu/~wanthro/babble.htm.

Wilmsen, Edwin N. 1996. "Introduction: Premises of Power in Ethnic Politics." *In* E.N. Wilmsen and P. McAllister, eds., *The Politics of Difference: Ethnic Premises in a World of Power*. Chicago: University of Chicago Press.

Wilson, Rob, and Wimal Dissanayake. 1992. "Introduction: Tracking the Global and the Local." *In* R. Wilson and W. Dissanayake, eds., *Global Local: Cultural Production and the Transnational Imaginary*. Durham, North Carolina: Duke University Press.

Wilson, Tamar Diana. 1994. "What Determines Where Transnational Labor Migrants Go? Modifications in Migration Theories." *Human Organization* 53 (3): 269–278.

Wolf, Eric R. 1982. *Europe and the People Without History*. Berkeley: University of California Press.

———. 1996. *Peasants*. Englewood Cliffs, New Jersey: Prentice-Hall.

World Bank. 1998. *World Development Report 1998/99*. Oxford: Oxford University Press.

————. 2000. *Entering the 21ˢᵗ Century: World Development Report 1999/2000.* New York: Oxford University Press.

————. 2001a. "International Finance Corporation: Pakistan." Retrieved January 7, 2001, from the World Wide Web: http://www.worldbank.org/ ifc/asia/sa2/pakistan.html.

————. 2001b. *World Development Report 2000/2001: Attacking Poverty.* New York: Oxford University Press.

World News Interpress Service. 2001. "Migration-Mexico: Making Big Bucks on Expatriate Remittances." Retrieved January 7, 2001, from the World Wide Web: http://www.oneworld.org/ips2/nov98/23.11_107.html.

Worsley, Peter. 1984. *The Three Worlds: Culture and World Development.* Chicago: University of Chicago Press.

Yanagisako, Sylvia. 1998. "Department of Cultural and Social Anthropology—Vision Statement." *Anthropology Newsletter*, October: 21–22.

Young, Philip D., and John R. Bort. 1999. "Ngóbe Adaptive Responses to Globalization in Panama." *In* W.M. Loker, ed., *Globalization and the Rural Poor in Latin America.* Boulder, Colorado: Lynne Rienner.

Index

About the Author

TED C. LEWELLEN is Professor of Anthropology and former Chair of the Department of Sociology and Anthropology at the University of Richmond, Virginia. He is the author of numerous books, including the Choice Outstanding Academic Book, *Dependency and Development: An Introduction to the Third World* (Bergin & Garvey, 1995). He is currently working on a third edition of *Political Anthropology* (Bergin & Garvey).